Dustin Diamond

Behind the Bell

Dustin Diamond

Behind the Bell

Behind the Scenes of Saved by the Bell with
the Guy who was There for Everything

TRANSIT
transitpublishing.com

Published by Transit Publishing Inc.

ISBN: 978-0-9812396-9-9

Editor: Timothy Niedermann
Cover design: François Turgeon
Text design and composition: Nassim Bahloul
Front cover: Wayde Peronto of Babboni Photography;
NBCU Photo Bank/ZUMA/Keystone Press
Inside front cover: NBCU Photo Bank/ZUMA/Keystone Press
Spine: Gary Null/NBCU Photo Bank/ZUMA/Keystone Press
Back cover: NBCU Photo Bank/ZUMA/Keystone Press
Inside back cover: Joseph DelValle/NBCU Photo Bank/ZUMA/Keystone Press

Transit Publishing Inc.
1996 St-Joseph blvd. East
Montreal, Quebec
CANADA
H2H 1E3
Tel: 1-514-273-0123
www.transitpublishing.com

Printed and Bound in Canada

Table of Contents

PART III: FAMOUS AS SHIT

PART IV: THE DENOUEMENT

EPILOGUE

Acknowledgements

I wish to thank Jennifer Misner, who has watched my many transformations both on and off stage. Without you my world would be dark, and with me being the darkest thing in it, it probably wouldn't work out so well.

Roger Paul—Without you this would never have gotten done. Thank you Roge.

Mark Bridge—You are a dirty rotten bastard . . . thank you so much. Smell my finger.

Loppy—Without you my face would never be down in the noodles.

Mr. Bungle, Frank Zappa, more metal bands than I can possibly list.

Everyone who loves horror, Halloween, and metal.

And all the supporters of this book.

If I missed anyone I'm sorry. It's late, and I'm tired . . . Scott "The Radman" Radmacher, Evan "Spaz" Hanson, Rob "Timmy" Simpson, Chad "Gggilf Hunter" Hooper, Eric "American" Oates, the Misner family, and many, many more.

For my fans you keep me going.

For my non-fans—you just don't know me yet.

For the man in my basement who is probably more than terrified right—soon.

P.S. Oh yes, and I want to give it up for B.I.G. Give it up for B.I.G.

INTRODUCTION

Hollywood likes to present itself through a glass darkly, with grace, poise, style, smoke, and mirrors. No question, there are still pockets of true dignity and elegance in Hollywood—authentic, creative people, comfortable in their skins and honest in their dealings. But that shit is rare, my friends. Honesty is the Pink Panther diamond of Los Angeles, so precious, it's practically a myth. And at the center of this mythology are those droll Hollywood tales of artistic whimsy, told with wit and charm at black-tie cocktail parties. Sorry to burst your bubble, but it's all horseshit.

I'm going to make an assumption, and it's this: the majority of people reading this book will not be current or former child stars of hit television shows. They will be regular folks who grew up in relatively normal childhood environments. They will most likely have attended local elementary and high schools, spent quality time with fellow classmates and neighborhood friends, eaten meals at designated time in their homes, were disciplined by their parents, and, at some point during the week, sat down and watched kids like me and the gang at Bayside High on the flickering boxes in their living rooms. They may have watched those pixilated versions of kids very much their own age, representating archetypes they were all too familiar with in their everyday lives (even if they didn't know what the fuck an archetype was), and perhaps entertained thoughts such as, *Wow, how lucky are those kids? They've got things so much better than I do.*

Yes and no. Yes, we probably made more money at ten years old than you did. We met lots of interesting people, were recognized and adored for a window in time, and went on adventures that would not have been possible if we hadn't been serendipitously plucked from relative obscurity one day in 1988 after several rounds of intense auditions. But on the other hand, no, our lives were not better than anyone else's in the sense that we were far from the perfect teens we portrayed in *Saved by the Bell*. In fact, truth be told, we were all pretty fucked up.

Celebrities are people, too. We're flawed like everybody else. We're just on television or up on a movie screen, pulling down more cash (when we're working). But as the warrior-poet Notorious B.I.G. once said, "Mo' money means mo' problems." The reality (in this age of reality-everything) is that working on film and TV sets is very cool—even more cool when you see the finished product edited together, complete with special effects, etc.—but underneath it all, it's just a job. None of the highly paid, glamorized, and glorified stars illuminated up on that wall of your local theater or in your little box at home is any different from you as a human being. If you work as a plumber or cop or software tech or at the phone company (like my mom did) or as any of the other millions of people that actually make the world go 'round do each day, you're no different (and in some ways, you're better) than your favorite stars, who have been placed up on false pedestals to be admired and emulated by the masses.

I think a problem with us human beings is that we want our gossip, dirt, and scandal in great detail. But sometimes the details aren't the best part of the story. What I mean is, details alone don't allow you see the whole picture. The questions are: Where does this information fit on a timeline? Why is it relevant? And what were the consequences of people's actions as they unfolded? For example, Tiffani-Amber Thiessen went from sweet, innocent, loveable all-American teen to *SBTB*'s set whore and Hollywood's pass-around girl. I wasn't a mouse in her pocket for each and every lay (thank God), but I can relate what I did see and put those reminiscences in their proper context.

A lot of the people I discuss in this book will not want to be depicted in the light I cast them in. Too bad. The things I write about are the things I've seen, the things I've heard from reliable sources, and the things I've come to know since starting work as an actor in Hollywood at the age of eight. People are going to deny that these stories are true, but I lived through them with my eyes wide open, and now I'm sharing them with you, fair reader. The stories actors and actresses *do* want told are the ones where they were honored with an award for their craft or chatted at a party with Tom Selleck and Jack Nicholson. Nobody cares about that shit. Not really. I believe that, at our core, what people crave most is to learn everything we can about others' human frailty, because it helps make sense of our own.

Hey, I'm putting myself out there on the block, too. Lord knows I've done some stupid shit (some of it on camera). But I also view myself—and I hope you will too—as an outsider, looking in on a popular clique I was never really a welcomed part of, reporting all I saw in stark black and white.

I moved to Wisconsin several years ago to get the fuck out of L.A. I loved the work, and the perks were fantastic, but I never cared about the fame. You don't make real friends in L.A., you make transactional friends, friends of necessity. In L.A., you meet a lot of middlemen (and middle women). In many ways, Los Angeles is not unlike the idealized version of Peter Engel's Bayside High, set in Palisades, California—except everyone in L.A. really was the actual star quarterback or captain of the cheerleading team at their real-life high schools with dreams of even greater stardom. So, each day from every metropolis and one-traffic-light Podunk in America a lot of hopeful, fresh-faced kids arrive in L.A., only to leave weeks, months, or years later, bitter and regretful as part of "The Used." But like moths to the fame flame, they keep coming.

Fuck fame. Allow me to tear down your allusions. My motivation in writing this book is to yank back the curtain and show you the wizard. I want some girl in an office building in Tacoma, Washington, to realize that she has more class than Tiffani-Amber Thiessen; that a dude slicing pastrami in a deli in Brooklyn has a better temperament than Mario Lopez; that, on balance, they'd all rather be Tom, Dick, and Harry than Zack, Kelly, Slater, Jess, Lisa, and Screech.

For my part, I've reached a point where I'd rather just be surrounded by good people. I'm a passionate student of the quirky and the obscure in all formats. I've always searched for influences that could help me grow and always tried to get to the real truth beneath. As you'll see, that's a search I've been on my whole life.

PART I:

THE BEGINNING

GOOD MORNING, MISS BLISS

I killed the Smurfs. What I mean is, I starred in the show that pretty much killed Saturday morning cartoons. In 1988, when *Saved by the Bell* settled into its regular 11:00 AM time slot every Saturday on NBC, it was the first live-action sitcom for kids— an instant hit, spawning a long succession of imitators—which meant that we had essentially killed all my favorite cartoons. And I had a lot of favorite cartoons because I was just a kid my-self. When I landed the role of Screech in *Good Morning, Miss Bliss*, the NBC pilot that would become *SBTB*, I was eleven years old playing an eighth grader. NBC and Disney were in early talks of possibly merging. That, of course, didn't work out. Disney's Michael Eisner eventually walked away from the deal in 1994. But NBC's chief of programming at the time, Brandon Tartikoff, liked the characters created by the show's executive producer, Peter Engel (by the way, Tartikoff was a *huge* Screech fan), and he felt the show shouldn't get lost in the shuffle just because the two companies never did reach a meeting of the minds. Disney had acquired *Good Morning, Miss Bliss* when NBC had passed on it, but when Disney cancelled the show after only one season, NBC reacquired the rights. NBC then to *Good Morning, Miss Bliss*; re-cast it, keeping Zack, Lisa, Screech, and Belding bringing in Kelly, Slater, and Jessie. The show was then renamed *Saved By The Bell*.

I auditioned six times for *Good Morning, Miss Bliss*, finally getting the part of Screech. After I was chosen I met a bunch of executives at NBC, including the vice president of children's programming, Linda Mancuso. Linda had always been there through all the callbacks, just another suit in the room, but I finally noticed her (I mean, noticed her-noticed her) at our first table reading. That first day was a whirlwind. Really exciting. "Dustin, here's your parking space at NBC (er, I mean my parents' parking space)," "Here's your dressing room . . ." There were all these fantastic hit shows going on all around me like *Cheers* and *The Tonight Show*. I'd bump into Doc Severinson walking down the hall. I got to work with Jeff Melman, who directed *Night Court* and later, *Frasier*, and who ended up directing *SBTB* at one point. It was a very cool time.

It wasn't until I entered Linda's office that I suddenly realized what she did: She was in charge of putting all my favorite NBC kids' programs on TV! Overall, the shows I was in love with at that age were programs like *Bugs Bunny*, *He-Man*, *GI Joe*, *ThunderCats*, *Transformers*, *Gobots*, and yes, *The Smurfs*. I was astonished to learn that Linda had access to tapes of all these shows, even though not all of them aired on NBC. Remember, this was long before DVDs were available; getting personal copies of television shows was unheard of. I quickly made a habit of going up to Linda's office all the time to feed my fascination because I simply couldn't believe the stuff she could pull down from her shelves. She handed me tapes of *The Yogi Bear Special* or *Captain N: The Game Master*, a brand-new TV show that I got to preview before the rest of the world. I had the inside scoop. Linda hooked me up with all the latest swag.

Once I got to know Linda, I realized she was so nice, so friendly, and so different from all the other network executives. Even though I was only eleven, I knew she was an important person, and we bonded over my viewing these shows that the success of *SBTB* would eventually drive off the airwaves. She had a soft, womanly approach to every challenge. I knew instantly that I could talk with her and trust her. She was like a big sister. Well, not exactly like a big sister. But I'm getting ahead of myself.

I was born in San Jose, California, about 370 miles north of Los Angeles. People tend to associate the entire state of California with the entertainment industry. but the area I hailed from was mostly like the Midwest. L.A. is its own universe with a personality (and smog-ridden weather system) all its own. These days I live in Wisconsin, and I consider the Midwest, the East Coast (where my family originated), and L.A. as three totally different vibes. In the Midwest, if someone doesn't like you, they won't speak ill of you, but they won't deal with you either. Midwesterners will be cordial and polite, but you're basically *persona non grata* to them. In New York, if someone has a problem with you, they will tell you right to your face. The culture in New York is too fast-paced to get bogged down in any horseshit. If there's an issue, you need to get it out in the open, mix it up, and move on. In L.A., if someone doesn't like you, they will kill you with kindness. They'll tell you they absolutely love you until you're out of earshot, then they'll start plotting your destruction. No one has the balls to tell the truth to anyone's face in Hollywood.

My family didn't come from old money or have much new money, either. My parents were a hard-working, middle-class couple that drove a Pinto (the no-air-conditioning, flickering-dome-light, non-exploding model). After it rained, we'd find mushrooms growing under the floor mats in the back of that car. Mom worked the graveyard shift as a computer operator for Pacific Bell, and dad taught digital electronics for one of the early Silicon Valley computer-processing firms. As the saying goes, "We weren't very L.A." As a result, I felt like we were kind of looked down upon by some of the other families of the *SBTB* cast. I don't think they'd ever admit it, but the vibe from my fellow cast members was pretty uppity and exclusionary, looking down their noses at my hand-me-down jacket or discount store clothes. I mean, I didn't dress as bad as Screech, but I didn't dress as well as Zack Morris or Lisa Turtle either. After all, Lark Voorhies, who played Lisa, came from a doctor's family, Elizabeth Berkley from a lawyer's. Most of my co-stars came from super well- to-do families.

My mom transferred her job, and my dad gave up his job teaching digital electronics so they could help me reach my goal of becoming an actor. I say acting was my goal and never my dream for a reason. I was just a kid who had no clue where my acting adventures would lead me. I started acting at age eight and early in my career appeared in between sixty and seventy commercials for products from Burger King to Post Alpha Bits and Fruity Pebbles cereals. The Burger King spot was for the "We Do It Like You Do It" campaign, which was based around the idea that they made flame-broiled goodness just like you grilled at home. In the ad, my TV dad can't figure out how to assemble his barbeque grill, so in exasperation he takes all his kids to Burger King. I take a bite of my burger, smile at the camera and say, "I knew he could do it."

I also made several guest star appearances on popular TV shows like *It's a Living* and *The Wonder Years*. On the *The Wonder Years*, I played what could be considered my first role as a nerdy character, even though that part was really more of an awkward adolescent, not necessarily a full-blown geek. I bounced around to different gigs and got to know all the Hollywood kids my age who were living the same lifestyle. Some went on to get their own shows or to appear on *SBTB*. It was just the way it was. We were kids, but we were also busy, hard working, professional actors.

In the beginning I just wanted to have fun, but the process of auditioning was a real drag. I have early memories of leaving school, seeing my mom or dad waiting by the car and thinking, "Aw, shit. Another audition." I knew I would have to sit in the hot, stale air of the Pinto's back seat doing my homework while we fought the freeway traffic for our forty-five mile, ninety minute commute into L.A. (or longer if we were stuck in beep-and-creep traffic). But when I arrived, I was all business. I would switch on my spotlight smile, ham it up, and try my hardest to book the gig.

For me, acting was always about the challenge. It's like, all my life I've enjoyed playing video games, but the thrill has never been about winning; it's more about meeting and facing down every obstacle that's placed in front of me. Speaking of video games, being a kid, the purchasing power acting provided me with was a huge motivator. I knew that as long as I kept booking jobs, I could walk into a toy store and buy whatever game system I wanted and every game that went with it (that was a long time ago, remember.) The first gig I ever booked was a commercial for Giant Eagle Food Stores, an East-Coast supermarket chain. The premise was that the food flew off the shelves so fast that they couldn't keep them stocked. Therefore, the only way to describe Giant Eagle's food, because it was always moving, was "busy." In the spot, all this food keeps passing by me piled high on plates, but every time I reach for something, a bunch of hands beat me to it, and the plate is picked clean. Finally, a giant hamburger is set down in front of me. The announcer says, "People say Giant Eagle food flies off the shelf so fast. How does Giant Eagle taste to you?" My response: "Busy." It was a national commercial, so it made me Screen Actor's Guild eligible, but I only had one line, so I didn't qualify.

I did bit parts on other shows and in movies before *SBTB* took off. Right around the time *SBTB* was starting, I played a character named Joey in two episodes of *The Wonder Years*. One episode featured a gym scene where my character was the last to be selected for the team—even after über-geek Paul Pfeiffer, played by Josh Saviano. The producers asked if another character could "pants" me, offering to pay more money in return. I was like, "Sure!"

Working on that set, I got an early taste of how kids can be when they're the stars of a big-time hit. Yes, I must sadly report that Fred Savage, the diminutive star of *The Wonder Years*, was another Hollywood douchenozzle. I watched Savage stick a pencil eraser in his nose, scoop out a booger, and stick it in a female extra's mouth. I also saw him go up to a director and kick him in the shin. WHAM!

In Savage's case, his dad had a lot of power over the production of *The Wonder Years*, which is extremely rare. Under those circumstances, it's understandable how a child actor could easily slip into a tiny prick suit—the whole set depends on them for their paycheck. And to be fair, years later, after they've matured and had time to reflect on those years when they had so little control over their daily actions—indeed, their lives in general—many of them mellow and transform into decent human beings. After all, Fred Savage did triumphantly warm our hearts again as the moley-moley-moley mole in *Austin Powers in Goldmember*.

I have a lot of great memories of my early roles and of my time on *SBTB*, and I wouldn't have changed anything. But looking back now, I do feel like a big chunk of my childhood was stolen from me. I think it's mostly because I never really fit into the *SBTB* family. Early on, I was oblivious to the idea that anyone could be looking down his or her nose at my family and me. But it didn't escape my attention long. I had a huge dad (6'1", a former martial arts instructor, and just a shade under

400 pounds) with a keen radar for snobbish slights. The span of my dad's back, from shoulder-to-shoulder, was as wide as our refrigerator. Dad was quick to let folks know they could go fuck themselves. There were times when I secretly cheered my dad's fearlessness and other times when I was horrified and humiliated, and swore I could never be out with him in public again. But that's just the way it was when you were the only one driving to the set in a Pinto.

* * * *

Good Morning, Miss Bliss starred the fantastic Hayley Mills. There is absolutely nothing I could write about that special lady that would approach the praise she deserves. What a beautiful woman. If she had stayed on with the show when it returned to NBC and was reformatted, it's hard to know what sort of show *SBTB* would have become. Would we have still been a hit? Impossible to say with any certainty. I could only speculate. When Hayley starred as Miss Bliss, we only taped thirteen episodes on a closed sound stage. Maybe the transition to a live studio audience would have been a major factor. *Miss Bliss* was a darker-lit show—different quality, lower budget. Who knows? The viewing public is fickle, and I would be a much wealthier man than I am if I could decipher its maddeningly mysterious likes and dislikes.

What I can say is that Hayley Mills exuded class. Given that fact alone, I wonder if the revamped format would have been able to fully celebrate its campy cheese factor to the extent it did for so many successful seasons and incarnations with the regal Hayley Mills at the head of our class. Remember, when we started we were up against the likes of *Bugs Bunny*, so a certain cartoonishness was expected from our scenarios and acting in order to lure away that show's viewership. Our executive producer, Peter Engel, worked hard to drive home his wholesome vision of the all-American teen: no cursing, no misbehaving, drink your milk, and everybody hug at the end. He took his mantle as the avatar of Saturday morning children's programming very seriously (never mind that he invented the concept of putting fresh-faced T&A on TV for kids first thing in the morning). When I ponder the alternative reality of a *SBTB* starring Hayley Mills, I'm inclined to say it would not have worked. Hayley would have convulsed against the material, not unlike a transplant patient's immune system rejecting an incompatible donor organ.

One day on the set of *Good Morning, Miss Bliss* we got a visit from Gentleman Gerry "The Great White Hope" Cooney, the boxer who was most famously defeated in 1982 by Larry Holmes with the "Punch Felt 'Round the World," in the biggest pay-per-view fight, with the largest prize purse ($10 million) up to that time. He was there to see Hayley because he had a crush on her. He was bouncing around backstage like a little boy. Cooney melted in Hayley's presence, his bashful eyes sweeping towards the floor, his voice softening a few octaves. Hayley was a very handsome woman who attracted many admirers—like Latino heartthrob A Martinez, who one day popped over from the set of *Santa Barbara*. He was so smitten with Hayley that he, too, instantly turned into a starry-eyed little boy in her presence. He was, like, "Do you think she'll talk to me?" But of course Hayley was eminently approachable. He threw out a cheesy opener like, "Hi, I'm A Martinez. Just 'A,' my parents couldn't afford the rest of my name." Har, har.

Cooney, the aging pugilist, though there to meet Hayley, spent most of his time off-set, regaling the male cast members, crew, and parents with tales from his life inside the ropes. Cooney had his arm wrapped firmly around my dad's neck (my dad, a massive guy, was dwarfed by Cooney). As he recounted the fight, blow-by-blow, Cooney kept jerking my dad's head down—unexpectedly and unwillingly—to mimic the technique Larry Holmes used to overpower him after twelve rounds. He described how, while hunched over in this headlock, he clocked Holmes below the belt. All the guys listening backstage doubled over in instantaneous empathy. "Good story, Champ," said my dad. "But please don't punch me in the balls."

As I said earlier, when *Good Morning, Miss Bliss* was cancelled by Disney after only thirteen episodes, the president of NBC Entertainment, Brandon Tartikoff, believed enough in the show's potential to bring it back to NBC with a new title and re-vamped cast and format. The story goes that Peter Engel wanted to change the name to *When the Bell Rings*, but Brandon convinced him to go with *Saved by the Bell*. A full season for most half-hour television series totals twenty-six episodes. But they only shot sixteen that year. That meant, in order to complete an official, full first season for syndication purposes, episodes from the original *Good Morning, Miss Bliss* had to be interspersed with the new one's from *SBTB*. That's why, when you watch that first season now, it appears so discombobulated. The way they attempted to solve the problem was by employing what became a signature narrative technique in *SBTB*: Zack's shattering of the fourth wall by talking directly to the audience Ferris Bueller-style, setting up flashbacks of what were supposedly the gang's junior-high-school experiences. He'd say, "I remember back in the day . . ." (twinkle, twinkle, twinkle), and the action would flash back to junior high. But really those are just the shows from our season as *Good Morning, Miss Bliss* at Disney. All those episodes were folded into the SBTB franchise for our eventual syndicated distribution.

In 1994, the planned merger between NBC and Disney tanked. This had the affect of hurting us kids on NBC shows when we tried to get roles in Disney projects. We were punished for not being pure Disney. It wasn't our fault, but we were made to somehow feel responsible. For instance, we would audition for in-house Disney projects and would be summarily dismissed just because we were the orphaned ghetto rabble from NBC still clinging to the railing of the ship. In my own experience with the Disney freeze-out, I lost the role as the voice of Flounder in *The Little Mermaid*. I was told at the audition that I had won the part. "We love you," they said. "It's yours." I leapt into the air I was so ecstatic! Then, in the next moment, someone shuffled some papers, leaned over and informed the director that, "Mmmm. He's one of those 'merger kids.' " So long, Flounder. So long unbelievably huge box-office success and Disney animation immortality. But I wasn't alone. Disney basically banned everyone from *Good Morning, Miss Bliss* from landing any Disney roles. As far as the studio was concerned, we were like Spartan daughters left alone in the hills to suffer and die.

Brandon was aware of all this and didn't like it. I can't say enough about Brandon Tartikoff. He was a decent man in a douchebag industry, an eagle among turkeys. I heard his daughter loved the show (she, too, was a big Screech fan), and that certainly didn't hurt Brandon's decision to give us another go at NBC with his full backing. Well, not full backing. Brandon initially only approved seven episodes for that first season back at NBC. Brandon liked us, but he was only going to dip his toe in the water. He wasn't ready to do a running cannonball into the pool. He was happy to wait and see how we fared with our new cast and format.

I have such fond memories of strolling into Brandon's office at NBC whenever I wanted. I thought I was hot shit plopping myself down in Linda Mancuso's office? Ha! Brandon was the Head Honcho, the Big Cheese, not only of NBC Entertainment, but of television itself in the 1980s. He played a personal hand in what became the most renown programs of that era: *Hill Street Blues*, *LA Law*, *ALF*, *Family Ties*, *The Cosby Show*, *Cheers*, *Miami Vice*, *The Golden Girls*, *Knight Rider*, *The A-Team*, *St. Elsewhere*, *Night Court*, *Hunter*, *Highway To Heaven*, *Matlock*, *Remington Steele*, *Punky Brewster*, *A Different World*, *Star Trek: Deep Space Nine*, and of course, *Saved by the Bell*. I mean, c'mon. Shepherding just one of these shows onto network television would qualify him for legend status, let alone all of them.

Brandon's secretary would smile as I walked straight into his office, unannounced and uninvited, any time I pleased. It was the prerogative of a precocious child. I realize now what a privilege I enjoyed being in proximity to the man while all these wonderful things were happening all around me. I would wander around his office, studying all the bric-a-brac on his shelves, or deposit myself in one of his deep, cushy chairs. Brandon was a busy man, but he made allowance for my childish impositions and always acted glad to see me. But there was always business for him to attend to, so after several minutes, he'd gently urge me back out the door.

I can't help but remember how, when *SBTB* first started, every critic and industry insider railed against it. They called us another craptacular show that was going to fall on its face and never make it. In *Entertainment Weekly*, television critic Ken Tucker, after giving the show a grade of "D," wrote, "Now in its second season, *Bell* is a ratings success, but that doesn't mean that it's edifying programming. *Bell* features stiff acting, cheap sets, and plots that seem lifted from *Happy Days* reruns . . . Forget intelligence or any talent beyond hip-swiveling as worthy attributes; in the world depicted on this program, superficiality is everything . . . High-minded and low-quality at the same time, *Bell* is depressing. Kids' TV should provide intelligent escapism, not dumb sanctimony."

Then, when we started to stick, gaining a fan base through the hard work and quirky style that eventually made us a worldwide phenomenon, those same naysayers started coming back around saying, "Congratulations. I said you deserved it. I believed in you all along. So, what's it like now to be famous?" *Fuck you, you two-faced slimeballs.* Then, the backhanded compliments started.

They would say, "Well, you've found your cornball niche in the marketplace, but it's not like you'll be nominated for any awards or anything." They fanned on that ball, too. From 1990 to 1997, *SBTB* and its cast and crew were nominated for twenty-six awards, winning six. But that's the thing about Hollyweird, everybody wants to be associated with a smash hit, but nobody knows what one looks like until it becomes one.

In 1991, Brandon left NBC after his daughter, Calla, nearly died in a car accident near their home in Lake Tahoe. Brandon was driving. Calla survived, after being in a coma for six weeks, but was severely injured. After that, Brandon pretty much shut down. Then, in 1997, at the age of forty-eight, Brandon succumbed to Hodgkins Disease, which he had battled, off and on, for almost twenty-five years. It was a sad day when that news was passed down. One thing is certain: if it hadn't been for Brandon, there would be no Screech today. You can love him or hate him for that fact alone. Of course, I love him.

Rumour had it that when General Electric bought NBC in 1986, the first order of business was to install GE light bulbs in every socket of every building at NBC. These were all perfectly functioning light bulbs that they swapped out. Before that, no one ever recalled a bulb going out. But thereafter, bulbs of all shapes and wattage blew with reckless abandon. But it was just like the days of the old monarchies when one king would immediately remove any trace of the previous regime.

The same thing, sort of, happened when Brandon left NBC Entertainment in 1990 (he would quit NBC totally the next year). Warren Littlefield, who replaced him, came in and promptly wiped out anything that might remind people of Brandon or any other fond memory of how we used to make entertainment at NBC. Littlefield and all the other new suits stalking the hallways were much less approachable than we had become accustomed to. There was definitely a pervasive new sense of fear and awkwardness. I recall thinking, "I hope I say the right thing. This dude can snap his fingers and end my show, or, at the very least, cut my role." The carefree days of strolling aimlessly into Brandon's office and flopping down into a chair had come to an end.

MEET THE CAST

St. Peter

No one wants to get caught saying something bad about the boss. We may have been working at a television studio instead of standing around the water cooler in some office complex downtown, but in most regards, every job is basically the same. We all have a guy who signs our checks and can paint over our parking space if we rub him the wrong way. And everybody likes to bitch about their job and dig up dirt about the boss. The cast, crew, and writing staff for *SBTB* were no different when it came to our executive producer, Peter Engel.

When *SBTB* first began I used to like hanging out with the writers, especially the writing team of Ron Solomon and Brett Dewey. I would bring around my Yorkshire terrier, Scooby, and Ron would help me train him. I was way into comic books, too, but I didn't like the little kids comics, I liked Marvel comics a lot but wanted to read something even more hardcore. When I'd visit with Ron and Brett in the writers' room they'd always have a cache of graphic novels and hard-to-find titles. They hooked me up with this one comic, *Boris the Bear*. Boris was a vulgar, violent, aggressive bear, and the series was a cult favorite, really hard to get, but those guys helped me complete the collection. I was around them a lot.

I remember sitting around one day with Ron, Brett, and the other writers listening to stories about Peter Engel's party days. I was stunned. Peter was a renowned born-again Christian and consummate straight arrow. His vision of *SBTB* was to create an idealized, goody-goody high school that "we all wished we went to." Saint Peter had been a party animal? Apparently so. It was one of those situations where someone offers a little tidbit, a morsel of scandal, and then, with a wink and a knowing nod, everyone agrees it's all true—but best to keep it under wraps, unless you're in a big hurry to get shit-canned from the show. It was all news to me, but apparently it was common knowledge that Peter, in his former life, had done a ton of blow and even nearly suffered an overdose. It was that experience that supposedly set him straight and on the path to finding God and salvation.

Many years later I made a comment to Peter, face to face, about his party-boy past. He turned red and didn't deny it. He simply acknowledged that "those days were gone." Which was basically an admission confirming that the stories were true. Must be nice to be born all over again. I'll keep that in the back of my mind as a possible option down the road. For now though, I've still got some partying left to do.

Every year, the cast and crew would be invited to St. Peter's Cathedral (that is, his house) in Bel-Air—which, for those who don't know, is the *rich* section of Beverly Hills—for a pool party and barbeque. Peter's house was swank, complete with a tennis court in back. I mean, a full-on Wimbledon tennis court, not some cracked-pavement parking lot with a shabby net stretched across it like you find down at your local rec field. The Engels had a daughter and two sons. I liked his sons, and they liked me and my character, Screech. Peter was enormously proud of them (*SBTB* trivia: They drew the heart logo for Peter Engel Productions). I felt a twang of sympathy though when I first saw them descend the stairs dressed in ascots, blue blazers, and short pants. I was, like, *Damn, St. Peter, let the kids be kids.* They invited me upstairs to see their toys, and I followed. After them, I was the next youngest person in the house. I was expecting to be led into a full planetarium complete with NASA telescope and real brontosaurus fossils. But no, it was just Legos. I was shocked and pleased. Plus, they had constructed a life-sized Lego statue of Screech. Just kidding.

Then the boys gave me a tour of the upstairs. We peeked into their parents' bedroom and, I kid you not, St. Peter and his wife slept in separate beds, Ozzie and Harriet-style. Peter was actually living the wholesome lifestyle he worked so hard to portray at Bayside every Saturday morning on *SBTB*.

Making this even more ridiculous was that Connie, Peter's wife, was a real beauty. A stunner. In my eyes, the original MILF. And in many ways she was very different from St. Peter. Eventually, they were divorced, which I suppose, if you're not even sleeping in the same bed, at some point just becomes a formality.

THE GOLDEN CHILD

When we moved back to NBC after our brief tenure at Disney, Peter Engel decided to alter the format from the teacher-centered storylines of *Good Morning, Miss Bliss* to the kid-centered stories that became *SBTB*. He also chose to focus the show on a main character. That main character was Zack Morris and that meant that henceforth Mark Paul Gosselaar, who played Zack, would be known as the Golden Child, enjoying all the rights and privileges that that title provided. Before landing his role as Zack on *Bliss*, Mark-Paul had made the Hollywood child-acting rounds much like I did in my early days, appearing in the usual fare such as *Highway to Heaven*, *Punky Brewster*, *Charles in Charge*, and *The Wonder Years*.

I won't lie, his coronation as the star of the show was pretty disappointing to me. I didn't expect I'd be the star, I just thought it would be a full ensemble cast. Over five thousand kids auditioned for the role of Screech, but I was the front-runner from the very beginning. During the audition process, we were each given a breakdown of that character's attributes and backstory. My character's real name was Samuel Powers, but he was called Screech because his voice was supposed to be high and crackly at all times. His very name was meant to evoke the image of nails screeching down a chalkboard. Can you imagine how annoying that would have been if I was emoting at that decibel level without any let up?

In one early audition, I asked the casting director and other gathered suits, "Do you guys seriously want me to talk this way the whole time?"

They said, "That's how the character has been envisioned."

"Well, isn't it gonna get kinda annoying for the viewers, really fast? I know I wouldn't watch that."

The suits sat back for a moment for a collective, "Hmmmmmm."

"Okay," they said, "Okay, can you just crack your voice every so often instead?"

I said (in my signature cracked voice), "Of course."

After that, I never saw another potential Screech at the callbacks.

For the role of Zack Morris, the Golden Child, the final auditions were between Mark-Paul and a dude with black hair (yes, in an alternative reality there could have been a black-haired Zack Morris). What I remember about the black-haired Zack was that he preferred to be off in his own world, doing his own thing.

Because I was the only Screech left and the final auditions were scenes with Zack and Screech together, I would approach him to see if he wanted to run lines and he'd say, "Please let me be. I'm trying to get my part down." So I went over to Mark-Paul to make the same offer. Mark-Paul was, like, "Sure. Let's do it."

They didn't seem to be able to decide between the two hair colors—which is amusing since Mark-Paul bleached his hair, even though he emphatically denied it for years. It's common knowledge now, but back in the day it would've been a scandal if word leaked out. No one was supposed to know. I don't know why it was such a big deal. *Dude, look at your eyebrows—you're not a real blonde.* But it was a huge ordeal one day when I popped my head into his dressing room to ask a question and spied his box of Sun-In Hair Lightener on the couch. Sun-In: that's how Zack Morris maintained his flaxen tresses.

When Mark-Paul and I went in for our sixth and final callback, all the network suits were there alongside as well as St. Peter Engel himself. Mark-Paul and I had run our lines together and had our timing down. Black-haired dude was on his own (and we all know how that panned out). It occurs to me now that those auditions were held in the same rehearsal hall where, years later, we would all congregate to eat our meals together during so many run-throughs and tapings of the original *SBTB*. Of course, I couldn't know that at the time. All I knew was that I was as nervous as I had ever been in my young life and that the judgment of that table full of grown ups held my future career as an actor in the balance. Fortunately, they loved us. When we got the parts, we didn't quite know how to celebrate with one another, being so young and our new kinship being so tenuous, based solely on the volatile vocation of landing a role on a new television program. The moment was amazing but our future together was uncertain at best.

I firmly believe it was the chemistry Mark-Paul and I shared that won him the role. We really fed off each other in those crucial late-audition callbacks, pushing each other to perform our best. I was Laurel to his Hardy, Costello to his Abbott, Kramer to his Seinfeld. I thought of us as a great team and figured the show would be centered on Screech as much as on Zack. But I was just an eleven-year-old kid. I had a lot to learn about the real world of Hollywood.

One of the first things the producers asked the main cast to do was to write down any special talents we had or hobbies we enjoyed. The questionnaire was designed to help the writers come up with new material. The writers had a tough job. The goal of any show is syndication and that required—at the time—at least one hundred episodes in the can (four seasons of twenty-six episodes). The were looking for any nugget of info that could help the writers spark ideas for plot lines or subplots to contribute to that steady march towards the brass ring of syndication.

Mario Lopez, who played A.C. Slater, was a California state wrestling champ and played the drums, so they worked some of those storylines into the show. Later, during *The New Class*, Natalia Cigliuti, who was a gymnast, had that talent worked into episodes. Anthony Harrell, also on *The New Class*, was a singer with his two brothers so they wrote an episode where he encounters two "strangers" whose lead singer has bailed on them. Anthony teams up with them to harmonize and save the day. If one of the *SBTB* cast members could do a standing back flip, they'd write it into the show.

I played bass guitar in a band, so naturally the writers had me play keyboard. I also played chess, enjoyed computers, video games, and martial arts—some of which they worked into Screech's character as well. Elizabeth studied dance, so she eventually portrayed that interest, and Tiffani wrote down that she liked beauty pageants and horses. Beauty pageants made it onto the show, but equestrian pursuits turned out to be a difficult hobby to work into a four-camera sitcom on a sound stage. Lark liked to wear expensive clothes in real life, so maybe that was her "talent."

I don't know what Mark-Paul wrote down, but whatever his off camera diversions may have been, they never found their way onto the show. I wonder how that conversation with the writers might have gone:

"Mark-Paul, buddy, can you sing?"

"No."

"Can you dance?"

"No."

"Play sports? Instruments? Can you juggle?"

"No."

"Do you have any interests outside showing up here and gelling your hair?"

"Um, I do have this cell phone that's the size of a loaf of bread. I like talking into that."

"And so you shall, my boy. *And so you shall.*"

When the cast for *SBTB* was finally assembled, everyone was fully three years older than me. Indeed, I remember walking along the hall in the offices at NBC on my twelfth birthday when Peter Engel stopped me and said, "Happy thirteenth birthday, Dustin!" When I told him I was only twelve, he was genuinely shocked. "Wow," he said. "If I'd known that, I never would have hired you." Thanks for the vote of confidence, dick. Glad I could help make your show a success.

Though the Golden Child did end up being a decent guy years later, I have to say that during much of *SBTB*, he was a douche. Clearly, he was a fan favorite (even though it was Screech who received the most fan mail—as many as seven thousand letters a week. And remember, this was before e-mail). Mark-Paul was a cute kid with bright (fake) golden hair and delicate, vaguely Asian features—a result of his mixed heritage (his dad, Hans, is Dutch, and his mom, Paula, is Thai). Mark-Paul's parents both had thick accents and could often be heard just off set, where Mark-Paul's mom hovered to watch with unbridled pride her genius thespian son working his onscreen mojo.

My dad would often hang out behind the scenes, too, mingling off-set with the other parents and crew. Like I said, Dad didn't suffer any bullshit. Unfortunately, rarely would he choose his battles wisely. He'd rather just shoot straight from his hip, telling people precisely how he saw things, and let the cards fall where they may. A propensity to rub someone's nose in their own B.S. isn't always the best recipe for forming fast friendships. No doubt, my dad embarrassed the hell out of me in front of other people many times. But sometimes his style was also pretty funny to behold.

One afternoon, my dad found himself standing beside Mark-Paul's mom, Paula, as she swooned over her son's innate craftsmanship in the dramatic and comedic arts, groaning ecstatically, "Oh, oh, my God. Mark-Paul's acting can move mountains."

Dad simply could not allow that one to hang in the atmosphere. "Mm," he said. "Mountains of shit."

In the early days of *SBTB*, everybody started jumping on Mark-Paul's bandwagon. For instance, if the Golden Child mentioned that he had just purchased a new CD, the next day everybody owned that CD and were bobbing their heads in rhythm to it. If he mentioned he was going out one night to see some classic piece of art-house Dutch cinema, all week long people roamed the halls raving about *Turks Fruit* or *Soldaat van Oranje* or *Spetters*. When he "discovered" a trendy Thai restaurant, suddenly for lunch everyone was going out for Tom Yam Kung and coconut soup. I'm sorry, but I just don't get excited over peanuts in every meal and a burning asshole all night long.

It just wasn't in my constitution to be such a conformist, bowing to someone else's whim and caprice. I was like, "You guys need a flashlight? It must be pretty dark so far up Mark-Paul's bunghole." They were crammed high and tight inside the nether regions of that Netherlander (well, *half*-Netherlander). Even the usually reserved, quiet and all-around boring Lark started claiming she too was of sturdy Dutch ancestry. *Dutch ancestry? Really? That's how you're choosing to curry favor with the Golden Child?* Just to set things straight, Lark is not Dutch. Her real surname is Holloway. Voorhies is just a stage name.

PUTTING THE KAPOW! IN KAPOWSKI

Tiffani-Amber Thiessen was cast as Kelly Kapowski, the pretty, popular girl, even though her character supposedly came from a big, struggling, working-class family. In real life, Tiffani had just won the Miss Junior America Beauty Pageant and *Teen* magazine's Great Model Search, so there was no question she was pretty. The problem was that she knew it. She was one of those attractive girls who think they are better than everybody else, walking around with one thought dominating her frontal lobe: "I'm hot."

Well, that's not entirely fair. When Tiffani first started, she was really sweet and humble. She would say things like, "Gosh, it's so nice to meet you. Isn't this so exciting to be on this show? I know you guys have already done the season before us, and I just hope this works out and we can all be great friends." She was just a wide-eyed young girl genuinely excited about the possibilities of the future. Everything was bright and sunshiny. That ended quick.

Once Tiffani started getting a taste of fame, she became the queen bee. I don't recall her ever actually saying, "All you bitches best avoid me when I walk into the room or I'll have you fired!" but I suspect she was thinking it. Put it this way: if she had said it, I wouldn't have been shocked.

But it was just another symptom of the disease formed by the Ultimate Situation, that being the moment St. Peter ordained Mark-Paul as the cast's Golden Child, hero of *SBTB*, and Peter's clear favorite. That's precisely when everybody did an immediate career assessment. "Hmmm," they thought, "Where's the hand that feeds?" Then they looked at St. Peter, swept their eyes down his arm and found his hand cupped firmly around Mark-Paul's Golden-Boy shoulder.

So Tiffani started taking cues from Mark-Paul right away. I remember once I made the grievous mistake of calling Mark-Paul "Mark." I got a dagger stare from the Golden Child, along with the admonition, "It's Mark-Paul, thank you." Tiffani started the show calling herself just that, but it wasn't long before she was "Tiffani Amber, thanks."

Eventually I got to know the Thiessen family, and they were all very nice to me, especially her mom, a sweet, lovely, and kind woman, who, to be delicate, was also a big woman. Knowing the apple usually doesn't fall far from the tree, I put two and two together when later, while we were on the beach in Santa Monica filming the "Malibu Sands" episodes for *SBTB*, St. Peter started to regulate our caloric intake based on TAT's genetic predisposition. (This is when Leah Remini was playing Stacey Carosi on the show, and we were filming on the beach. Leah's character had a summer-romance storyline with Zack, but there were no off-screen sparks between Leah and Mark-Paul that I knew of.)

During those Malibu Sands beach episodes, Tiffani was sporting a one-piece bathing suit and walking around with her hands casually shielding her ass. St. Peter took notice. He told her she needed to start watching what she was eating. Then, to cover his tracks, he decreed that the entire cast had to begin eating healthier. He ordered that the Kraft Food Service (which provides all the food for most Hollywood productions) stop providing any junk food like donuts, candy bars—you know, all the good stuff. From then on it was all healthy shit like whole wheat bagels, radishes, carrots, and kale—whatever that is. I hated it. Why was I made to suffer for Tiffani's fat ass? I was thin as a rail. And frankly, Tiffani's ass wasn't even that big. But this was television, and the camera really does add fifteen to twenty pounds.

This is why I say that Tiffani should have been a much nicer person than she was. She had no business being so mean because she knew that, deep inside her DNA, there was a gathering storm. I always thought that, years later, as soon as she found her true Prince Charming and said "I do," it'd be like pulling the ripcord on a life raft.

But as long as her ass was still tight, Tiffani wasn't shameful about spreading it around. In 1991, on the day we taped the "No Hope With Dope" episode, Tiffani's real-life boyfriend, Eddie Garcia, was on-set to play Hollywood heartthrob Johnny Dakota. Johnny was at Bayside to film an anti-drug public service announcement (or PSA, as they're known in the industry). Eddie was starring on another NBC comedy series called *The Guys Next Door* and had been a back-up dancer with Michael Jackson during his *Bad* album days. Eddie was a good-looking, talented kid, in addition to being probably the nicest guy in the world. He adored Tiffani and treated her like a teenage fairy-tale princess. But I felt terrible for the guy because I knew that, behind his back (and sometimes right in front of him), Tiffani was shuttling between Mark-Paul and Mario's dressing rooms.

I could even smell a certain "smoke" wafting from the crack beneath Tiffani's dressing room during one of her pit stops. She would materialize from Mark-Paul's room, pop a mint, spend some time chatting up and nuzzling Eddie, then slip away, disappearing into Mario's room. Poor, sweet Eddie. Johnny Dakota was oblivious.

That shit went on throughout the week, until Eddie finally caught Tiffani in her dressing room all tangled up with Mario. From the set, we heard Eddie explode on her, devastated that she'd been so conniving right under his nose. She had embarrassed him in front of the dozens of cast, crew, and ever-hovering network suits who, sadly, had known all along that it was Eddie who was really the one with no hope because he was being made to play Tiffani's dope. It came as no surprise when they broke up immediately following the taping of that episode.

The irony and hypocrisy behind the scenes of that episode are staggering. Johnny Dakota, the supposed "bad influence" that descends on Bayside with his wicked Hollywood ways, was played by Eddie, the nicest, most steadfast dude you'd ever want to meet. While innocent Kelly Kapowski, who was in danger of being corrupted by the lure of Johnny's reckless life in the fast lane, was played by Tiffani, who in real life was dashing between Mark-Paul and Mario's dressing rooms behind Eddy's back, toking between takes. Gotta love it.

It took many years of intense lobbying by advocates for *SBTB* to tackle any of the most pressing teen issues of the day, like drunk driving, drug use, and suicide. St. Peter was firmly against it. But at the end of "No Hope with Dope," Brandon Tartikoff spoke directly into the camera about the dangers of dope, and the episode ended up being a huge hit. I just can't help but think of all the off-camera drinking and recreational drug use being indulged in by the cast members during that time. The only place the gang at Bayside was fulfilling St. Peter's vision of the world's goody-goodiest high school was in the scripts being handed down from the writers' room.

And, boy, was Tiffani different in real life from Kelly. Rena Sofer (who recently played Marilyn Bauer on *24*, among many other TV roles) was in the cast of *SBTB: Hawaiian Style*, our one-hour special episode, which aired in November 1992. When Rena hit the set, she and Tiffani formed an instant friendship, like peas and carrots. I mean, they got spooky close. My radar told me that those two had immediately become a situation to be avoided. Rena was like Tiffani's long-lost half-sister. Every night after shooting they'd hit the Hollywood party scene. Mind you, guys aren't any different, especially guys who have an edge with a little fame and a fat roll of cash in their pockets. But, unfair as it may be, the situation is viewed much differently when it comes to the ladies. When a guy hits the late night scene, it's "What a stud." When a girl does it, it's "What a slut."

Tiffani was daddy's little girl, just on the periphery of blooming into full-blown womanhood, and her family, who were all sweethearts, were no match for her party-girl ways. It's hard enough for any parent to rein in their teenage daughter or have any influence on her personal decisions. It's damn near impossible when that teenage girl makes fists full of her own money, can buy whatever she wants, has a red carpet rolled out in front of her wherever she goes, flies and stays everywhere first class, and enters every room to a delirious chorus of "I love you."

A.C. Makes the Ladies Scream

For television hunks, the lucky ones shuttle around from gig to gig for decades. Remember those "Milk, It Does a Body Good" commercials? In one of them, there's a little Latino kid who looks into the camera and says, "Hey, Mr. Moo, whadya say?" He tosses a basketball over his shoulder, and it swishes through the hoop. "Fresh moo juice makes my day." That's Mario Lopez.

The first time I met my new cast mates for *SBTB* was when we were all ushered into a small, bare, windowless room at NBC Studios containing a single table. Mark-Paul, Lark, Dennis, and I sat on one side, and Tiffani, Elizabeth, and Mario sat on the other. It was a typical, first-day-of-school kind of moment for all of us. Sort of a non moment, actually, though I do recall staring in rapt wonderment at the permed mullet of the swarthy Latino in the neon, sleeveless tank.

Mario was a man-whore. I mean, so was I eventually, hell, so are most guys at some point in their lives if they can get away with it. But Mario's vain sexcapades during his years on *SBTB* culminated in a weird, twisted scandal that ended with a team of NBC attorneys quietly paying off one of his numerous sexual conquests.

Mario was a womanizer from day one. He made it blatantly obvious that he was on an eternal quest for fresh tang. He got a lot of mileage out of those dimples and that winning smile. Even before he would go out in front of the audience for opening bows—for all the underage girls to scream and cheer for him (which sounds pretty amazing, but don't forget, this was concurrent with New Kids on the Block, so really, what the fuck do little girls know, anyway?)—Mario would be on the floor backstage doing pushups to juice his arms and pecs, summoning a patina of perspiration to accentuate his chiseled physique beneath those big, 20K studio lights. *Dude? Dude? Do my arms look bigger?* Yes, Mario was *that* guy. The funniest part about that is that Mario started working out *waaay* too early in life—when he was twelve. So, as he aged, he developed these weird, saggy, old man boobs that looked like Ziploc bags half-filled with water. It started in the area beneath his pecs, like the muscle was starting to tear free. I don't know how exactly to describe it. I would glance over while we changed between scenes and say, "You getting a little boobage there, buddy?" That pissed him off. He was clearly aware and self-conscious about it. He said, "Leave me alone, man." I don't know if he had plastic surgery for it but I do recall him going away for a while, and when he returned, his man boob conundrum had improved dramatically.

Other than a fierce interest in the ladies, about the only thing Mario and I had in common was a head of thick, curly hair. There's not much you can do with curly hair. For each of the original cast members on *SBTB*, their hair on the set wasn't much different from the way they wore it in real life. Everybody looks back at previous hair styles (the 1980s, for instance), and we say to ourselves, "God Almighty, what was I thinking?" My hair today is shorter, but relatively the same as it always was. I also have facial hair today, and always wanted to grow it years ago, but that was a major no-no while playing Screech. (Too bad we never did an episode where Screech holes up in a cabin deep in the woods, writing his manifesto.) I did let my beard grow during our off-weeks and hiatuses, but would promptly shave it before arriving back on set. The girls wore their hair in bangs, except for Elizabeth, who couldn't really pull it off (once again, that unruly challenge of naturally curly hair). Well, maybe not bangs in her hair, but later, when *Showgirls* was released, we learned she could certainly pull off the bang lifestyle—on screen, at least. But nobody's hairstyles went through more changes than those of the phony, pretentious Hollywood-douche-squad duo of Mark-Paul and, in particular, Mario.

Mark-Paul sported that golden, feathered mop jutting out like the deck of an aircraft carrier. But Mario, he took first prize with that Menudo-inspired permed mullet. I should thank Mario for allowing me to experience such enjoyment: viewing that hairstyle every day provided me with greatly satisfying laughter for many years. I kind of hope that Mario loses his hair up top but grows it out long again in the back as he ages. A skullet would be the only way he could top his *SBTB* hairstyle.

Despite his unfortunate styling, Mario was a bully. On the other hand, his parents were the salt of the earth—truly cool, sweet people. He grew up in Chula Vista near San Diego, where there was a lot of gang activity in the neighborhoods near his home. Some of his buddies from those neighborhoods were bangers, and when we would appear at events in Oceanside or on the outskirts of San Diego, friends of Mario's would show up, and he would get plenty brave in numbers. Mind you, Mario was a state wrestling champion, so he was comfortable getting in some dude's face if the dude mouthed off at him—or even if he hadn't. Mario did enjoy making his snide comments, and if you objected, he got right up in your face. *What? What'd you say? Say it again, I dare you.* That sort of shit. The writers even started working some of that real-life aggression into episodes of *SBTB*. Better to go with the flow of a hard-charging river than try swimming against the current, I guess.

All Mario's aggression and anger issues made me think, "Man, you're a TV star, you can't be going around getting into fist fights. One of these days you're gonna get jammed up. You're gonna lose your cool and punch some dude who was mouthing off, pushing you over the line, just so he could sue the shit out of you." Or, I thought, Mario might punch the wrong dude, get his ass handed to him, and lose his cushy TV job as a result. I think St. Peter would have frowned upon Slater missing all his front teeth. Hell, this was L.A.; he could even have wound up stabbed fifty times in an alley or shot in the face on the freeway. But Mario was always confident that there was no trouble too big for him to handle. He was sure he could manage anything that came his way. Until, of course, he was accused of rape.

Mario used to hit on every co-star, every extra, every production assistant, and every fan he found himself standing next to. It was a game of averages, but the truth is that most of these girls were so dumb they would hook up with him without much effort on his part. Mostly this was because they were expecting to get somewhere in their "acting" careers, but that was a very silly notion indeed. You could always tell when Mario had finally banged the chick he was after because it was like flipping a switch. He wouldn't have anything else to do with her. Just like on TV when the girl finally gives in, allowing the school stud to deflower her, only to have him stroll right past her in the hall the next day while she stands at her locker, humiliated.

We had a lot of guest stars over the years that went on to bigger work. Hot chicks like model Kathy Ireland (who, after she was cast as a nurse, didn't work out at the Monday table read, so the producers replaced her the next day) and Bridgette Wilson, who played Ginger for five episodes in the original *SBTB*'s senior-year season then went on to star in *Last Action Hero, Billy Madison, Mortal Kombat,* and many other feature films before settling down with tennis legend Pete Sampras. Mario usually took a run at all these-type chicks, and often he succeeded.

Denise Richards, of Bond-girl and Charlie Sheen ex-wife fame, appeared in one of the beach episodes where A.C. Slater saves her from drowning. Mario's lip-locking resuscitation technique also extended back to his trailer after taping. Just another notch on

Mario's bedpost. These girls kept cycling through Mario's revolving dressing room door, and after a while you just had to feel bad for them. Another one lured in by Mario? How can they not see through his cheesy game?

In his heyday, Mario even had the balls to bang one of the female executives from Rysher Entertainment, the company that distributed *SBTB* in syndication. She used to show up at the set all smiles and touchy-feely. Obviously their relationship was supposed to be a secret, but we always knew who was banging whom. That bootie call was an angle Mario worked for a long time, weaseling his way into solo invites to all kinds of cool events through the distributor. In 1994, I think Mario landed the role as host of the Family Channel's *Masters of the Maze* as a direct result of his relationship with that Rysher exec. Sometimes that's just how Hollywood works: you calculate who you can schmooze in bed to get your next job. People will refuse to admit it, they'll deny it up and down, but that's the way it works. It's the underbelly of the industry. It often comes down to, not how talented you are or even who you know, but who you bone. Sex greases the machine. Tiffani starts to date Brian Austin Green, and BAM! . . . she's on *90210*. (And she didn't get the TV show Fast Lane for her awesome acting ability, either.) It's especially difficult for the girls (or easy, depending on your perspective). As the story goes, as soon as Marilyn Monroe inked her first big studio contract, she turned and announced, "Well, I'll never have to suck another cock again!"

Learning from Mario the Master, this Machiavellian approach to the business bang later took root in my own sex-addled brain during *The College Years*, when I started hooking up with a girl in our production office at Sunset-Gower Studios. She handled the checks for all the talent and staff, so I was able to learn what everyone else was making for salary. Very interesting.

But if you're playing a game of averages, it's just a matter of time before you get burned. For Mario, that day arrived in the form of a girl who claimed she was lured back to his pad, which was not really his pad but a guest house in the yard behind his parents' house, and was forced to have sex against her will. She claimed she screamed no, and Mario wouldn't stop. She claimed she had the marks and bruises to prove her allegations. She also claimed she'd had a vaginal clock exam administered. That's a test that measures whether or not vaginal muscles have been forcibly damaged by penetration. The name derives from the clinical stance that mild bruising at the ten o'clock and two o'clock positions tends to indicate consensual sex, while bruising at the seven o'clock and five o'clock positions is more consistent with rape. No bones about it, the tune she was singing was full-on, "Mario raped me."

Everyone was shocked that Mario had been accused of such behavior. I was like, "Huh? Excuse me, this dude is the ultimate poon hound." Mario often made it known through his physical intimidation that he was ultimately going to get what he wanted. He didn't take no for an answer. Had no one been paying any attention to how he was spending his leisure hours?

Like an army of red ants, NBC's lawyers materialized out of every corner and crevice. NBC quickly decided it had to protect its interest, which was Mario. The image NBC wanted portrayed was one of glitz and glamour, and this bit of squalid behavior definitely did not fit with that. So when the girl threatened to file formal charges and go to the press, the lawyers at NBC decided to settle with her fast, in cash and out of court. Essentially, they paid her off to keep her mouth shut. And my understanding is that it wasn't a boatload of cash, either: somewhere in the neighborhood of fifty grand. Not a very big payday for such strong allegations against a famous television star. But at least one person was very happy. That stiff, westerly breeze you may have felt in the early '90s was most likely Mario Lopez's giant sigh of relief.

So the matter was hushed up successfully and completely. Even in 2002, when the E! Entertainment Network's *E! True Hollywood Story* episode on *SBTB* came out, they never mentioned Mario's rape accuser or the cash payoff that kept her quiet.

The Showgirl

Elizabeth Berkley played the gawky, nerdy chick Jessie Spano, and today she's most remembered for two things: (a) going from *SBTB* to showing her tits in *Showgirls* and (b) her landmark acting performance in the episode "Jessie's Song."

That episode was another example of *SBTB* taking on the hard-hitting issues of the day. In that case, it was the rampant epidemic of teen addiction to caffeine pills. Remember the congressional hearings back in 1990? I sure do. The episode resulted in the most quoted line in *SBTB* history, delivered by a twitching Elizabeth Berkley: "I'm so excited, I'm so excited . . . I'm so scared." *How ridiculous was that scene?* I was on set saying, "Okay, lemme get this straight . . . she's had the equivalent of three Mountain Dews, and we're carting her off to the Betty Ford Clinic?" I may have been laughing, but Elizabeth, and everyone else on set, was deadly serious.

Elizabeth Berkley's performance in that caffeine-addiction episode is completely without irony or insincerity. She did not secretly believe that the plot or the dialogue she had to deliver was corny or unrealistic. She truly put her all into the severity and gravitas of that moment when Zack held, then shook her, on her aggressively pink bedroom set. It was Elizabeth's full-court press for a daytime Emmy nomination. The firm consensus afterward was that she had nailed it and that she was a fine actress indeed.

Am I shitting you? My friend, I shit you not.

Acting aside, Elizabeth, like everyone else, was extremely sweet in the beginning, but the Hollywood bug soon bit her, too. That's not to say we didn't have our share of fun times together. Like the time I showed her my humongous dong.

Mark-Paul, Mario, Elizabeth, and I were hanging out on-set one day, joking around with each other. The guys were saying things to Elizabeth like, "You couldn't handle my junk, it's in 3-D" and "One day they'll build statues honoring our man bags." Stupid teen stuff like that. Elizabeth laughed it off and made a dismissive comment, something like, "Well, I'll be holding auditions later. Just forward me your 'head' shots and resumes." That was all Mark-Paul needed to hear. He promised her we'd take pictures of our tackle and deliver them to her by the end of the business day. She laughed us off, assuming we were full of shit.

The three of us huddled up and decided to each take a Polaroid of our dick and slide it under Elizabeth's door. We convulsed in hysterics, convinced this was the greatest plan ever hatched. Mark-Paul snatched a camera, and we handed it off to one another, retreating to our private, yet well-lit, areas to snap a shot of our one-eyed goblins. Then, one-by-one, we slid our photos under Elizabeth's dressing room door. Except that, afterward, Mark-Paul and Mario informed me that they were just fucking with me. They didn't actually do it. *Holy Fuck!*

Imagine reconstructing poor Elizabeth's thought process when it began to dawn on her that little (well, as it turns out, not-so-little) Dustin Diamond—Screech—had slid a Polaroid of his angry flesh baton under her door for no apparent reason. How's that for a calling card? *Um, Elizabeth, will you be my Valentine?*

Elizabeth (eventually) threw away the photo, strategically tossing it on top of the garbage in the trash bin of the communal rest room. It wasn't long before everyone backstage had gotten a good look at Dustin Jr. Afterward, Mark-Paul and Mario—through tears of laughter—were happy to fill in the details for anyone who would listen. Around the set, it became a big running joke. I guess if I'd been a smaller man I would have been mortified. But I felt comforted that Elizabeth spent those crucial first moments puzzling over why she was staring at a photo of a naked man with three legs.

I found out later from a girl I knew that, while she was on an audition with Elizabeth, she had recounted that whole penis Polaroid episode in veiny detail. In fact, I learned from various sources that it was a story she enjoyed telling her girl friends. Glad to make such a big impression.

Showgirls was released in 1995. We all went to see it and were eager to support Elizabeth, but there was no getting around the fact the film sucked. After its immediate thrashing by the critics, no one had the heart to point out that people were only paying to see the tits and crotch of that tall, "feminist" chick from *SBTB*. Including us. To put this in its proper generational context, if today the Olsen twins were to pose together nude in *Playboy*, it would be the best selling issue ever. I kid you not.

Weirdly, *Striptease*, starring Demi Moore, was released the following year and was almost as—perhaps even more—horrific. How could Hollywood spend a combined $100 million on two films packed with beautiful naked chicks and turn them into turkeys? If *Showgirls* was Elizabeth's *Armageddon*, then S*triptease* was Demi's *Deep Impact*. Same shit, different actress.

But us guys on the cast saw the girls naked all the time—it was the *theater*. Technically, we weren't supposed to be able to see anything, and the girls and everyone in wardrobe tried their darnedest to hide them from us, but when you're walking backstage between scenes, and the girls are doing quick changes, you can only do your best to respect their privacy. But sometimes your best just isn't good enough. There was a black curtain to shield quick costume changes, but after years of constant familiarity with the same people, such Puritan decorum eventually breaks down. So no, for me it wasn't that big a deal; *Showgirls* was not the first time I'd seen Elizabeth naked. For the crew, network suits and staff though—especially St. Peter—I'm sure it was a much different viewing experience. For her part, Elizabeth became much more comfortable with her body after *Showgirls*. She talked about having to be naked in front of dozens of people all day on the set of the film. She definitely never tried to hide her figure on the set or behind the scenes of *SBTB* after her first big movie-making experience. She wasn't walking around with her tits hanging out, but her demeanor and her attire had definitely changed. She had become a woman.

There wasn't much of an official NBC response to Elizabeth's decision to do the film. Mostly, it was just a lot of awkward moments in the hallway, "Hey, Liz. Great, uh, movie. Definitely gonna watch it again more closely on home video. Frame by glorious frame." I guess it's worth mentioning too that I never heard St. Peter breathe a word about *Showgirls*. Then again, he never really had to tackle *Showgirls* head-on. It wasn't long after it premiered that Elizabeth refused to renew her contract to complete the final season, and she was gone.

Recently, Elizabeth popped up on *CSI: Miami* as Julia Winston, Horatio Caine's love interest (once more, a slutty temptress.) I just heaved a heavy sigh. After *Showgirls*, she was typecast as the skank: *Any Given Sunday* (prostitute), First Wives Club (skankity skank skank), et cetera. But *CSI: Miami* kind of bugged me. This was the number-one show in my rotation—shit, the number-one show in the world. There she was, invading my home screen. I'm sorry, I just can't watch her as a serious actress. I was just a few feet away for that "I'm so excited . . . I'm so scared" performance. I still wake up in cold sweats.

And I'm so familiar with all her backstage escapades, like when she fooled around with Mark-Paul and Mario as Tiffani's sloppy seconds. Elizabeth had a whole different approach from Tiffani's. To compare her and Tiffani, I would say that Tiffani was the I'm-better-than-everyone-else, chick-with-an-air-about her, Paris Hilton-style girl, living in the Hollywood spotlight. Whereas

Elizabeth seemed to party around more for attention—to be want-ed, or more accurately, needed. There was a desperation to Eliza-beth's ho'ing, like she had a lot of catching up to do. It wouldn't have surprised me if Elizabeth walked in one end of the dressing room while Tiffani was exiting out the other. Like down at the corner deli: "Take a number . . . Next!" But on the Royal-Party-Girl scale, Tiffani was most definitely the queen, while Elizabeth was more like a minor duchess, living off somewhere in the hill country.

ME, SCREECHING TRUTH TO POWER

I was always something of an outsider on the set. The biggest reason was that I was a few years younger than everyone else. When *SBTB* started at NBC, I was twelve, and Mark-Paul, Tiffani, and the others were all around fifteen or sixteen. At that age, a few years makes all the difference. They were fully teenagers, living like adults, and I was still a kid. But the source of the biggest rift between me and the rest of the cast wasn't my age. It was my lack of interest of kissing the ass of the Golden Child.

Because everybody knew Mark-Paul was St. Peter's favorite, everybody wanted to be best friends with Mark-Paul. Just because we were kids doesn't mean we were immune to the rules of Hollywood—or the rules of any actual high school, for that matter. Theory: Proximity to powerful and popular people helps one rise quickly up the ladder of life. But if someone was being a douche, I didn't want to hang out with them. And Mark-Paul was usually being a douche. Simple as that. I always thought that was a good way to conduct myself, but behind the scenes of *SBTB* that attitude made me Public Enemy Number One.

Once I took up opposition to the Golden Child, I instantly became the cast's whipping boy. A lot of it was stupid shit when I think about it now, but at the time, being so much younger than the others, being ostracized by the group really stung. I remember one stupid encounter right after M.C. Hammer's megahit, "Can't Touch This" had just come out. Everybody was singing it; it played on the radio ad nauseam—Hammer's ubiquitous shimmy-shammying back-and-forth in his gold lamé genie pants. Anyway, I was on the school set playing the song on my boom box. Elizabeth was sitting there singing, "Dum-da-da-dum, Can't help it!"

Huh?

At this point I was administering a sort of self-imposed silent treatment with the rest of the cast for what I had perceived as efforts to keep me at a distance as the odd man out, like when the cast would buy gifts for each other and all conveniently forget me. I'm not trying to paint a whole "woe is me" portrait, I just feel that, if you're going to watch a play, you need to know who the players are. But the silent treatment never lasts very long. You find yourself talking again in no time flat, rambling on until you suddenly catch yourself and think, "Shit! I'm supposed to be giving you assholes the silent treatment."

That was the situation when I heard Elizabeth mangling the lyrics. I just had to set her straight. Politely, I said, "Uh, 'Can't touch this.' "

Elizabeth said, "What?"

"M.C. Hammer's song. The refrain is 'Can't touch this.' "

"No it isn't."

"I think that . . ."

"I don't give a fuck what you think. It's 'Can't help it.' "

Then Tiffani chimed in, "Dustin, you're so stupid. Everyone knows it's 'Can't help it.' "

So I played it again, over and over, certain that would settle the matter. Surely their ears functioned properly when they were fully focused on a single task. They continued to deny me. It reached a point where I wanted to beat them over the heads with my boom box. I thought, "They can't be this stupid!" And maybe they weren't. Probably they weren't. They were just fucking with me to make me feel small and insignificant—to remind me of my proper place, far outside the group.

Sometimes the shit they babbled on about was positively mind-boggling. I had to wonder if they were being serious or just choosing to be obstinate because banding together behind a contrarian viewpoint was more interesting or amusing for them than being friendly. But I have to say, in all honesty, I thought they were just idiots. Like when the first *Nightmare on Elm Street* flick came out and everyone was talking about how scary Freddy Krueger was. I loved the film and was a big fan of the franchise, but what threw me for an absolute fucking loop was the aspect of Freddy they found most terrifying. Let me put it to you: When you picture Freddy Krueger, what characteristic of that character frightens you the most?

That freaky leather hand contraption with the razor knives

gleaming from each fingertip? His horrific melted face? His penchant for stabbing nubile teens?

Mark-Paul, whenever anyone on the set would ask about the movie, would say, "I just couldn't watch it. That sweater . . . That sweater! It was horrible."

Really?!

You thought the most terrifying aspect of Freddy Krueger was his *sweater*? But sure enough, everyone fell in line with this opinion, and would shudder at Freddy's sartorial horror. . It's like saying that the most terrifying thing about Jason was that he couldn't swim . . . idiots.

Another time, on Lisa's bedroom set, Mark-Paul was sitting with Tiffani-*Amber* and Elizabeth during one of the breaks. I tried to mosey up to the group and Tiffani snapped at me, "Why don't you go fuck yourself?" Strict as St. Peter was, profanity on set was obviously the ultimate taboo. I said, "Aw, that's real nice. Why don't I go tell Peter what you just said? I'm sure he'd love to hear how his darling child is choosing to structure her sentences with such colorful language."

Tiffani said, "I'll say it again: Go fuck yourself. Go ahead, tell him. Who's he gonna believe? You? Or us?"

Us?

That wasn't the last time one of the cool kids got away with something I could never pull off. Like the time in one episode when Zack was supposed to nail Screech with a water balloon. The problem was, Mark-Paul kept hitting me with the balloon, but it wouldn't burst. The director and crew came up with the idea of me holding a sharpened pencil in my hand, trying my best to angle it towards the point of impact for maximum splatter. It didn't matter, though, because in the next take, while Mark-Paul was menacingly holding the balloon, the thing exploded in his hand. That kind of mishap was a big deal. It meant the whole production had to shut down while Mark-Paul went through hair and make-up all over again and, hopefully, wardrobe had an exact replica handy of every stitch of clothing he was wearing or we would all have to sit even longer while his costume tumbled around in the dryer. Perhaps Mark-Paul immediately grasped the gravity of this blooper the instant it occurred because he blurted out, "Oh shit!" in front of a live studio audience.

He showed instantaneous remorse, apologizing profusely for the gaff, which probably ameliorated St. Peter's wrath—that is, after the audience's hysterical laughter subsided. After all, he was the Golden Child.

Moments like those really brought it home for me. That's when it was perfectly clear that a line was drawn between the rest of the cast—the older, cooler kids—and me. If I really was Samuel "Screech" Powers, the character I played on TV, I would've just hung my head and slinked away as we mixed sad music and cut to commercial. But in real life I've never been the kind of person who turns the other cheek. I'm a big fan of what I call justice.

And the cast weren't the only ones who would feel my wrath. There was this extra, turned bit-part actress, on *SBTB*. She was a real skank. She thought she was, super hot because she was slender with long, dark hair and exotic features, the kind of chick that in Hollywood is a dime a dozen. She was a slut. Her goal was to fuck Mark-Paul and/or Mario and/or anyone else she could screw into wrangling her a regular role on the show. She made that plan perfectly known. One day we were all hanging out on set during a break. She turned and said something really insulting to me. I thought, "Bitch, you're a fucking extra. I may play the nerd, but I'm one of the stars of the show. You can be replaced in a heartbeat."

The worst part was that Mark-Paul and Tiffani laughed, validating her comment and her attitude towards me. It appeared that I would have to take matters into my own hands. Sometimes, you just have to show people where they fall in the pecking order. So when the extras went to lunch in the NBC commissary, I grabbed her purse, took it into the restroom, and pissed in it. The punishment, I felt, definitely fit the crime. So beware. Don't rub me the wrong way, or I might hide a turd in your pocket.

Lisa Turtle and Her Shell

Lark Voorhies played Lisa Turtle, after whom Screech would endlessly pine. But practically the only time I heard Lark speak was when there were lines for Lisa Turtle in the script. Lark was bizarre. She was always extraordinarily low key and pretty much kept to herself, which was no doubt due in large part to her strict faith as a Jehovah's Witness. In fact, she could possibly be in the room with you right now, while you're reading this book, and you wouldn't even know it. Lark was also very beautiful and came from a nice, upper-class family. On top of that, she was soft-spoken, so much so that the director would often ask her to repeat her lines more loudly. "There's an audience here, Lark. They can't hear you in back."

Lark started coming around and hanging out more towards the end of *SBTB*, around the time her character began to take an interest in Zack. From my perspective, Lark's time on the show broke down like this: She came in and said, "Okay, I'm surrounded by sin but, I'm a good, wholesome religious girl. I'm not going to get sucked into the temptation and evil of this Hollywood world. I'll do my job, get my work done, get in, and get out." Then she probably thought to herself, "Hm, clearly there is a hierarchy here. To smooth my path, I'm going to get close to those I see are the favorites." When she started to feel she was being accepted into that group, she thought, "Hey, I've been living a little uptight for too long. I think I might stretch my wings, just a bit, to see how it feels. Nothing crazy. Just test the waters." She started off by having her little hissy fits directed at me, always when the others were around. Finally, she came all the way around with the inevitable sucking up to Mark-Paul. They went off and tried to have their own little relationship, only by that time, Lark was sloppy thirds. And that's sloppy. There didn't seem to be any real spark or attraction there anyway, no real desire between them. They were just going through the motions.

The writers worked it into the show that Zack was horning in on Screech's girl. Screech catches them kissing backstage at Lisa's fashion show as the audience purrs, "OooOOOooo." I knew that the relationships in front of the camera often continued after the red light turned off. It's like my cast mates couldn't separate reality from their characters on the show—clearly the mark of truly gifted actors. Not. If you ever want to know who was with whom off-camera on *SBTB*, it's easy: just go pick up the DVDs.

Unfortunately, what comes to mind these days when I think of Lark was the bizarre experience of meeting up with her again after so many years when we came together to do the audio commentary for the DVD version of *SBTB*. Since I'd last seen her, Lark had been briefly engaged to actor and comedian Martin Lawrence (he gives a dedication to her on one of his comedy albums). Unfortunately, that engagement abruptly ended when, on the *Arsenio Hall Show*, Martin announced his plans to marry another woman. At the DVD commentary recording session, I was happy to see Lark. I said, "Hey, what's going on?"

Her response—her whole body language—was freakishly distant. She was weirdly aloof and had no desire to engage in any form of communication. When we were all miked up and rolling on the DVD commentary, Lark never uttered a word. The sound technician in the booth gently suggested, "Lark, could you add something?"

When he spoke, she flinched.

After the recording session, I was concerned. I called Lark to see if she was feeling all right. Almost every answer was, "Uh huh" or "Mm hm" or "Okay." She told me she had started a production company and that she was doing fine. I acknowledged that we'd fallen out of touch over the years but encouraged her to call me anytime. "Oh yeah," she said. "Sure, sure."

Now you can take from it what you will, but here are the facts.

A) She flinched whenever a man was near her or a man's voice was suddenly projected toward her.

B) She rocked back and forth mumbling to herself in a very disturbing fashion, as if in her own world.

You can draw your own conclusions from that but, for some reason, Lisa Turtle, never that outgoing to begin with, had completely retreated into her shell.

THE PRINCIPAL

The principal of Bayside High was, of course, Mr. Belding, played by Dennis Haskins. He also appeared with me in *SBTB: The College Years* and *SBTB: The New Class*, so I got to know the man well, and I'm still good friends with him. I called him "The Man From Everywhere."

Why? you ask.

At NBC, the *SBTB* cast had adjoining dressing rooms separated by sliding pocket doors that were by no means soundproof. I could hear everything going on next door. For an entire season, Den had the dressing room adjoined with mine. I love Den, but the first thing I learned was that he was a very ambitious opportunist. Whenever he saw someone cruise past his door that he thought could help his career, he pounced like a predator from the tall grass. I don't blame the guy for it. In Hollywood, you need to seize every chance you get to expand your network of contacts. You're your own best salesman in a business where you're the product. But Den had a pitch that I've never heard before or since. He must have spent his leisure hours researching inane facts about every city, town, village, and hamlet in America. No matter the place, he knew something—however minute—about every bustling metropolis or stagnating backwater the person he was talking with could mention. I would overhear him talking to people on the phone and in the hallways. Den engaged in one of these typical conversations with *Wings* star Crystal Bernard, whom I knew from when I appeared on the sitcom It's a Living as a young Paul Kreppel (I had a huge crush on her back then). Crystal was appearing on *The Tonight Show* (we shared a soundstage with them). Her conversation with the Man From Everywhere went something like this:

DEN: Hey, Crystal, where you from?

CRYSTAL: Garland, Texas.

DEN: Garland, Texas?! That's my hometown!

CRYSTAL: Really, because it's kinda small . . .

DEN: Hey, did they ever wind up restoring that old church steeple? I hope so, because it was so beautiful.

CRYSTAL: Um, yes actually. They did.

DEN: Good. Good. That holds such a special place in my memory. Hang on a sec, I'm gonna give you a head shot.

Of course Den wasn't from Garland, or Baltimore or Detroit or Minneapolis St. Paul or American Samoa or wherever else the person he was talking with said they were from—unless it was Chattanooga, Tennessee, which is where I'm pretty sure he's actually from, but I can't be one hundred percent certain. That was just his "in," his conversational icebreaker, but the Man From Everywhere was bullshitting everybody.

At one point Den got married, but he didn't invite anybody from the show to the wedding. He may have done it in Vegas. He brought his new wife to the set and introduced her to everyone, feeling pretty good about himself. "Excuse me dear," said Den, hitching up his trousers, "I've gotta get to work."

The harder Den worked, the more money she got because they were soon divorced. She took him for everything. That definitely jaded him against chicks for a long while. Ours was a weird relationship because it went from Den only knowing me as a little kid to, at the end, us becoming buddies.

One more thing on Den: the dude had no game. Every television show has stand-ins who take the place of the actor during certain aspects of blocking, lighting, and scene setup. We had many stand-ins over the years of *SBTB*, some who stuck around for a while and some who were just passing through. There was one girl I always liked named Penny Nichols. At the time, if I had to guess, I'd say Penny was in her mid-twenties. She later played Roxanne Rubio in a 1994 episode of one of Peter Engel's other NBC shows for tweens, *California Dreams*. Penny was a pretty, pale-skinned redhead with sort of elfin features. She was normal-sized, though some stand-ins in Hollywood, particularly for shows featuring children, are little people.

Penny always wore black clothes with boots, but she wasn't

some Emo-Goth by any stretch. We shared an interest in horror flicks and obscure metal bands, so I was drawn to her. There was no physical or romantic relationship, I just enjoyed spending time with her. And, I thought she was really hot.

After his divorce, Den was never very lucky in love. He used to offer Penny impromptu backrubs without much willing acceptance, much less reciprocity. Den was never real smooth with the ladies. His massage technique was more akin to that awkward rubdown President George W. Bush gave Angela Merkel, the chancellor of Germany, in 2006. I wasn't privy to all the gossip, but I do remember one day, when Penny and Den were sitting together up in the stands, Penny screamed at Den, "Fuck off!"

In all the years she worked on *SBTB*, no one ever heard Penny talk like that. She was crying and very upset. She didn't want to be anywhere near Den. I asked Penny what happened, and she said everything was fine and didn't want to discuss it. Everyone was staring up at Den seated alone in the stands. It was an extremely uncomfortable moment. Den rose slowly and tried slinking out the stage door. Later, when I asked him what happened, he said, "I don't know, she just freaked out and started acting weird." That's as far as he would go towards an explanation. After that explosion, Den would never be seen anywhere near Penny again.

Taking It to The Max

Ed Alonzo played Max, proprietor and magician-in-residence of The Max diner and all-purpose hangout for the gang at Bayside, in nineteen episodes between 1989 and 1992. Ed was an accomplished magician in real life and shared an enormous magic and prop studio warehouse with that wordsmith of male pattern baldness, that prankish pummeller of picnic fruit, Gallagher.

Ed also used to perform on Michael Jackson's private stage at Neverland Ranch. When I heard that Ed performed there, I begged him, "Dude, can you take me with you next time?" He agreed, but when the day arrived, for some reason I can't explain except to regard it as pure intuition, I decided to back out and stay home. There was a powerful voice in the deep recesses of my gray matter that boomed, "Don't Go!"

I recall traveling with Ed and one of his hot wives (perhaps

his second) to Missouri, I think St. Louis, for a charity event. All
I remember is that it was God awful hot and sticky. I also remember that I was instructed to zip Ed's wife into her sparkly stage
costume, during which I enjoyed a panoramic view of her spec-
tacular breasts. I was, like, *Dude, I'm looking at your wife's rack.
Doesn't this bother you?* But Ed was in his own magical world,
preparing his implements of deception to delight that night's audience.

Later, I was on stage to assist Ed in one of his tricks, where he
made a bird suddenly appear in an empty cage. Ed presented an
egg for the wide-eyed children, who crowded the stage to inspect.
He then smashed the egg into the cage. This released a trap door,
which sprung open, depositing the bird into the cage. At this point
let's just say the bird in question had had difficulty with the Midwestern heat and humidity inside its secret hiding space. I held
the cage aloft for all to ogle as, in a grand gesture, Ed opened the
tiny door and in a practiced flourish called out, "It's magic!" The
dead bird thereupon fell to the stage like a feathered paperweight.
Realizing what had happened, Ed, the consummate pro, took advantage of the audience's momentary disorientation by smoothly
scooping up the carcass and handing it off to wife number two. He
then moved quickly on to his next illusion.

In 1987, I played Big Z in a film called *The Purple People
Eater* alongside Dr. Doogie Howser himself, Neil Patrick Harris, who, by the way, was an asshole. He strode around set like
the cock of the walk; the de facto star of the picture—sort of like
a poor man's Mark-Paul Gosselaar. Look, I'm not trying to hate
on Neil Patrick (another member of the Hollywood Two-First-

Names Club), but a lot of these child stars were incredibly full of themselves and their overblown accomplishments (admittedly, I include myself in that category, but only on occasion).

But what's important to this story is that Neil Patrick Harris loved magic. Loved it! Hey, I'm not knocking it—I loved magic, too. My dream was to learn every card trick in the magician's repertoire then hop a plane in a full assault on the tables at Vegas. I was, like, ten years old. If magic was the drug, Ed Alonzo was the dealer. He had what Neil Patrick and I were jonesing for. Ed would perform many of his stage tricks on the set of *SBTB*, which was cool because he allowed us to see behind the action where all the trickery came into play. Another joy of having Ed on the set for his episodes was that whatever wife he had at any given time was fucking smokin' (his first wife especially). But despite Ed's matrimonial status and his overt flirtations with his magician's assistants, there was always something, I don't know, shall we say, flamboyantly enthusiastic about his demeanor.

One day, Ed invited my dad and me to his magical warehouse. Wandering around the cavernous space we saw Gallagher's over-sized tricycle, the giant couch, his octopus suit, etc. Ed even gave me one of Gallagher's beer guns—a device wherein you load a can of beer or soda, puncture it with the trigger and direct your stream of carbonation at some hapless victim. My dad and I had a great time, and I made plans with Ed to come back for another visit. But later Ed cancelled, informing me that he had accidentally scheduled over some quality time he was spending with his new best pal, Neil Patrick Harris.

The D-man getting passed over for the Doog? Say it ain't so!

Ed wound up spending a lot of time with Neil Patrick Harris. A lot of time. For a while they were inseparable, going away to perform magic together, conjuring their mystical spells of enchantment.

It wasn't until years later that Neil Patrick Harris announced that he was gay.

PART II:

HOW THE MAGIC HAPPENED:
A WEEK IN THE LIFE OF *SBTB*

MONDAY

Monday morning, around 8:00 or 9:00 AM, everyone would shuffle in one-by-one, wiping the weekend haze of booze and drugs from their raw, sleep-encrusted eyes (or, in St. Peter's case, the remnants of inspirational scripture passages) and take their seats on stage for the week's first table read. The table was sectioned into four folding tables shaped in a long "T." Peter, the director, assistant director, and line producer situated themselves at the head, while the cast, guest stars, and stand-ins (who read the guest-star parts if they weren't yet cast) seated themselves opposite one another along the length. The lovely Linda Mancuso and the network suits sat in the stands, where the audience would normally be, while the writers sat further up the bleachers, enveloped in shadow.

After everyone had consumed their bagel and coffee and

Tylenol and gotten themselves situated, we would read through the entire script. We acted out the gags, hamming up the laughs as best we could, while everyone scribbled their notes for changes.

After that, we kids were off to three hours of set school with Sidney Sharron, our teacher, while everyone else took a break. Sidney also occasionally played Mr. Klopper, the janitor, on the show. During the break, the execs and writers disappeared upstairs into their offices to make notes. The writers would fervently call their agents to see what was the buzz around town on their new spec script, pleading for a better writing gig than *SBTB*. Set school was administered under very rigid guidelines. We had to be in class for a mandatory number of hours each week. So, if we were pulled out of class to be present for some complicated set-up onstage (which was rare), Sidney would dutifully clock us in and out to insure we adhered to all the government's standards. Set school was only three hours per day, but consider that we had two designated teachers as well as various language tutors. Though our set-school hours were much briefer than public school, they were way more intense, with a lot of personal instruction. Instead of one teacher for thirty to forty students, we enjoyed a ratio of two or more teachers for six kids. When you have that many teachers per student, there's not much opportunity to get away with anything. It's not like regular school where you spend most of your days goofing off, daydreaming, or shielding your spontaneous boners with your Trapper Keeper. I was a typically antsy kid. I got easily bored and felt cooped up in the small room where they conducted set school. It was so quiet in class most of the time that you could actually hear the seconds ticking away on the wall clock. Sometimes I would ask for a quick break and when I would eventually wander back Sidney would say, "Uh, Dustin, you've been gone fifteen minutes."

"Really? Huh."

When we returned to our scripts from set school, there might be a bunch of revisions sent down for material that didn't work in the first read-through. We would then head over to the sets and start blocking out the scenes for the actors. Blocking is when we would run through the lines again on set with full cast, guest stars, stand-ins, and the director. We would rehearse our movements and camera positioning and mark off our stationary positions for each scene. We ran through each scene multiple times. What a tragedy it would have been if, say, Mark-Paul hadn't known exactly where to dive in order to catch Screech's mom's treasured Elvis bust when Slater tripped and sent it sailing in the "House Party" episode.

As the show progressed, this process took considerably less time, until we could basically just phone it in. Sometimes there were instances when we wanted to hammer through and get things done, but during those early years the network had to adhere to strict child-labor laws. You could be sure that, when the second hand hit the twelve, Sidney would jump up and say, "That's it, work's over." In those early days of *SBTB*, we were required by law to maintain an extremely strict education and work schedule. Years later, when I had graduated from high school and we had all mastered many of these pre-production steps, we were allowed to come in as late as noon or after to run through new scripts. But until that time, the Monday table read started first thing in the morning and rehearsal and blocking took until 5:30 PM. Then, pulling away from the studio in our Pinto, dad and I had our hour-and-a-half commute back home to Anaheim to look forward to.

TUESDAY

Tuesday we started on the set with scripts in hand for another full read-through. We rehearsed each scene three, four, seven times—whatever it took. The crew would begin to work with the cast to figure out all the props and special effects. For instance, if Zack says, "Y'know what? I'm gonna get us into that concert," and pulls out that shoebox-sized cell phone, at this time during rehearsal he would have the actual prop phone in hand. Every day was a step closer to the finished product before a live audience, so every prop and effect was hammered out with meticulous detail. We'd break for lunch around 1:00 or 2:00 PM and return to set an hour later to run through everything all over again.

At 4:30 PM every Tuesday and Wednesday, we would commence what was known as "network run-through." This was a big deal. It was when all the suits and bigwigs convened, descending from their corner offices to sit in their comfy director's chairs in front of a personal rolling table (for their brilliant note-taking and random musings) in the area between the stage and audience, where the cameras would normally be. We ran through each scene in chronological order, from scene one to scene twelve or thirteen in a typical script, which translated into anywhere from forty-two to forty-four pages on average.

The length of the script usually depended on how much business we had in the episode. "Business" was the crew's shorthand for creative problem solving, defined as any effect that needed to be designed and activated in the successful execution of a scene. For instance, if there was something in a scene that Screech wasn't supposed to touch but he touched it anyway before exiting, then that thing falls over, hitting another object, causing a chain reaction, etc. Or a scene in an episode where Zack is selling Lisa's clothing designs in the hallway, and there's a gag where all the lockers are supposed to open simultaneously when he pushes a button on a remote control. The arrangement and execution of all those effects that were out of the cast's direct control were known on-set as "business."

We would perform the network run-through, front to back, including as much of the business as we could so the execs and writers could see how it looked in live action. The run-through usually ran about an hour. It's a half-hour show, but it took twice as long to set up all the scenes. At this stage, things were still very primitive—no hair, makeup, or wardrobe—and we were still holding our scripts. When you had memorized all your lines and could recite them without your script, it was known as being "off-book."

Regardless of anyone's skill level as a performer or back-stage shenanigans, one thing everyone was pretty equal on was memorizing their lines. It was the one, major requirement of us, and we all approached it like professionals. People got their lines down fairly quickly, but I was usually the quickest. Especially later, during *The New Class*, even with all the notes that would be passed down throughout the week, Den and I would be off-book by Thursday, while the kids still had their heads buried in their scripts. Getting off-book was also a practical matter for the blocking. If your face was facing down towards your script during run-throughs, it made it hard for the lighting and camera guys to set up their shots and get their angles.

Dustin Diamond in full Screech Powers mode early in *SBTB*

Dustin Diamond

The cast in year one of *SBTB*: Lark Voorhies as Lisa Turtle, Ed Alonzo as Max, Tiffani Thiessen as Kelly Kapowski, Mark-Paul Gosselaar as Zack Morris, Dennis Haskins as Mr. Richard Belding, Elizabeth Berkley as Jessica Spano, Dustin Diamond as Samuel 'Screech' Powers, and Mario Lopez as A.C. Slater

And more relaxed shot of the SBTB cast in year one: (l-r)Tiffani Thiessen, Mario Lopez, Lark Voorhies, Dustin Diamond, Mark-Paul Gosselaar, and Elizabeth Berkley

Screech in *SBTB: Hawaiian Style*

SBTB cast members Tiffani Thiessen, Lark Voorhies, Mark-Paul Gosselaar, Elizabeth Berkley, Mario Lopez, Dustin Diamond, with Tori Spelling as Screech's girlfriend, Violet Anne Bickerstaff

Behind the Bell

Dustin Diamond and Lark Voorhies in an undated photo.

Dennis Haskins as Principal Richard Belding and Dustin Diamond as Samuel 'Screech' Powers in *SBTB: The New Class*

Dustin Diamond

**NBC Entertainment president
Brandon Tartikoff**

**A young Mark-Paul Gosselaar
as Zack Morris**

Behind the Bell

The cast of *SBTB: The New Class*, season 2: (top row) Dustin Diamond as Samuel 'Screech' Powers, Dennis Haskins as Principal Richard Belding; (middle row) Sarah Lancaster as Rachel Meyers, Christian Oliver as Brian Keller, Jonathan Angel as ''Tommy D'' De Luca, Natalia Cigliuti as Lindsay Warner, Bianca Lawson as Megan Jones: (bottom row) Spankee Rogers as Bobby Wilson

Dustin Diamond

Mario Lopez, May 2009

Behind the Bell

Tiffani-Amber Thiessen, October 2005

Dustin Diamond

wenn.com/wenn.com/KEYSTONE Press

Mark-Paul Gosselaar, May 2009

A grown-up Dustin Diamond in 1998, toward the end of *SBTB: The New Class*

Kathy Hutchins/ZUMA/KEYSTONE Press)

Elizabeth Berkley, February 2009

WEDNESDAY

Wednesday was exactly the same as Tuesday, just more refined. We arrived in the morning, ran through scenes, broke for lunch, then came back and ran through more scenes.

On stage we had a refrigerator always packed with our favorite beverages. There was the Kraft Service table, where we could get sandwiches made or pile up on the snacks (until Tiffani's ass relegated us almost exclusively to fruits and vegetables). The ladies who worked for Kraft Services were always very friendly and fun to be around. We could go to the NBC commissary and bring food back to our dressing rooms, where I'd spend most of my time playing video games: Nintendo, Super Nintendo, Sega Genesis, Sega Saturn, Neo Geo—all the finest game systems of the 1990s.

There could be long stretches of downtime—sometimes as much as two or three hours at a pop—where content was being rehearsed that didn't involve my character. If the extras were around, I always had something to do. One extra in particular, named Sherry, was the object of my desires for a while. She was in her late thirties and played a background teacher for a while. She had Ann Jillian-style blonde hair that was almost white, and she always smelled like vanilla beans. I flirted with her for a long time but could only muster some smooching. I always regretted that we never sealed the deal. Aside from those adventures, downtime Monday through Wednesday could get pretty boring. The only thing on the television in my dressing room was basic cable and all the live feeds from the other sound stages. Even though I was technically at work, I was essentially getting paid good money to chill.

But with all that free time, it was inevitable that us kids were going to get into trouble. That usually meant pranks. We started out with stupid stuff like moving around the tape on the floor of the set so that actors would fuck up their marks. Each mark was in the shape of a "T" and all different colors (for each character). You don't usually see the marks on the floor in live action, but they're there. We also took gaffer's tape, tore off strips, and left them sticky-side up outside people's doors so they'd walk on it and drag it onto the set. Not to mention the old favorites of slapping tape on someone's back or seeing how many clothespins we could pinch on various parts of people's clothing throughout the day.

Then we moved on to the big stuff, like when I messed with Bobo. Bobo's real name was John Deitrich, and he was head carpenter on the set. He supervised the building of all the sets and, over time, became friendly with my dad. In the morning, dad and I would bring in our breakfast from Astro Burger, which included, of course, a giant chocolate shake.

We'd hang out in an area backstage at Raleigh Studios where Bobo had set up a Nintendo. We'd eat and play video games, get called to set, do our table reading, and come right back for another fifteen-minute break, more fast food, and more video games. Except for one time when I came back to discover Bobo had eaten half my breakfast and was still drinking my chocolate shake. I'm said, "Bobo? What the fuck?"

"What?" said Bobo. "I saved you half."

My dad just sat there, laughing. Okay, fucker. Lesson learned. So the next day I ate my breakfast fast, but left my chocolate shake, irresistibly alone and vulnerable, right under Bobo's nose. When I returned for my break, Bobo had of course polished off my shake, which I had, of course, filled with Ex-Lax, that old chestnut of a prank. Problem was, I had no idea you were only supposed to mix it with a normal dosage. I had emptied the entire bottle into my Astro-shake. Poor Bobo.

While Bobo groaned and hollered at me from the shitter, he plotted his revenge. Later, when we were shooting before a live audience, Bobo went into my dressing room (this is why it helps to be friends with the janitor), gathered up every stitch of clothing I owned, stuffed it into a clear garbage bag, climbed up into the rafters and hanged it from a cord, swinging back and forth just over the heads of the audience. It was during a scene where I was seated in Mr. Belding's office. Screech was supposed to gaze off dreamily, like, "I can see it now . . ." But what I saw was all my fucking clothes dangling from a rope.

And that wasn't all. When we wrapped, I returned to my dressing room to find it completely bare—every stick of furniture and every fixture, gone. Bobo had enlisted his fellow Teamsters to cram everything into my closet and bathroom—the bathroom I shared with Mario, whose dressing room was on the other side.

After I got all my shit resituated, the pranks continued. Always a fan of the classics, I decided I was going to get Mario with the old cellophane-stretched-over-the-toilet gag. Mario liked to stay hydrated throughout the day, so I knew I could nail him on one of his frequent potty breaks. Sure enough, before long he started heading up to his dressing room. I rushed up, secured the cellophane across the bowl and waited listening on my side of the door. I thought perhaps I might get lucky, and Mario would go in there to drop a deuce, A.C. Slater-style (a term coined by fans for facing backward on the toilet, in the same fashion Mario sat on every chair on the *SBTB* set). Mario's bathroom door opened; it closed. The fan clicked on, whirred. So far, so good. Then . . . a woman screamed! It was Mario's mom, Elzia. *Ah, Dios mio, la madre!*

When 4:30 PM rolled around on Wednesday, we'd perform our second network run-through, then head home. We were home in time for prime time, so, in case you're wondering, here's what was available for our viewing pleasure on Wednesday nights starting at 8 PM, circa 1990: on ABC: *The Wonder Years* (with that douche, Fred Savage), *Growing Pains*, *Doogie Howser, M.D.* (with Ed Alonzo's magical tickle-buddy, Neil Patrick Harris), *Married People*, and *Cop Rock*; on CBS: *Lenny, Doctor Doctor, Jake and the Fatman*, and *WIOU*; and, on NBC: *Unsolved Mysteries, The Fanelli Brothers, Dear John*, and *Hunter*.

Years later on Wednesdays, after our run-throughs, the producers would buy a bunch of pizzas and set up a screening room where we could watch the upcoming episodes after they'd been edited together, but before they were broadcast on television.

"MUST-SEE" THURSDAY

On Thursdays, I woke around 5:00 AM for my hour-and-a-half commute north because on this day, things began a bit earlier than usual. This was a high-energy day. It was when the crew finalized its camera blocking. This was also the day that all the extras were on set, officially known as "Ladies Day." There were also a number of male extras who I enjoyed hanging with. It was like TGIF a day early when my buddies would show up to joke around, then we'd all go play pretend. We spent Thursday blocking all the physical action in each scene, ad nauseam, until we knew it by rote.

This was the day when the cast would visit wardrobe for any final touches on special costuming that the script required. Like the dream sequence where Screech has to wear a Robocop-style outfit. Wardrobe had to hunt down all those materials and fashion the costume so that it both fit me properly and met the approval of the producers, writers, and network suits.

Thursday ran very similarly to Tuesday and Wednesday, only now we were rehearsing "live" with people in the booth. The booth was the hub of the show, the control center where all the monitors were located and where the director, producers, and writers sat. *SBTB* was a four-camera show. That meant there were a lot of shots that needed to be timed and called perfectly by the director in the booth. Each camera—just the top camera part and not even all the mobile apparatus that comprised the base—was worth over $250,000. The cost of each camera total was in the neighborhood of half a million dollars. When they set up shots, there would be one camera for wide shots, one for close ups, and one each for two shots or three shots (where there are two or three actors in frame). Then there were cross shots. Cross shots were necessary if, say, Zack was on the far left, Kelly was on the far right, and the rest of the gang was arranged side by side, facing front, in a sort of police line up (because you never want to show your back to the audience). That held true even if you were seated in a booth at The Max. You always wanted to have your body half-turned towards wherever the camera was located so it could get the most "coverage." For instance, if Zack and Kelly were seated at The Max and Zack was on the left, his camera would be located on the far right, shooting across, to get his half of the coverage in the back-and-forth of the conversation between the two characters. It would be the same, only opposite, set-up for Kelly.

Remember, this was being taped before a live audience, so it made for high drama inside the booth. The director would have to anticipate camera changes and call for a new shot the instant it occurred in the natural flow of the scene, which wasn't easy. The director would call for a shot, then ready the next shot, calling for the cut with a snap of his fingers.

For example, take the scene of that conversation between Zack and Kelly in their usual table at The Max. The director has cameras one and four trained on the actors in the scene. Camera one is up on Zack while camera four is ready on Kelly. Then you have a variety of different angles and shots blocked out for cameras two and three. From the booth, the director communicates through headsets with the camera operators, calling out a sequence such as, "One ready, four (*snap*). Four ready, three (*snap*). Three ready, one (*snap*). One ready, four (*snap*)." And on and on. In fact, I can't watch a television show to this day without counting the snaps in my head—sometimes scenes with as many as twenty-five cuts or more. "Wow," I'll think. "That scene had a buttload of snaps."

Let's say camera one has Zack, but Zack has to leave. That means the director instructs camera two to be ready to take the wide shot, picking up Zack's movement through the set as he exits. Now camera one has to cut over to someone else, say, standing by the jukebox. Camera one has to spin around, zoom in on the jukebox, and be ready for the next shot when the director calls, "Two ready, one (snap)." Sometimes these camera guys had to move like lightning to get the shots.

In addition to the cameramen, you had crew members moving yards of loose and coiled cables as thick as nautical rope. Then there were the booms—long sticks that hovered over the action with a microphone dangling from it. The main booms (there were two) were not entirely operated by hand; they were each a crane with a platform attached to a sturdy metal base that was basically a three-wheeled vehicle with a chair and steering mechanism on the back. This tool had its own tangle of wires running from it, adding to the off-camera pasta bowl of cables we were all constantly stepping over. If you decided to wander around between your scenes to where the cameras were in play, you were taking your life in your own hands. We didn't use wireless microphone packs like you'd find on the set of a feature film, so sometimes, very rarely, we would also have microphones coming up from below the floor of the set—a sound tech with a mike pack and a smaller, hand-held boom. This was all done at breakneck speed to maintain the flow of a live production and to offer the maximum entertainment experience to the studio audience.

Backstage there was a special TV rack fashioned with a cube of monitors and a larger monitor divided into four smaller screenshots on which you could view the angle from each camera. There were makeup tables, quick-change rooms, and curtains just off set as well as cast members and extras waiting for their cues. In all that controlled chaos, our crew never tangled cords or crossed cables to the detriment of the performers on stage. That's why camera guys never stop working. A show gets cancelled, they just go camera another show. Many of our guys worked over on *DOOL* *(Days of Our Lives)* or *The Tonight Show* every day while we were rehearsing for tape day—and they kept on working the four months we were all on hiatus. Those guys worked all over NBC. No doubt, camera guys have steadier jobs than most actors. It was a highly coordinated ballet, performed each week by masters of their crafts. A dance I took completely for granted.

There is a second language the makers of a television show speak fluently. It's an industry-wide language of acronyms and pidgin English that every veteran actor eventually has ingrained into his or her psyche. *Cheating*, for instance, is not only what Tiffani was doing on her boyfriend Eddie Garcia during the filming of the "No Hope Dope" episode, it is also a term for rotating your body towards the camera for maximum coverage in a shot. The direction will be, "Okay, Dustin, we need you to cheat to camera. Open up left to camera." This evokes another set of terms, this time directional. There's *stage left* and *stage right*, and *camera left* and *camera right*. The camera's left and right are from the perspective of the audience either in the studio or at home, the actor's left or right is from his own perspective on stage, looking out at the audience. So, an instruction for me to cheat left is an instruction to cheat camera left (known as *house left* in the theater), which means to my right, or *stage right* (sometimes also referred to as *actor's right*). This sounds confusing (especially for kids), but after complete immersion in this world for many years, this backwards, cryptic style of communication is wholly unremarkable. In fact, after a while, the direction would simply be, "Cheat a little bit." The presumption was that the actor now knew where his camera was and which direction he needed to turn.

An actor must always be conscious of where the camera is because on television you don't converse with people like you would in the real world. From an observer's perspective in real life, one participant in a conversation might be turned fully to the side or have her back to the observer. On TV, both actors must cheat toward the front. Encountering this style of communication for the first time, a visitor to the set might presume we were all windtalking. Try this one if you're scoring at home: "Okay, the gang enters sans Belding. Dustin, we need you go up-stage a bit. You're gonna cheat then pull a POV TTC." Translation: Screech, Zack, Kelly, Slater, Jess, and Lisa enter without Mr. Belding. Screech needs to walk away from the camera (to the rear of the stage, making the front of the stage down-stage) then turn so we get a Point Of View Towards The Camera. Easy, right?

Another Thursday process was to get the monitors upstairs "color keyed." I never knew much about this mysterious procedure. All I did know was that for all the years I was on *SBTB*, there was a woman upstairs in an office whose only job was to make sure that certain patterns and colors were avoided so they didn't strobe or clash on television. There's probably some elaborate technical reason for this effect occurring, but I have no idea what that undoubtedly excellent reason might be. She probably had a tough job making sure Screech's ridiculously loud outfits didn't fuck up the color palette, or whatever.

We wouldn't always go to the NBC commissary when we broke for lunch. Sometimes we'd walk to Johnny Carson Park, which is located right across the street from the studio in Burbank. For us, it was a lovely haven from the hectic confines of the production studio: shaded trees, a babbling brook, nature. Another benefit was that most of your fellow park wanderers were also fellow actors, so there was no one bugging you. It was just a nice place to relax for an hour. In the first years of the show, the network and producers made a deal to publish *SBTB* books, one of which featured a photo of Screech sitting on the limb of a tree wearing his rainbow-colored pants and all that other crazy shit they used to make me wear. Come to think of it, that's the same outfit they used to dress the Screech doll. In the photo, Screech is pulling down his glasses, looking over them. That picture was taken in Johnny Carson Park. Many of our press and promotional photos taken out in a natural setting were taken there.

Back in the studio on Thursday evenings, depending on the earlier call time for the underage kids (i.e., me), we would do a 6:30 PM run-through on camera that would typically last about an hour. This was a dress rehearsal. We were not in full hair and makeup, but we would all be in wardrobe, including the incorporation of our quick changes backstage. By the way, here's another tip if you ever star in your own television show: don't wear a ball cap on the day you're in wardrobe without having your hair done in character, especially if you have a curly bird's nest like mine crowning your melon. You'll have all-day hat hair worse than a drifter's.

We referred to the Thursday run-through as "camera day" because everybody got to see how things looked on monitors in preparation for "tape day," Friday's big performance in front of the audience. Tape day was for all the marbles. The director and crew paid close attention to how all the business went off on camera day in case they needed to make any last minute adjustments. Some episodes called for much more business than others. Was everything working the way it was supposed to? Sometimes we wouldn't even see the business in action until this late Thursday run-through. The carpenters would have been instructed on Monday or Tuesday that such-and-such a prop needed to be constructed to do such-and-such then they'd disappear to construct the business required for that week's episode.

When the Thursday camera run-through was complete, we were free to go home. When I was younger, that meant the long drive home with dad, dinner, TV, etc. When I got older, that meant it was time to reconnect with the ladies I'd chatted up all afternoon, go out, have some fun, maybe spread some Screech lovin' around. Yeah, Thursdays were good days.

FRIDAY: SHOWTIME

Monday, Tuesday, Wednesday . . . *Meh*. Thursday was full of life. But Friday . . . KA-POW!!! Friday was tape day. Friday was HUGE.

On Friday, the stage jumped to life: the camera guys, sound guys, lighting techs, grips, carpenters, all the friends you've made in the pool of extras, the *ladies*, all the network suits, the producers, director and assistant directors, stage managers, hair, makeup and wardrobe, the full cast, and a live studio audience.

But before we get to the action, one crucial aspect I have yet to discuss is "pages." All week long, we would have been handed pages from the writers. These were ongoing writing changes to plot, dialogue, setting, business—you name it. Small changes in dialogue were also called "sides." Sides is the common term for the scene an actor would be asked to read at an audition. It refers literally to the sides of conversation in the dialogue of the scene. More involved revisions to the script were known as pages. On the set, we would be notified that, "Pages were coming down." New pages were color-coded. The annoying part of this process was that there was no industry standard for the color coding, making it difficult to keep track of which pages had been handed down to you when. Obviously this was critical, because you always had to be on the latest pages, not still memorizing lines that had already been cut or rewritten. I carried a three-ring binder that I clipped new pages into. For a long time white pages were our original script, first revisions were usually pink (revised lines had an asterisk next to them), followed by green, blue, yellow, orange, etc. I can't remember the exact order anymore. You'd even start to get pages to replace your pages. So instead of just pink pages replacing the white pages from your original script, now you had green pages to replace the pink. You really had to keep your shit straight to be on the color of the day. Sometimes people would fuck up and not have their pages or be reading from the wrong script, but that was rare. For the most part things ran smoothly. Our line producer had production assistants who would walk around pushing a wheeled cart with extra scripts stored in the bottom. And if someone was delivering the wrong line, rehearsal stopped immediately, and the dipshit was handed the new pages. We were operating within the comfort of a pretty fail-safe system.

Pages were necessitated by gags that fell flat at the table read, business that didn't come off in live action like it read on the page—any number of reasons, really. Writers would disappear into their room and, as a result, you could be handed down no pages, one page, twenty-eight pages, or anything in between. You never had any idea when changes might be called for. They could come down multiple times in one day; it was always a surprise. Here was an excellent guide: if St. Peter didn't laugh at a joke, there were going to be pages. As actors, we just sucked it up, memorized the new lines, and moved on; it was all part of being a professional. Keep in mind, I was a professional actor from the time I was eight years old, working full time. Nobody was down my throat to make sure I was memorizing the correct color pages or that I had my lines down at all, even though, technically, I was just a little kid. It was simply expected of me. By the end of the week, our script binders resembled rainbows.

Friday was the confluence of all these disparate pieces coming together to create *SBTB*. Every single scene you see, whether on reruns or DVD, was filmed on a Friday. It's worth noting that when viewers watched the character Screech in all the incarnations of *SBTB* over the course of a decade, they are watching the real-life Dustin Diamond grow up one Friday at a time.

Fridays usually began early, 7:30 or 8:00 AM, but sometimes, if our scenes began deeper into the first taping, we would receive a later call time. That was a nice treat, since I lived so far from the studio. I would look at the day's breakdowns and see that the first scene to be taped called for Zack, Kelly, Jessie, and Slater, and I'd be fired up because it meant I could sleep in. Those odd moments were the source of perhaps one of Hollywood's least known paradoxes: Actors looking forward to scenes they weren't in.

Now, here's something you probably didn't know: Every Friday, we would film the entire show, front to back, twice: First on an empty sound stage and second in front of a live audience. The reason was for safety. We had to be certain we had each scene in the can before taping live in front of an audience to hedge against mishaps, disasters and—not insignificantly, running long and coming up against child-labor laws. I believe the window for the live audience taping was from 5:00 to 7:30 PM. To make the early, audience-less, taping go faster, we would film the show out of order. If the script called for four scenes total in The Max, we would film all four scenes before moving on to the next set-up. In the live taping before the studio audience, we taped the show front to back in the correct chronology. The continuity benefitted the audience so they could follow along with the story, supplying appropriate responses to the plot as it unfolded. But no matter what happened during the live performance, the producers and editors knew they had every scene on tape and could cut the final broadcast together in post-production, if necessary.

We had to be very careful at lunch on Fridays not to get food stains on our wardrobe. Some people changed or wore a smock over their clothing. Den and I donned robes like the true men of leisure that we were. And we didn't wander far from set to eat. Often, Friday meals were catered with a sit-down meal in a nearby rehearsal hall or studio, usually, in fact, the same rehearsal hall where our very first auditions for *SBTB* were held. Parents, friends, cast, guest stars, crew, producers—everyone—would eat together in the same space. We would end our meal with any last-minute notes from the director for the live taping and a little pep talk from him or St. Peter to keep our spirits and enthusiasm high.

Backstage we would sit for makeup touch-ups and twirl for final wardrobe inspection. Here's a tidbit about stage makeup for television: the lighter your skin, the more orange it must be made in order to even out the color scale. I'm not talking about fake-tan orange, I'm talking Chester Cheeto orange. We called it Cheeto makeup because everyone who had to wear it was the spitting image of that smudgy, curled, cheese-flavored cornmeal snack. If you were very fair-skinned, then every Friday you'd walk around set looking like Otto the Orange, the Syracuse mascot. Lark, obviously, was spared this indignity each week. Mario was also saved by his swarthy Latino complexion. But me, Mark-Paul, Tiffani, Elizabeth, and Den would get Cheetofied. You absolutely cannot tell on television how orange our faces were, but if you had bumped into us backstage you would have been horrified by what was clearly a tragic mishap at the Frito Lay factory—producing a mutant squad of oranginators. And as much as that sucked, sometimes there were scenes where I had to wear swim trunks or have my shirt off, and so I had to have my whole torso slathered in orange. That stuff is thick as pan-cake batter, and if I were to smear my finger across my cheek, I'd scoop off a little mound of what looked like whipped cheese. Once the basic Cheeto effect was achieved, the makeup artists toned the orangeness up or down as needed with puffs of powder like KT 1, Golden Dew Amber, and Bronze Tone. You might be thinking right about now, "Most guys don't know what sort of makeup they require." But trust me, in the entertainment industry, especially after you work on a series for ten years, it's your job to know what makes you look good on camera. Don't believe me? Just ask the ghost of Richard Nixon.

Then, it was *showtime*.

Hanging over the crowd during taping (just like that plastic bag filled with all my clothes, thanks to Bobo) were a series of directional microphones outfitted with tight cones to make them very specific sound receptors for different areas of the studio audience. All the applause and laughs and hoots and jeers and oohs you hear are real. But the directional microphones also allowed the sound editor to zero in on zones where clowns just wanted to act like asses because they thought they'd be heard on TV (i.e., "Wooo, Kelly, suck it baby! I'm right here!"). That hosebag would be wiped from the final soundtrack. The sound editor would just turn down the cone over the problem area and fill the space with more sound from surrounding microphones.

From backstage, we could hear the audience being loaded into the studio. The set was hidden from view by a large wooden framework suspending long, black tarps. We would invariably poke a tiny hole or peel back a corner to peek at the audience as they found their seats. I would also locate the friends, family, and lady friends I had reserved seats for during the taping. My first girlfriend, when I was twelve and she was fifteen, was a fan of the show who sent me letters, which included very tasteful personal photos. We used to talk on the phone for hours. She only lived about fifteen minutes away from me in Diamond Bar, California. Ah, young love. She was a big fan of stuffing all our correspondences with silvery confetti that would scatter everywhere each time I opened her latest letter. She thought it was hilarious. Me, not so much. But she was hot, and I was horny, so I put up with it. I invited her to a Friday taping with her mom with a promise to host a first-class tour of the *SBTB* set after we wrapped. We ended up dating for a long time. Corny as it may sound, it also helped when I—or any of the cast members—knew there was a guest in the audience who we could perform for. For me, it was a little added incentive to stay focused and do my best work, not unlike live theater.

The audience was seated by NBC pages (i.e., Kenneth on *30 Rock*). The pages also monitored the audience and guarded against any unruly behavior or crazy people storming the stage. I enjoyed performing before a live audience. It exuded a terrific energy, an immediate feedback from an intense, communal vibe created by a room full of people all hanging on your next line of dialogue. And the explosions of roaring laughter were very satisfying, though of course I also liked it when people laughed at the actual jokes written into the script.

Sometimes, when I would peek at the audience throughout the show, I would pick out a hot chick and ask one of the pages to approach her after the taping and tell her that I'd like to invite her backstage for a tour of the show. This technique was always a crapshoot, but it often worked marvelously. Girls would be thrilled to be invited backstage. If things were proceeding nicely, I would end my tour in the set graveyard (the place where all the old set walls, stage pieces and some props were stored) where we could spend some quality time alone, getting to know one another. I don't remember any of my cast mates ever singling out au-

dience members and inviting them backstage like I did. Strange
as it may seem, it was I who developed into the real off-camera
ladies' man on *SBTB*. I was undercover for a long time; my reputation was very slow to catch up with my exploits, which was fine
by me. I like to think I approached the backstage hookup with
style, whereas Mario was just an unabashed slut, hitting on anything with a respiratory system. Mark-Paul, for years and years,
was never seen with a girl on set. I was the true Super Pimp.
Hand me my wide-brimmed hat with the snow-leopard trim, my
gold-capped cane, and my chalice. *Pimptacular.*

When the audience was loaded into their seats, they were first
entertained by our long-time warm-up guy, Phil Stellar (he was
the main one, we had others). A warm-up guy is a comedian who
gets the crowd laughing and in good spirits by involving them
in his silly, often cheesy routine. *SBTB* was a kid-friendly show,
so Phil couldn't be too risqué with his material. He would tell
jokes and pick out people for some good-hearted ribbing, basically keeping their enthusiasm high leading into the main event.
He ended his set with instructions for the audience on how loud
they needed to cheer and laugh and "ooOOOOOooo" in order to
fill the studio space with a big sound that would resonate on TV.

When Phil had finished and the cast was ready (and Mario
had done his push ups), we all came out for an opening bow. After that, we took our places, the tarps were lowered, and the first
set was revealed. Then we dove right into filming from the top of
the show. As I mentioned before, we moved through the script in
chronological order for the benefit of the audience, even though
it was more complicated and time-consuming to film that way. If,

however, there was a scene that was more complex or involved a lot of intricate business, quite often we would not perform it live. Instead the scene as it had been taped earlier would be shown to the audience on large monitors while we set up for the next live scene.

When we transitioned, the end of each scene was indicated by an applause sign. It's a common misconception that the applause sign blinks and flashes after each corny gag to encourage the audience to laugh, even if they're not amused. Really it was to signal to the crowd that the scene was over, but without the aid of music. On the screen, transitions from scene to scene or from scene to commercial are accompanied by music. But in fact, all of the music was added later, in post-production. Without music as a guide, we had to rely on the applause sign. For instance, if a scene were to end on a long pause, say Zack staring out into an uncertain future, without the aid of musical cues it's difficult for the audience to know when to applaud. And you don't want them starting early, ruining the take. That's where the applause sign comes in. At a given, pre-planned moment, the applause sign turns on, and the audience applauds as if on cue. Simple as that. In the final edit, the music is mixed in with the applause mixes, and you get the full transition effect.

As you can see, sound had to be managed carefully to avoid anything spoiling the scene. As a wall of defense against jack-asses in the audience purposely trying to ruin takes, there were directional mikes on the ceiling. So, if while Zack is holding his pause some dipshit calls out, "Yeeaaahh," he can rest assured he won't be featured in the final cut.

The producers of *SBTB* also employed a company called Audiences Unlimited, whose sole job was to fill the seats for every episode. They guaranteed to find an audience no matter what. Even if they had to drag homeless winos off the streets of Burbank, that studio would be full for tape day. So, even if your show blew—and I make no accusations—there would be a warm ass in each and every seat.

Everybody thinks bloopers are hilarious. Not so much. Keep in mind that, in 1990s dollars, it cost something like $10,000 an hour just to light the set for *SBTB*. Keep in mind also that every time we fucked up a take and had to do it over from the top, the production got that much closer to losing some of its younger actors due to child-labor laws. This was a formula that rendered the higher-ups most unhappy when bloopers occurred. They didn't want to be viewed before a live audience as sticks in the mud, but at the same time they did tend to get pretty aggressive when things were lagging behind schedule. The show's creators weren't such big men and women that they were above leaning in and whispering a threat of punishment if we couldn't get our shit together and stop laughing. We were kids. Trying to make each other laugh—through the use of funny faces or by whatever other means at our disposal—was practically a full-time job. For example, Screech might bid farewell to Slater as he walked off set, but Mario would linger, making faces and offering up lewd, suggestive body language in an immature attempt to distract my attention from the task at hand. An attempt that often worked wonders. Of course the classic rule applies: The more you don't want to laugh, the more you will.

In one scene, Screech had to stand up in front of the class to deliver a speech. I was holding a piece of paper that, in theory, was supposed to have the speech written on it, but really I already had the lines memorized. More often than not, the prop guys would write something on the page like, "Just a friendly message from the prop guys: don't crease this paper, we're going to need it later. Thank you." Or more interestingly, sometimes you'd sit down at your desk on set and flip open your algebra book to find a picture of the prop guys mooning you. One week there was a Polaroid frenzy of full moon shots. Mark-Paul opened Zack's locker to discover an impressive array of prop guy ass taped inside. These sorts of pranks made it all the more difficult to hold it together and get through your scene with the suits breathing down your neck.

So there I was, standing at the head of the class holding a prop page to deliver this speech. Mario started me laughing, and I couldn't stop. The director walked over and said, "What the hell's going on?" I said, "He's making me laugh." His response was, "You're an actor. Get through the scene." But the giggles can be infectious. That particular time, St. Peter descended from the booth to administer a stern warning to me, Mark-Paul, and Mario, threatening to dock our pay if we couldn't pull it together and get through it. My point is, I was also a kid. I know we were all there for our big-time jobs that were stuffing everyone's bank accounts, providing them with those sporty convertibles and mansions in gated communities but, ahem, I was thirteen years old! So bloopers were not always fun; in fact, they chapped a lot of asses.

That makes me think of the least-aired episode in *SBTB* history. At least it held that distinction for many years. These days, with its insane syndication schedule, it's probably just melded in seamlessly with the others. I heard at one point the ratio was like one hundred to one, meaning every other episode would air one hundred times before this one. At the time, the episode was quietly swept under the rug. It's called "Slater's Friend," and it featured Artie, Slater's pet chameleon. Spoiler alert: Artie dies. We all knew on the set that this episode was incredibly cheesy. At the end, gathered around Artie to mourn his passing, the gang sings, "Oh, Artie Boy" to the tune of that timeless Irish dirge, "Danny Boy":

> Oh, Artie Boy,
> The bugs, the bugs are buzzing.
> There's gnats and ants, mosquitoes on the fly.
> And they'll be there for breakfast, lunch, and dinner,
> In that big, chameleon banquet in the sky.

It doesn't get much cheesier than that. What made it more ridiculous was that Slater was directed to cry during Artie's funeral elegy. This had the effect of making us all quiver with barely repressible glee. We couldn't help ourselves. We kept busting up in laughter. It was impossible to get through the song because the entire scenario was so incredibly stupid.

We shared that "Oh, Artie Boy" scene with the fat, jolly Mr. Tuttle, who appeared in a few episodes as the driver's ed teacher, the conductor of the Glee Club, and as head of the teacher's union when they struck during senior year. Mr. Tuttle was apparently next in line at Bayside for the principal's position. He once called Mr. Belding "Mr. Balding" and intimated that he already had the new colors of his office picked out. Mr. Tuttle was played by Jack Angeles, who was a real-life accountant who worked in the accounts department at NBC. He was the actual guy who cut our real-life checks. Mr. Tuttle's signature line was, "Hup-hup-hup, everyone! Pushy, pushy, move your tushy. Now that's not the way we do it!" Oftentimes, names that were used for teachers— particularly teachers you never saw, like Mr. Testaverde—were throwbacks, homages, and inside gags for the writers. There was reference made to a teacher named Mr. Tramer, alluding to our longtime head writer, Bennett Tramer. *SBTB* was loaded with those kinds of inside jokes.

If you look closely at the Artie-death-dirge scene in "Slater's Friend," you will notice each of us trying to hide from the camera as we labor to get through the song without exploding into hysterical laughter. For my part, I was swallowing what amounted to an infarction. I'm lucky I didn't suffer a brain hemorrhage. These giggle moments were, of course, compounded by our fear of wasting costly production time with bloopers and outtakes. Knowing we were pissing off everybody up in the booth only made us laugh harder, spasming and convulsing. One might assume that our reactions to the scene would eventually be viewed as appropriate. The gang probably would giggle through that ridiculous song because the moment was so absurd. But if that's what one might assume, one would be wrong. St. Peter and the writers were steadfast in their opinions that the scene was a somber one and should be acted as an authentic moment, honoring the passing of a noble reptilian soul, a soul that had brought Slater many hours of friendship and solace. In the end, we could never fully get through the scene. We always fucked it up, and that's the footage they were forced to go with after many takes. That's why "Slater's Friend" became notorious as the least-aired episode of *SBTB*.

Even though we were kids, we knew when something was lame-o. Allow me to sample a line for you: Screech knocks a turkey off the counter in the kitchen and goes to get it only to be stopped by Zack. As Zack lifts the bird from the floor, Screech says, "Okay, but don't gobble it!" Truly, this was not exactly Pulitzer-worthy material we were working with. But what could we do? We groaned on the inside. Sometimes we would try to sabotage lines we knew were more stupid than our normal level of stupid. The corniness did exact its toll over time in our personal lives. No one wants to go to school and have kids go out of their way to get in your face and say, "You're fucking stupid, man. Your jokes are dumb, and you play an asshole." Thanks, chum.

I had most of the stupid lines that needed to be delivered in each script. Sometimes, when feeling bold, I would try to submarine a particularly onerous slice of dialogue. The only thing I could really do was to deliver the line flat so it didn't get the laugh that was intended. This required subtlety. I couldn't appear that I was tanking the line; it had to look like the flaw was inherent in the writing. The best approach was to nail it all day until run-through, then tank it so St. Peter wouldn't laugh, and it would get tossed out or kicked upstairs for a rewrite.

The writers did not tend to welcome our suggestions for line changes. Our flashes of inspiration were definitely viewed as an insult. Sometimes I would try a new line out during run-through only to receive a note later from the director because the writer bitched. "Look," the director would say, "just say it the way the writer wrote it." No matter how big a laugh my new line got during run-through, I would be asked to revert back to the script. It's a weird dance that develops between actors and writers. From the actor's perspective, I knew that if I wanted a change in dialogue I would have to present it in such a way that the writer thought it was his own idea. I needed to lead him to the banks of the river and, once he started drinking on his own, say, "Wow! Great idea, dude!" If diplomacy failed, though, I could also be devious.

On tape day, I would deliver the line how it was written then gauge the reaction of the audience. I felt like, after playing Screech for so many years, I had the best sense of what sort of lines coming out of my character's mouth would get the strongest reactions from the audience. If the line landed with a thud on the first delivery, on the second take I'd just do it my way. What were they going to do at that point? Especially when my line, as it invariably did, brought down the house. Even then, the call would come down from the director in the booth to Maria, the stage manager and she would tell me, "The director wants you to stick to the dialogue in the script." Fine. At that point it was a moral victory anyway. I had proven my way was funnier. As the years went on and Screech had transitioned into *SBTB: The New Class*, I got bolder with my opinions and ad libs. Den and I had put our time in and had proven we knew our characters well.

But things started getting weird between us and the writers during *The New Class*. The writers started fucking with Den and me, inserting a whole undercurrent of gay innuendo throughout the scripts between Screech and Belding. I'll dive into that in more depth when I discuss my time on *The New Class*, but suffice it to say, as a result, Den and I started to deliver a lot of our own improvisational material in an effort to sidestep all that horseshit. I think Den and I eventually developed into a very in-sync comedy duo. From Screech's early days as straight-man Zack's goofy sidekick, I transitioned into Mr. Belding's. Den would set the gags up, and I'd knock 'em down. We knew our characters so well we could feed off one another, even finish each other's sentences. The crew grew to love Den and me and our scenes together because we did our jobs. They called us the One-Take Champions.

There were different styles of *SBTB* shows. Sometimes they would air "clip" shows, which I always thought was lazy television, just a way to buy some time while new scripts were hammered out. That's my theory, anyway. I don't know why they became so popular. Clip shows are exactly what they sound like, just an editing together of old clips introduced and narrated by Zack in that style of, "Do you remember when . . .?" Cue dream-like music and wavy transition. Basically the same deal as how the network handled integrating the *Good Morning, Miss Bliss* episodes with the original *SBTB*. In my opinion, clip shows suck. They rob the audience of new content.

Occasionally, we had to do a wrap-around show. A wrap-around show is an extra episode squeezed into the normal one-episode-per-week taping schedule. Wrap-arounds were rare, maybe once per season (I can hear the snickering). We would film two or three weeks in a row and then get a week off. Three weeks of work would usually mean that we were taping three episodes, but for a wrap-around show, that meant we were filming four full episodes in those three weeks.

How it would work was like this: with there being around twelve scenes per script, that meant that, in order to complete a fourth episode in the course of three weeks, we would have to tape four extra scenes each week. During rehearsals, we would run through all the scenes of that week's episode then turn to those extra scenes (with a totally different storyline, obviously), which would eventually be cobbled together into a complete episode at the end of the month. It was normal for the writers to hand us just the pages of the extra scenes we were doing, not the entire script for the wrap-around. Sometimes this would make it difficult to get the gist of the plot, so we'd just guess at what the fuck was going on, pros that we were.

Granted, we weren't taping an episode of *The Wire*. The plots were pretty basic, and there were only so many ways the gang could fall into mischief at Bayside. Every show had its *A* theme and its *B* theme. That's the basic structure of a half-hour sitcom. The *A* story would be, say, Zack cheating to become valedictorian in the graduation episode, while it's really Elizabeth that should have been awarded that title. The *B* story is that they're having problems writing the song for graduation, and they need to get it right in time for the ceremony. Nothing against the writers, but we did reach a point in our mastery of our characters where we could pretty easily reach a resolution to the dual themes of each show, complete with gags, without much plotting.

At around 7:30 PM, we would come back out on stage, do our final bows, and the audience would be ushered out. That's when we would normally say our goodbyes and head home. But if it was a wrap-around show, that meant a whole new round of wardrobe, with hair and makeup touch-ups. Everybody was pretty beat at that point. Plus, we had to have another third of a script memorized along with blocking, cues, etc. Wrap-around shows were considered rather tedious and definitely screwed with our internal clocks. My internal clock, for instance, would be telling me that I was supposed to be sitting in L.A. traffic, not still standing on-set. Unless of course I got lucky and Screech wasn't in any of the wrap-around-show scenes that week. Again, that little known paradox of the joy actors feel when they learn there are scenes they're not in.

Another drag about wrap-around shows was that, in the course of that month, we were forbidden to do pretty much anything extracurricular. We couldn't go outside and skateboard, for instance. There was no bike-riding, no horse riding for Princess Tiffani, no activity of any kind with the potential for physical injury. And we couldn't alter our appearances in any way (i.e., a new haircut, a suntan, etc.). Think about it: I needed to look exactly the same on last day of taping in the month as I did on the first. In those wrap-around episodes, there could be a scene where Zack says, "I've got to get outta here." Cut to a scene in the hallway that was taped a month later. Mark-Paul can't have a scratch on his face, a smudge on his shirt, a missing belt, a hair longer or shorter than it was in the last instant of the preceding scene. To ensure that this would be the case, Polaroids became an omnipresent fixture on the set (and not just of my epic dong). The crew and departments took hundreds, thousands of Polaroid pictures to ensure continuity. Polaroids were used for all the cast, the props, the set dressing, the wardrobe, hair, makeup. The prop guys would take pictures of every table at The Max, where every ketchup and mustard bottle was situated, every napkin and salt shaker, how the books were stacked, etc.

When we taped wrap-around shows during the seasons of *The New Class*, there was no getting out early anymore for me. The kids' scenes were always taped first to get them finished and headed home before they came up against the clock under child-labor laws. That meant it was always the scenes with just Den and me that were scheduled to tape last. This is when Den and I endeared ourselves to the crew and earned our reputation as the One-Take Champions. Den and I were so comfortable with each other's style and rhythm of working that we would fly through those wrap-around scenes on Friday nights. Once, we filmed all the Screech and Belding scenes in a block at the end of the day and were out of there in half an hour. The crew loved us for this.

Because they were quilted together at the end of the month, wrap-around shows were not taped before a live audience. So, mixed in with all the other episodes of *SBTB*, are shows that were spliced together at the end of those three to four weeks of piece-meal tapings, then edited with a soundtrack to provide canned laughter and all the other necessary cacophony of a living, breathing audience.

After we wrapped the show on Friday, we all came out for a final cast bow to a thunderous standing ovation in celebration of our collective brilliance. The lead-time to air for the episode we had just taped was anywhere from three to four weeks, some-times longer. After the ovation, we were handed our scripts for next week. We were expected to read them over the weekend to be prepared for the Monday table reading. Then, it was time for the weekend.

WHERE THE MAGIC HAPPENED

The Sunset-Gower Studios, where we filmed many episodes of the original *SBTB*, were old. So old, in fact, that it's where the Three Stooges committed many of their slapstick heroics to celluloid posterity. During World War II, a rabbit warren of subterranean tunnels was created that crisscrossed yards below the studio floors so that studio executives, movie stars, politicians, and dignitaries could move around in secret and in safety. I don't know how vast the network of tunnels is in its entirety, but I do know from my own wanderings that it's pretty elaborate. I remember walking from beneath one of the banks, straight under Sunset-Gower, to a recording studio at least a half-mile away—all underground.

The tunnels were notorious for being haunted. They said that there was the apparition of a young girl who roamed the tunnels.

And that there was an old man, perhaps an actor from a bygone era, who could also be seen peering from the shadows every now and again. I'm skeptical of all that paranormal boogie-man stuff, but I often went searching for it nonetheless. If a ghost existed, of course I wanted to see it; I still do.

The studio definitely had a creepy, haunted-house feel to it. There was one room upstairs with an angled ceiling like an attic. I don't know what it could have been used for: there were no windows, and there was no room to stand fully upright, not even space to set up a desk. The first odd thing about the room was the complete absence of ambient sound. Usually, in any industrial space, you can hear faint street noise, distant voices, or the drone of florescent lights and air vents. But the air in this room had an eerily perfect silence and stillness. There was one spot in the room that was ice cold, but the room was windowless and had no ventilation whatsoever. Even so, as you passed through this one spot, the temperature would plummet, sending a rippling chill shivering through your body.

There was another spot in the Sunset-Gower Studios complex, in the back of Studio 11, a storage area where props were kept and where there was a trap door in the floor. Mark-Paul and I decided to pry the trap door up with a crowbar. To our delight, there was a ladder leading down into the bowels of the tunnel system. We reached the bottom and found ourselves in a small dirt room that, as far as we could see, led nowhere. We had brought along flashlights and a hammer to pry nails or locks or to dig or to bang for help if we got trapped somewhere. Searching around behind a dirt pile, we discovered a crawl space we could worm through on our bellies in the dirt, wriggling along to emerge into an adjacent area. On the other side, we could stand again. Through the dank, stale air we spied more tunnels snaking down black corridors and one passage that had been bricked off. Waving our bars of light into the darkness, we discovered a huge steamer trunk. The inside was filled with Civil War-era clothing and rifles, keys, and buckles. It was impossible to discern if they were authentic antiques or long forgotten props and wardrobe. This was not an easy area to access. That shit had been sitting down there undisturbed for a long time. It definitely wasn't from the set of *F Troop*.

Mark-Paul and I decided we'd explored far enough for the day and turned back. Just as we started to retrace our commando crawl through the low dirt tunnel, we heard Bobo, the head carpenter, holler, "Who left this fucking door open?" We knew the crew was diligent about locking down all tunnel access because they would get their asses chewed by the producers if any of the cast were caught exploring beneath the studio. We started crawling as fast as we could to where the ladder was when suddenly the light in the outer room was snuffed out, enveloping us in darkness. Then, above our heads, we heard the sickening thunk of the heavy trap door falling shut. Next came the whine of a hand drill as Bobo zip-screwed down into the door's perimeter, sealing it. Mark-Paul and I hollered in terror, certain we were being buried alive, entombed below our own television studio like some cornball Edgar Allen Poe-tribute episode. We screamed at the tops of our voices, shimmying as fast as we could through the cold dirt, fumbling with our flashlights. Staggering into the outer room, we emptied our lungs in desperation at the black ceiling. The trap door flew open. Bobo and friends, like Cheshire Cats, grinned down at our grimy, fear-stricken faces. They knew we were down there the whole time. They were just fucking with us.

Later, one of the crew told me that, since I liked to explore, there was a space in between the walls in the backstage area of the sound studio where, if I looked straight down, I could see something freaky. I took a look, and sure enough there was something weird just beyond my sight. I asked our special effects guy, Chuck Hughes, what he thought it might be? He handed me a flashlight and urged me to check it out. I scooched along inside the narrow space between the walls of the studio expecting to encounter a corpse or something, the bones of some long-dead mistress who threatened to topple a mogul's empire. When I got a few dozen yards from where I entered, the flashlight began to flicker, and then it went out. I was alone in the dark. I started to freak a little, turning back, I called to Chuck, "This flashlight is out. I'm coming back." "Oh," said Chuck, "maybe the batteries are going dead."

I start backtracking until the flashlight suddenly popped back on again. "There you go," encouraged Chuck. Then he shut the door as the flashlight went dead again. Chuck had rigged the fucker with a remote so he could control its flickering and cutting in and out. I told you, never mess with the crew.

* * * *

We were taping at Sunset-Gower Studios one time when we were shaken up pretty good by one of California's many earthquakes. It was a good-sized rumble, and the old building felt like it was going to cave in. Some of the massive 20K lights over our heads fell smashing to the floor. It was chaos as all the buildings were evacuated. Those 20K lights were dangerous enough without a major seismic event along the San Andreas fault. When those lights blew, they didn't just fizzle or pop, they exploded, sending glass and dust spraying and raining down on the set. Everyone would run for cover, shielding their mouths to avoid breathing in the hazardous particles. That shut down production for a few days.

The only other time I remember things getting shut down at Sunset-Gower involved Johnny Carson and a robot.

Disneyland used to have a display for children where a performer would speak into a near-invisible radio headset and their voice would emerge from a robot. Parents would secretly feed the performer information, and then the robot would suddenly come to life as a little boy walked past saying, "Hello Bobby, I hear it's your birthday today. Are you really six years old? *Does not compute.*" The kid would shit a Disney mouseketurd. Then the robot would launch into all sorts of personal info that would cause the kid to completely freak out, thinking that he had a robot stalker living at Disneyland.

That guy's act (and voice) became Kevin the Robot in the first two seasons of *SBTB*. I have no idea how he got the gig, but however it happened, his time on *SBTB* wasn't without incident. Once, during a Friday taping, we were informed that the radio-control frequency being used for on Kevin was fucking up a sketch that Johnny Carson was rehearsing on the stage of *The Tonight Show*. Apparently Johnny was delivering a stand up routine dressed as Lincoln. In the skit, people in the audience start booing and heckling until someone fires a pistol at him, knocking off his stovepipe hat. To that, Carson says, "Jeesh. Tough crowd." Or something like that. Well, the radio-control frequency they were using to zing the hat off Johnny's head was the same frequency the operator was using for Kevin on the set of *SBTB*, and the signals were getting crossed. But instead of someone from Stage 1 at *The Tonight Show* simply popping over quick to ask us on Stage 3 to hold off for a few minutes while they got their take, Carson unilaterally shut down production of *SBTB* until further notice. We all sat with our collective thumbs up our asses, costing the network untold thousands of dollars, until someone strolled back over from Stage 1 and gave us the go-ahead. I guess I should just be grateful that was the lone time we irked Johnny Carson at NBC.

PART III:
FAMOUS AS SHIT

The Malls of America

We used to travel all around the country, appearing at hundreds of events and signings in malls and amusement parks. There'd be twenty thousand kids in a line that snaked all through the park, kids dangling from the railings of the second tier inside some giant Midwestern mall. It sounds crazy now, but sometimes it felt like we were like the Beatles. Teenage girls would even go so far as to tear our clothes off. Seriously. Chicks wanted a piece of the Screech.

At one mall event, there was a security breech from the sheer volume of crazed people. Up on stage were Mark-Paul, Elizabeth, and I. Kids broke through the line, stormed the stage, and swarmed all around us. Girls attacked Mark-Paul, ripping his shirt, yanking off his necklace. We had to escape the building under protection from armed security, hurried into a waiting limo like the president being evacuated from imminent peril by the Secret Service.

It might have been more of a burden—even terrifying, sometimes—for the rest of the cast, but remember, I was the youngest. For me, these excursions were a lot of fun, especially around 1992, at the height of *SBTB*'s popularity. I was still under sixteen, and the law stated that I had to have a parent or guardian with me at all times, but my parents wouldn't always go. That was when I had the best time. My de facto guardian was our set teacher, Sidney Sharron. Sweet, wonderful Sidney—very grandfatherly, very cool, and very brilliant. Sidney didn't just teach me my math book, he wrote it, for Holt and MacMillan. Sidney even appeared on the show for a while. Fans will recognize him as Mr. Klopper, the Albert Einstein-looking janitor. But the same endearing qualities that made Sidney so trusting are what also made him the perfect guardian on road trips. Sidney went to bed early, allowing me the opportunity to sneak out while he snored away.

I'd head over to the amusement park where we had staged the day's event, meet a girl, hook up on the rides, and, later, head back to the hotel. "Hey," I was thinking, "I'm fifteen years old, and I'm staying in a suite paid for by NBC." It didn't take a ton of game for me and my amusement park sweetheart to find ourselves back at my hotel, pre ordering room service for breakfast.

One disastrous morning I had to appear solo at an event in some small town in South Carolina. Along was my friend Mark, who came to most of these gigs. We were just kids traveling around the country having fun. On the plane, Mark and I were able to score some drinks, so we were feeling mighty fine upon arrival. Then, our handlers for the event—some good ol' Southern boys—took us straight out to a bar for a few more drinks to loosen up even further. The event was a no-brainer autograph session scheduled first thing the following morning at a downtown convention center. There would just be a table with a line, and I'd wave and sign photos and other *SBTB* promo materials for a few hours. We had a good time the night we arrived, drinking hard and picking up a pair of hot Carolina chicks. We brought them back to the huge, multi-room suite that was provided so they could ride our gamecocks.

The next morning I awoke to discover that my California non-driver's ID card and wallet chain were missing (don't give me grief about the damn wallet chain, okay? It was the style of the day). The chicks we banged had stolen them. They didn't steal my money; they just appeared to have made off with a couple of mementos from their night with Screech. Still, it was a pretty big deal to have my ID stolen. But that wasn't the worst of my troubles. My main concern that morning was that I had the bells of fucking Notre Dame going off in my head and wanted to vomit out my pancreas. I was so hung over I was pleading for death. And Mark looked worse than me. Our handlers from the night before showed up at our hotel door, still hammered themselves, and said it was time to go down to the limo. We were running late for the event.

Inside the limo, I pled illness to the other, more adult organizers of the event. But they could smell the alcohol seeping from my pores and were not happy at all. I said I felt like I was coming down with a virus, like I thought I might get sick; maybe it was something I ate. Their eyes shot back, "Tough shit, kid. You're hung over. The show must go on."

We rolled up to a red-carpet entry leading into a giant convention arena packed with people. Before I exited, they informed me there was an RV trailer in the parking lot for my use during breaks. I stepped out into what had to be the brightest daylight on record. I felt the sun burning three inches from my eyeballs. There was press there from every corner of the state. That small town was treating my Screech appearance like the friggin' Cannes Film Festival. Mark felt zero compulsion to suffer with me, and made a straight beeline to the RV, where he immediately fell asleep. Meanwhile, I made my way along the red carpet through the microphones and flash bulbs of what constitutes the paparazzi south of the Mason-Dixon.

Inside the convention center was even more mayhem. Thousands of people were gathered with hundreds more formed into lines snaking towards a giant, raised dais like the throne of King Xerxes. The organizers led me up the steps, my ass dragging the entire way, and deposited my sunken carcass at the signing table with a little stack of pens. Clearly, my body language conveyed that I was not having a good time. To channel Raymond Chandler, I had a face like a collapsed lung, and I looked like a bucket of mud. The event staff definitely picked up on my reluctant vibe, which made for a very uncomfortable morning and afternoon. The feedback was not good: *This is a complete disaster, the kid is drunk off his ass, he's miserable and not smiling at anyone, he's hurrying people through the line . . .* On top of that, I was still stressing that some chick had stolen my ID and personal items. The promotional event had shaped up to be a catastrophe of epic proportions.

On the bright side, before Mark and I left for home, it was such a small town that those handlers who took us out and got us wasted the night before had tracked down the chicks that stole my stuff. My possessions were passed along to me in a nondescript manila envelope.

Safely, mercifully, back in L.A., Linda Mancuso was selected to scold me for my poor performance in the public sphere. "Dustin," she said, shaking her head wearily, "what happened?"

"What do you mean?" I asked innocently, finally sober again.

"The local NBC affiliate in South Carolina has dropped *SBTB* as a direct result of your visit to their community. They claim you were drunk and practically catatonic. So again, what happened?"

What could I do? I knew that I could trust Linda to tell her anything. So, I lied.

"I wasn't drunk. I had food poisoning or something. I was deathly ill but went ahead and completed the event as best I could. The show must go on, right? Mark was with me. He can vouch."

"That's right," said Mark, conveniently nearby. "Dustin would never arrive drunk to an event, Linda. He's a professional."

Technically, we were telling the truth. I wasn't drunk at the event, I was hung over. I was drunk the night before and into the wee hours of the next morning, carousing with some hot chick who boosted my ID after we made sweet love back at my hotel. I always felt badly that I didn't come clean with Linda, especially years later when she wouldn't even have cared. But I really was embarrassed. I had cost the show through my unprofessional behavior. I started to wonder if I was becoming part of the troubled Hollywood youth culture. But then I looked at my co-stars, with all their problems, and I decided, "No, I'm fine." That realization was a fitting epilogue to my southern fried clusterfuck.

I did another solo show in Miami, where I signed a bunch of promo material for a very excited young girl and was immediately approached by some Tony Montana-looking, scar-faced Cuban dude. He was surrounded by an entourage of grouchy Cubans sporting shoulder holsters filled with an array of large-caliber weaponry. Tony Montana sat down next to me and in a thick Cuban accent said, "You do that show and make my daughter happy. I have a gift for you." He led me out back to the trunk of his black Mercedes and offered me, from a pile of white bricks, a kilo of cocaine. I gracefully declined . . . though I can think of some other cast mates who might possibly been tempted.

The entire cast appeared once at a mall in Arizona. Again, Sidney Sharron was along as our guardian. We were riding to the event in our limo when Mark-Paul announced he needed to go to the bathroom—immediately. We pulled into a 7-Eleven and Mark-Paul ran inside. The clerk decided to be a dick, telling Mark-Paul that the restroom was for customers only. Mark-Paul offered to buy something, but the clerk said, "Too late." This minimum-wage Arizonan obviously didn't know, or care (or maybe he did) that he was dealing with the Golden Child, star of NBC's top-rated sitcom for kids. He told Mark-Paul, "Too bad, so sad. Beat it."

His bladder reaching critical mass, Mark-Paul decided to piss behind the dumpster. It wasn't the world's best-secreted dumpster either, with a clear line of sight from the interstate, but desperate times call for desperate measures. As his stream pounded the pavement, an acrid steam rising to his nostrils, Mark-Paul exhaled a grateful sigh of relief. What a picture: In the background, the grand desert vista of the American Southwest. In the foreground, *Saved by the Bell*'s Zack Morris grinning with satisfaction as he micturated on a 7-Eleven dumpster.

Returning to the limo, Mark-Paul caught a flash of strobing lights and heard the blurp of a siren. A police officer had been seated in his car just a few yards away, watching him the whole time. Spooked, Mark-Paul dashed inside the limo, scurried to the far end and tried to make himself as small as possible. The cop tapped on the window, Sidney lowered it a crack.

"Can the gentleman who just urinated in public please step outside the vehicle?"

Huh?

"Sorry officer," said Sidney, "you must have the wrong vehicle."

"No," said the cop. "I don't."

"Mark-Paul," whispered Sidney, incredulous, "did you do what the officer is suggesting?"

Mark-Paul, from his fetal ball, whispered back, "Please make this go away."

It's a good thing Mark-Paul had at that point already relieved himself or he would have been pissing in his pants. Poor, sweet, old Sidney shook his head and stepped out to see what the hell was going on.

A few minutes later, Sidney returned, and we were back on the road to our event. He had taken care of it. Not only was Sidney a kindhearted, gentle math wizard, now he had graduated to the role of fixer!

That wasn't the only time that Mark-Paul fucked up. One summer we were all participating in a *SBTB* cast-and-crew softball game played in some local public park. It was introduced to us as a regular bonding event meant to strengthen our sense of teamwork through the rigors of physical exercise and the spirit of competition and fair play. It was so lame I never went back.

The only moment worth recounting was a particularly stellar at-bat by the Golden Child. *The ol' Dutch-in-the-clutch. Thai Goes to the Runner.* Mr. Amster-slam. He spit into his batter's gloves, clapped his paws together, tapped the plate a few times with the stickeroo, knocked dirt from his wooden cleats (just kidding), took a couple of practice swings, kicked up some red dust, then stood, bat on his shoulder, shifting from his back foot to his front, waiting for the pitch. Then came the wind-up, the pitch, and . . . TWANK!

Oh, wait. One thing I forgot to mention is that way beyond the end of the left-field line, a family was having a lovely afternoon picnic. It looked like a birthday celebration for one of the little tikes—balloons, presents, crêpe paper, and all the fixin's. From the family truckster, the dad was approaching all those beaming faces, in his arms a giant sheet cake. I know some stories sound made up, that they could never have occurred so perfectly, but trust me.

Back to Zack at the bat. The softball exploded off the barrel, filling the expanse of the park with the teeth-rattling resonance of a hollow thunderclap. The fat ball sailed high into the almost cartoonishly blue sky. Higher and higher, over the left field fence and . . .

Dad was traversing the fresh-cut grass, skipping along as he smiled, holding aloft the beautifully decorated birthday cake for all to see, when the softball smashed him squarely in the face. Yellow cake and frosting detonated in his hands like a box of pineapple grenades. Children started screaming, howling in terror; women were wailing. Dad crumbled to the turf where he convulsed acrobatically for several heart-stopping moments. It was horrific or hilarious, depending on where you were standing. Then nothing. Motionless.

"He's dead!" a woman shrieked. "They killed him!"

But he wasn't dead. Only knocked cold; his clock thoroughly cleaned. Mark-Paul, the half-Asian for every occasion, was completely freaking out. If there were a limousine nearby, he would have made a mad dash for it to hole up while Sidney Sharron administered CPR on his beaning victim. But this was not a seedy 7-Eleven in Arizona, this was Southern California. The classy thing to do was to go to the man, determine if he was alive or dead, and apologize. Perhaps even to his wife, apoplectic children, and other stunned family members and party guests.

Which, I've got to hand it to the guy, is exactly what Mark-

Paul did. Turned out the dad was okay. He sat up, knew most of his name, what day it was (roughly), and he appeared to vaguely recognize his wife. Mark-Paul apologized profusely for his galactic home-run-hitting display, brought about by his steroid-induced mondo manliness. He told the guy that if he ever found himself in Burbank—or Holland or Thailand—he owed him an autographed headshot. No, fuck that, *two* autographed headshots. The man smiled woozily; it wasn't clear if he understood what the words meant.

Around 1992, Lark and I were asked to appear at the Nickelodeon Kids' Choice Awards. They wanted us to come out and do a little Screech and Lisa Turtle bit where Screech pines for her attention and is rejected yet again. Technically we were there as Dustin and Lark, but our scripted dialogue was peppered with a few lame tongue-and-cheek Screech and Lisa jokes.

"So, Lark, how about after this you and I go . . ."

"Unh-uh. That is *never* gonna happen."

At the time, the show *Double-Dare* was popular, as was its signature gag of "sliming" people. The producers asked backstage if it would be okay if they slimed me. I didn't have a problem with it—it was all in good fun for an audience of children— but I had borrowed the shirt I was wearing from wardrobe at *SBTB*. It was an expensive shirt, and it was a nice thing for wardrobe to offer, something they were definitely not required to do. Whenever I went to them and explained that I had an event I needed to look nice for, the wardrobe department would usually offer to very generously let me borrow cool clothes (not Screech clothes) for the event. They would go out of their way to deck me out in something classy. The condition was that we take care of the garments and return them in the same condition as when we borrowed them. Which is just a good life rule to live by in general. So I said to the Nickelodeon producers, "Sorry guys. These clothes aren't even mine, and, not for nothing, my curly hair doesn't really agree with a bucket load of slime."

There were lots of performers and recording artists milling around backstage, including the Atlanta teenage rap duo Kris Kross—Chris "Mac Daddy" Kelly and Chris "Daddy Mac" Smith. You know, the little dudes who wore their clothes backwards. Their big hit, "Jump" was popular at the time. They were strutting around like big-time gangsta rappers.

That's the thing: anybody who experiences the slightest taste of fame in Hollywood feels like they've finally made it. They just don't realize how fleeting it all is. The moment you recognize that you've achieved some measure of fame, it's already running away from you. Some people are involved in the entertainment industry solely for the craft. That's admirable and can be fulfilling, but you can't drive around in craft. Craft doesn't keep you dry during a thunderstorm or feed your family. So you try to use your craft to earn money. After securing a decent income, the next step is recognition and, perhaps, fame. The danger is when you take a straight moon shot to fame. You lose touch with reality. Holding on to that fame, whatever the price, becomes more important than the money, the craft, or even the people you love.

I introduced myself to Kris Kross. Based on their clothing, I was confused as to where I should present my hand for shaking. Predictably, they blew me off. I said, "So, what are you guys gonna do when your song "Jump" plays itself out?"

"We gotta whole album, yo," said Kris or Kross.

"Mmm," I thought. "A whole album, indeed."

I wonder what they did when that song *did* play itself out... a few weeks later.

Either way, I'm still waiting on that second hit from that *whole* album.

In addition to our road appearances and events, another commitment we were required to perform back in the Burbank studio was known as "affiliate days." These were marathon sessions where we sat in a tiny room at NBC and did literally hundreds of fifteen- to twenty-second meet-and-greet promotional conversations, rapid fire, with all the network affiliates across the United States. It was just the cast members (rotating in and out throughout the day), a few chairs, a camera, microphone, and earpieces stuffed into our ears to hear the questions. Those days were a bear, but we had to keep our spirits high and be fresh for each brief interview. Almost as annoying as the task itself was sitting all day next to Mario, who was a total microphone hog. He was incapable of shutting the fuck up. Typical interviews would run like this:

(From earpiece: *Okay, you're on with WAFF-48 in Huntsville, Alabama*)

AFFILIATE NUMBER ONE: Hi gang! So Dustin, what do you think is the secret of your show's success?

DUSTIN: That's a good question. I think it's . . .

MARIO: Hey guys, Mario Lopez here, I think that's a really good question, too. In my opinion, the best thing about *Saved by the Bell* is . . . *Blah, blah, blah.*

Boom. Fifteen seconds is over. On to the next interview.

(From earpiece again: *Okay guys, this is Channel 11 in Atlanta, Georgia*)

AFFILIATE NUMBER TWO: We have Dustin Diamond, a.k.a. Screech Powers, here. Dustin, what's it like playing the comic relief on such a hugely popular children's television show?

DUSTIN: Well, I tell you, it's a blast . . .

MARIO: Y'know, Dustin, it is a blast. Isn't it? And I like watching you, man. Let me tell you something about this guy. By the way, is it hot today in Atlanta? *Yada, yada, yada.*

All day long, that's how affiliate days would go, sitting next to Mario. The dude would constantly speak over whichever cast mates were seated with him. It was all televised, so we had to keep our smiles painted across our faces, and we could never let off a whiff of conflict between the principal cast members. But after a few hours of this, I did want to scream, "Mario, buddy, shut the fuck up before I stab you with a railroad spike." Mario was older and larger than me, but nobody is spike proof.

Another way we interacted with the public was through our mail. We all got our share of wacky correspondence from cool fans, shut-ins, creeps, the mentally unstable, and a wide variety of stalkers-in-training, like the weirdoes who would send Tiffani gold necklaces, diamonds, naked photos, and such. I got this one letter that had a dead spider smooshed inside. The fan wrote, "This is my favorite spider. He means a lot to me. Please take care of him and send him back." I don't know if the guy was going on vacation and needed me to spider-sit or what, but I was like, "Whatever, fruitcake," and tossed it in the trash.

But then take the case of another guy who wrote me frequently. The content of his letters read like they were from an adult, but the handwriting and spelling looked like there was a developmental-disability issue involved. The letters were in big, fat, balloon handwriting like that of a child. He was a big fan who wrote often, and I wrote back. It was touching, having an impact on his life. Swinging back to the other end of the spectrum, there was a chick who sent me a letter requesting four things: a personal possession, a piece of my clothing, a lock of my hair, and a bodily fluid. She wanted to make a fucking voodoo doll of me! "Yeah, I'll get right on that, you crazy bitch. Wait by your mailbox. The package is on its way!" Oh yeah, I received everything from fan mail to chain mail.

And things could take an even more serious turn. During the early years of *SBTB*, I had my first stalker. The situation was so frightening at my house that I had to move in for a few weeks with Tiffani-Amber Thiessen and her family. The stalker made it clear that his goal was to kidnap me. He had it in his mind that if he could just take me, be close to me, he would wind up rubbing elbows with celebrities and producers and become famous himself. It escalated to the point where it was not safe for me to play in my own neighborhood. One afternoon, the guy actually tried to snatch me off my bicycle.

After I'd moved in with the Thiessens, my terrier, Scooby, proved his worth as a great watchdog for one of the scariest encounters my family had with that demented psycho. My dad had taken to sleeping with Scooby and a gun under his pillow. One night, Scooby started barking like there was an intruder. Dad saw movement outside, and hurried through the back door as a dark figure ran away into the night.

Dad smelled gasoline. Our home had been doused, and that fucking whack-job was only moments from setting it ablaze. The full tale behind my stalker episode opens an ominous door into the dark, twisted aspects of my life at home—away from the set of *SBTB*. That's the story behind-the-scenes of behind-the-scenes. But it's a story for another time. Trust the Dust, there's enough weirdness and violence there for a whole other book.

I'M GOING TO DISNEYLAND . . . TO GET LAID

During most of the time I was on *SBTB*, I lived in Orange County, located about an hour and a half south of our Burbank studio (in good traffic). That meant I was a neighbor to the best-kept secret for picking up girls in the history of the modern hook-up: Disneyland.

Long before my short-lived stint as a pseudo-employee of the Disney Network during our first season of Good Morning, Miss Bliss, I had a history with Mickey and Minnie and the rest of the gang. When I still lived up in San Jose, every year before we moved, my folks would take us on a six-hour family trek to the Magic Kingdom. It was a big deal. My dad loved Disney, Walt Disney in particular. Dad was born in 1954, and when he was a boy he once got lost at Disneyland. Lillian Disney, Walt's wife, found him, reassured him and brought him up to Walt's office, where he sat and chatted with the great man while park workers located my grandparents.

I would often make my trips to Disneyland with my buddy Brian. I met Brian when I invited a girl I liked to Tori Spelling's birthday party at Bar One in North Hollywood (the same bar where, years later, Tori's *90210* co-star Shannen Doherty's infamous fight went down). The girl's mom didn't want her going on a date to some Hollywood party without a chaperone, so she required that her older brother Brian go along. At first I thought that was pretty lame, but it worked out in the end. When the girl and I clearly were not making a love connection, I let her drift her own way to mix and mingle at the soiree while I hung out and joked around with Brian, both of us hitting on chicks together. Later on, Brian worked at Diz—Disneyland—and joined me in many of my magical adventures scoring chicks there. Another of my trusted wingmen was my best friend—and, coincidentally, Ron Howard doppelganger—Mark.

I became a regular at Disneyland and actually purchased an annual pass. I also made it a point to quickly get to know all the workers; you never know when you need well-placed friends. Disneyland soon became my neighborhood haunt. You need to remember that, sure, during the summertime the place was packed with little kids. But when school was back in session, the little kids disappeared, and I had the park practically to myself to prowl around. Plus, I was set schooled and enjoyed a four-month hiatus after we wrapped each season, a hiatus that never fell within the normal public school vacations. And even when we weren't on hiatus, we filmed three weeks and then had a week off. So, during that week off, I went to Disneyland and found nobody there. Nobody, that is, but hot chicks on international holiday from places like France, Switzerland, and . . . Sweden! Fifteen-, sixteen-, seventeen-, and eighteen-year-old, big tittied Swedish girls! Happy to be in America, happy to be at Disneyland, and *very* happy to meet a TV star they instantly recognized from his worldwide syndication in one hundred and six countries, sixteen times a week. I learned fast that overseas customs were very different from our own. Those European girls were way more physical when we first met. They liked to talk real close. I had no problem with that.

As I grew older, there was a stigma attached to Disneyland by my friends and fellow cast members on *SBTB*. They thought the park was for adolescents. The cool thing to do at the time was to use your fake ID and go out to the L.A. bar and club scene to meet girls. People don't realize that Disneyland in the early '90s was the perfect place to meet and hook up with chicks. If you were a teenage guy looking for a no-attachments blow job, to get laid, or even just to score a nice stinkfinger (or, as it later became known: Disneyfinger), Disneyland was where you wanted to be. It was perfect for a guy like me, that is, too young to drive. Every possible amenity for the typical date was there at our beck and call.

And let's talk about the rides, shall we? Fifteen minutes, uninterrupted, on the People Mover (or as we called it back then: the People Maker), late at night on four linked trams, high walls below the windows, no cameras. Fifteen glorious minutes of guaranteed alone time. The Haunted Mansion: a totally dark, nine-minute ride. Pirates of the Caribbean: a little more open, a little more exciting, but, if you timed it right (or knew the staff as well as I did) and could get into a boat that had empty boats at the bow and stern, eighteen minutes. And the best first-move ride to take a girl on: Splash Mountain. Why? Because it was a log-flume ride where you would sit, legs spread, behind the girl with your arms wrapped around her waist, fingers interlaced, with just a short jog north to cupping her boobs. If she didn't slap you away, it was nine to eleven minutes of soaking wet squeezing. Then, if that went well, it was on to the darker, more private rides. It was a practiced courtship, progressing in intensity, compressed into the span of a single day at a fun park. Yes, I have a many fond memories of my skirt chasing days at Disneyland.

Years later, when I was twenty-one, I realized I hadn't been to my old haunts in ages. My buddy Mark and I decided to make a triumphant return to see if we could relive the dream, conjuring the old magic. To prep for battle, we chilled in the parking lot before heading in, killing a couple of forty-ouncers. The plan was to pound them as fast as we could, get a good buzz going, then enter the fray.

Needless to say, it wasn't the same. Inside the park, everybody looked like a little kid, especially the girls. *Yipes! Did we really used to hook up with chicks this young?* It didn't even matter that, at the time, we were the same age—or younger. It was just plain wrong. It was such an odd, foreign sensation: being bored at Disneyland. Or even more so, feeling *old* at Disneyland! I even started to complain, like an old fogey, that my feet were hurting. Truth be told, we were pretty bummed out.

Suddenly, across the promenade, we spotted two beauties, and my old hook-up routine came flooding back. First, we would tag along behind the girls who, of course, knew we were following them. We would wait quietly in line behind them until casually striking up a conversation. We'd ask if they would enjoy going on the ride together, and then we'd split up, each with our respective girl. I'm not saying this was a foolproof approach. More often than not, the clear icebreaker was when the girls recognized me as Screech from *SBTB*. If that was the case, I'd ask their names, and BOOM! . . . we were off and running.

The difference this time was that these two chicks were working their game on us. Mark and I could sense that we were being followed, so we did all the little things to smoke them out: we'd stop, then they'd stop; we'd get a drink and stand along the fence, then they'd do the same. We were like, "These chicks are checking us out. Please God, let them be legal." Mark and I decided to get in line for the Haunted Mansion. The chicks got in line behind us. It was bizarre having my own hook-up tactics used against me. I felt so dirty, in a good way. We turned and said, "You girls here with anyone?"

"No."

"How old are you?"

"Nineteen."

"This may sound forward but, um, can we see some ID to that effect?"

Yes, indeed, they were nineteen, and Canadian to boot. Mark and I spent the rest of the afternoon and into the evening hitting all the rides with them, fooling around. When dinnertime rolled around we said, "What're you girls up to now? You want to grab something to eat at Denny's?" (Mark and I were first class all the way.)

"We thought we'd hang with you guys tonight," they said. "Maybe go back to your house."

Ka-ching!

"All right," I said. "That could work. You guys wanna follow us in your car?"

"Oh, we don't have a car. We got dropped off. Let's go back to your house. Where's your house?"

"That's weird," I thought. Plus, my guard was always up for possible con artists, gold-diggers, and leeches. I didn't know anything about these chicks. A harder look at them revealed shades of sketchiness in their mannerisms and appearance. I definitely sensed *the sketch*. I started thinking we could get these chicks back to my place, and they could rob us, or worse. Mark was stoked, but my radar was at DEFCON 4. I was wary of those chicks. But still, per usual, my monster was doing most of the thinking.

We piled into my car, and I circled the parking lot, making sure there were no sketchy-looking dudes tagging along, giving us the eyeball. The coast looked perfectly clear. Then I drove a long, roundabout, circuitous, and confounding route back to my house. If they were truly Canadian and had no local knowledge of the area, I figured they'd be oblivious. And they were. There was nobody behind us in the rear-view mirror. I thought, "As far as my horny, half-assed investigations are concerned, these hot little Canucks are stone-cold legit."

Back at my place, we popped some beers and got right down to some freaky business. Once again, my meat stick had trumped my better judgment, and it had paid off in spades. These girls were good to go. Mark stayed with his chick on the couch while mine led me into my bedroom. After our naked hockey brawl under the sheets we reclined for some pillow talk. Turns out our two maple leafs were runaways. Disneyland had been their golden, American beacon of hope—their West Coast Statue of Liberty— as they escaped the domestic problems of their troubled homeland. It was a beautiful tale: leaving home with the dreams of meeting Mickey Mouse but meeting Screech instead and sucking his hairy sack. I get a little weepy thinking about it. Call me a sentimental patriot.

The best part about those chicks was that afterwards they were so chill. They finished a couple more beers and prepared to journey along on their aimless way again. I asked where they were headed. They said they had no clue. Ah, the open road. I called them a cab, gave the driver a $20 bill and bid them adieu. That was how I tied a big, fat, red bow on my adventures at Disneyland.

SCREECH IS A BORN COUGAR HUNTER

Because of the show, sex started for me way earlier than it would have otherwise. And from the very beginning, it was usually with older chicks. I fumbled through my first clumsy sexual experiences with girls sometimes two and three years older than me. I knew I was lucky to have the advantage of my fame when it came to dealing with the ladies. But even though they had a few years on me, they were still just schoolgirls. In my mind, nothing compared to the lure of a woman. A mature woman could teach me all the things those young girls couldn't. The fantasy consumed me. It was intoxicating.

Around 1992, when I was fifteen and after four years of friendship, I started to discuss my sexual escapades with NBC vice-president Linda Mancuso. I would watch a wry smile spread across her face, empathetic but proud. It seemed to say, "Aw, the

D-man is growing up." I knew that, no matter the issue, I could talk with Linda, no holds barred. When I think about it, at that time Linda was around the age I am now: early thirties. From my perspective, it was an ocean of time and experience that separated us. She was so mature, so exotic.

I mentioned earlier that when I was twelve, my first official "girlfriend" was fifteen. This made me a hero to my pals, a true man of the world. "You're dating a girl three years older than you?" they'd say. "Dude! She's got boobs!" She did indeed. I'd bring girls to the set, and Linda would approve or disapprove of whom I took a romantic interest in. She was watching out for me. She didn't want me to get hurt or taken advantage of. Over the years, she continued to develop into my confidant, my friend, and my protector. No matter how bad things got, Linda was my go-to person. I could tell her whatever was going on and not have to worry that it was going to get spread around as the latest dish (you know, sorta the opposite of what I'm doing in this book). Except for that one time I showed up hungover to the signing in South Carolina, Linda would usually say, "Don't worry about it, Dustin. We'll take care of it." With Linda, I never had a moment where I thought, "Shit, I shouldn't have told her that."

As opposed to St. Peter, the super-born-again Christian. Peter wanted to be your buddy, but he was still the boss. You couldn't get too comfortable with Peter because if shit came down (and shit always came down), you could guar-an-damn-tee that Peter was going to slip on his asshole hat and bring down the hammer. You could be sure you weren't going to see the friendly, buddy-buddy St. Peter. No, you were going to be dealing with the get-in-my-office-now, piss-in-your-pants, going-to-the-real-principal's-office, Executive Producer Peter Engel. In fact, St. Peter could be so strict, he once punished me for handing out Halloween cards to the cast and crew because, to him, Halloween was tantamount to devil worship.

Linda was a beautiful, powerful woman, widely respected throughout the industry. She had a personal secretary scheduling meetings for her all day with influential, important industry people—and I could just waltz into her office whenever I wanted. I would wander in, plop down into a chair and hang out. Just chill.

We would sit in her office and talk for a couple of hours at a time. After, we'd always kiss goodbye. It wasn't anything romantic, everybody did it. It was, and still is, a Hollywood thing. Just a hug, peck on the lips, "Okay, see you later" kind of deal. But after one particular talk, there was a moment where we paused, and the kiss lasted just a teensy bit longer. It was just a half-second more, but you have to remember, my hormones were raging, and I was breaking down every move with fierce scientific analysis. Half a second longer was half a second longer. I thought, "This is definitely something different. Something new."

After that day, that talk, that kiss, I started thinking, "Man, Linda is a sexy woman." I was starting to think I really liked her—as much more than a friend. But I couldn't say anything. I was sure I was picking up signals, but it would have been devastating if I were to learn I was wrong. As it happened, that wasn't my most immediate problem.

In California at the time, you could get a learner's permit to drive at the age of fifteen and a half and, if all went well and you passed your test, you were awarded a driver's license at sixteen. But lucky me, I got fucked! Just when I was about to qualify for my learner's permit, the state changed the law, raising the age of eligibility. But the Golden State wasn't done having its way with me. After I lost two years of cruising around L.A. on my own, they lowered it back down again once I was finally legal. None of this would have mattered if those two years weren't the exact years in my life when I wanted to show Linda how grown up I was by driving, alone, over to her house.

Did I mention that Linda started inviting me over to her house?

It began one day in the studio when we stopped to talk in the hall. She asked me if I was free for lunch. I felt giddy, sneaking away from the world of *SBTB* to spend time with her. That's when I really started worrying about whether or not I was picking up signals of a sexual vibe or if I was just a clueless idiot. I was suddenly acutely aware of every micro-movement in Linda's body language. In set school with Sidney, we were studying psychology. Of course what interested me most was the pre-mating dance, the subtle dynamics between a man and a woman. For instance, I learned that some studies suggested it was a subliminal invitation for sex from a woman if, when she sat, she pointed her knees facing inward toward you. So, I had that kind of crap and a whole bunch more amateur, first-year-psych bullshit swimming around in my head, colliding with the surging testosterone coursing through every corpuscle. What can I say? I was nervous and hunting and pecking for it.

Was Linda really interested in me romantically, or was I allowing a fantasy to cloud reality? The last thing I wanted to do was fuck up the relationship we did have. I treasured our friendship and didn't want to ruin it. That's when I decided, if something was ever going to happen between us, she would have to make the first move.

We continued to meet, talk, and go out to lunch. One day I told her, "Y'know, I tell you everything I do. What do you do when you're away from the set?" She said she was a homebody. She liked her privacy, preferred hanging on the couch watching a movie to the bar scene around town. Besides, the Hollywood bar scene, for all the mystery and fascination it holds in the imaginations of celebriphiles (thanks almost exclusively to the paparazzi), it's pretty boring. Places like Bar One and the Viper Room were filled with mostly young—often underage—douchey kids making way too much money, peacocking around, making sure to get noticed. When I went out, I would just hang back, drink my drink, observe, and fade into the wallpaper. Years later, Lindsay Lohan, Paris Hilton, and their ilk came along and managed to make an already bad scene fucking unbearable.

I understood why Linda wanted to avoid all that L.A. bar-scene bullshit. So she invited me to stop by her house any time and gave me her address. I couldn't believe it: yes, I had a fake ID and could get into any club in L.A. but when Linda said, "Stop by my house," all I could think was, "Holy Shit, I can't fucking drive! I need a chaperone!!"

That's when things stalled. I tried working every possible angle in my mind on how I could look cool getting dropped off at

Linda's house by my buddy Brian (who was a few years older) or—horror—my parents. It just wasn't going to happen. I wanted to draw any attention away from my age and hone in on any real feelings that might be there. I didn't want to do anything that might wake Linda from what I could only assume was a dream in which she found me interesting, maybe even attractive. I was determined to not do anything that might make her say, "Whoa, what am I thinking?" if indeed that's what she was thinking at all.

So I never did drop by Linda's house. Not then, anyway. We wrapped up our twenty-six-episode season and headed our separate ways for a four-month hiatus.

During those hiatuses, the cast, crew, execs, and everyone else involved with the making of the show didn't keep in real close contact. It was a real hiatus in every sense—from the show and from each other. Think about it: working long hours together, day in and day out, collapsing once you got home to be back early in the morning to do it all over again with the same people. It was almost too much like actual work. As far as I was concerned, when hiatus rolled around, I didn't even want to look at my cast mates again until I had to. In a way, that's really the sadness of Hollywood and being a child star. I'm just as guilty of it as anyone. People you've worked closely with, cared about, and shared experiences with for years lose touch the instant they've moved on to new projects, barely batting an eye. There's almost a sense of relief to leave an acting job in the past as you build credits and move on to new opportunities. In my experience, it's very rare to maintain friendships with fellow actors beyond that

intense window of the creative project you came together to pro-
duce, whether it's a three-month film project, a television pilot,
or even over a decade on a hit show together. I say it's a sad thing,
but that's not entirely true. I never really liked any of them very
much anyway.

Any of them, that is, but Linda.

* * * *

When you're under contract as an actor on a network television show, you do a lot of events. The network calls and says,
"You're going to (insert city)." And you say, "Okie, dokie." You
don't get paid for the gig, but you fly first class, get put up in a
penthouse suite, and they pay for all your food and expenses. Top
shelf all the way. At least that was the world I lived in when *SBTB*
was a hit show on NBC. I don't know how things work these
days, especially on cable and especially since the world financial
markets crashed and everybody's assholes pinched shut. On this
particular trip, towards the end of the original *SBTB*, the network
called and said, "Dustin, you're going to New York City." And I
said, "Okie, dokie."

St. Peter always stayed in the best hotels. He was never one
to just crash at the airport Marriott. When we traveled with him,
we stayed in "his kind of hotels," like the Rega Royal, the Omni
Berkshire, The Mark (one of Peter's favorites), and The Time. St.
Peter was wealthy beyond belief, so when we were with him, it
was always the finest accommodations. My suite in New York
City had a living room, a kitchen, and an honor bar! Woo hoo! I

was hanging out in Manhattan, drinking from tiny booze bottles and living like a rock star. I had a hotel room better than most people's apartments.

Best of all, just a few doors down from mine, was Linda's room. By the time of this trip, Linda had become St. Peter's producing partner and had been made president of Peter Engel Productions.

That night, we returned to our swanky hotel from the day's event. My cast mates and some others wanted to go out and party in the city. I had a fake ID at the time, but it was pretty lame. Here's how clever I thought I was: I figured everybody gets a fake ID that says they're twenty-one, but that's just too obvious. I insisted on one that announced my age as twenty-three. I reasoned that the obscurity of the number would throw off any suspecting bouncer. The only problem was that, even when I actually was twenty-one, I still looked like I was twelve. It took a long time for it to dawn on me that I wasn't swift at all, in those days I was just benefitting from a lot of cool people who looked the other way so I could fully enjoy my time on the scene.

I didn't feel much like hitting the town and, fortunately, Linda decided to hang back, too, since her mom had joined her on the trip and was staying with Linda in her suite. Linda's friend and assistant, Robin, who also worked on *SBTB*, had traveled to New York also, but she was staying in a separate room.

I shuffled down to Linda's room, and Robin was there, which was awkward because she was like, "Hey, it's the little Dust Man. How're you doing. It's getting kinda late, huh?" All I could think was, "Alright, Robin, don't fuck this up for me."

Linda's mom had already gone to bed. Linda's suite was big with one of those separate, French-door-type-deals where, on the other side, her mother was fast asleep. Linda and Robin were sitting on the couch, drinking wine. Unremarkable enough, until I noticed that on the television was one of those soft-core chick movies with some Fabio-looking guy dispensing his rough, yet tender, brand of seduction. You know, the kind of thing with a loose semblance of an actual plot before the woman gets ravaged. I found the background moaning kind of encouraging. When I asked what they were watching, Linda and Robin just giggled. After a while, Robin said she was tired and excused herself. I have no doubt that she was oblivious to any sexual energy between Linda and me. I know because Linda was two different people when it came to me. Around other people, she was the network executive; when we were alone, she was the honest, beautiful listener whom I couldn't stop thinking about. As I matured, I realized why it had to be this way.

After Robin left, Linda offered me a glass of wine. I already had a drink in my hand, one I'd brought from my honor bar. I was playing every angle I could think of to appear mature in her eyes.

I made my way over to the couch. Linda was wearing one of those silky, button-up executive blouses. Every time she leaned forward I stole a glance of the heavenly view between her buttons. Linda was in terrific shape. So beautiful. Fireworks exploded behind my eyes (and that's not the only place). I knew I'd swore to myself that if anything was ever going to happen between us, it had to be her that made the first move. But in that moment, I knew I had to act. It had to be something subtle, something suave, something I could quickly back away from to save myself from crushing humiliation if all these signs I thought I saw, all these signals I swore I recognized, were nothing more than my own hormonal delusions, just boyish fantasy. "But look!" I thought. "Linda's knees are turned inward. Isn't that another sign? A subliminal invitation for sex? Isn't that what my grandfatherly Yoda, Sidney Sharron, taught me in our unit on psychology and human behavior?"

The couch could easily seat four, but I positioned myself on the same cushion as Linda. My eyes searched her body for any invitation. Whenever her gaze wasn't directly on me, mine was on her. But I was nowhere as smooth as I imagined. She caught me looking at her chest, her legs, her hair. Then Linda, after gesticulating to emphasize some point she was making, placed her hand on my leg. And left it there.

I started thinking, "If something happens here, this is no notch on my bedpost. No quick bang on the road. Far from it." Linda had been there for all my formative years. I'd shared everything with her. She was someone I truly cared for.

I leaned forward, inhaled. "Your hair smells good," I said, leaning back again.

Linda removed her hand from my leg. She rearranged something on the coffee table. My worst fears had been realized, I'd read the situation all wrong. *I was so stupid, stupid, stupid.* I leaned forward again, setting my drink down. Backpedalling, I said, "I really do think your hair smells good, I didn't mean to . . ."

We kissed. Slow and romantic. The kind of kiss that builds, rising to a fearful elation, cresting, then ending with a smiling sigh. My heart was like a crazed wolverine trying to tear free from inside my chest. Sure I'd kissed girls before, but this was a woman, one of the most powerful women in network television. I thought about her mother sleeping in the next room. I knew instinctively this moment was not going to proceed to the next step. But while it lasted, it was magnificent. Still, I was a guy. I was making out with the woman of my dreams. I had to try pushing the envelope. I moved my hand to her waist. I thought, "What now? Do I do the same stuff I do with the girls I pick up at Disneyland?" With those girls it was easy. With them I'd settled into a comfortable level of cockiness. With them, I'd just go for it, make a move. If they shooed me away, I'd say, "C'mon baby, I'm a TV star!" With Linda, everything was different.

When the kissing subsided, there was a long moment of *Okay. We just did that. Now what?* I found myself upright again, arm slung over the back cushion of the couch, hyper-aware of every movement I was making. "It's getting late," she said, matter-of-factly.

Next thing I knew, I found myself standing in the doorway telling her I'd see her tomorrow. She gave me a kiss—short, soft, and full on the lips. I thought, this must be what it's like when a woman kisses her man goodbye. Someone she really cares about. She closed the door. In the hall, I leapt in pure joy. But I knew I couldn't tell anyone. Not a soul. Not until now.

And that was only the beginning.

* * * *

My first vehicle was a brand-new, $35,000, 1993 Ford Bronco, Eddie Bauer Edition, deep forest green with mocha trim, bug shield, tow package. It was the shit, and I loved it. The reason I remember it so well is because this is the car I used when I finally took Linda up on her offer to stop by her house "anytime." Anytime had finally arrived. We were taking things to the next level.

I parked in her driveway, killed the ignition, and just sat there. Since New York City and the weeks that followed, there wasn't as much uncertainty anymore about Linda's feelings towards me. The trip to New York had been on a weekend. When we returned to work that Monday things were completely different yet still exactly the same. Different in my head and my heart. Different in the way I looked at Linda and the way I searched her eyes for any glance in my direction. But the same in that it was time to get back to work. The show must go on. We sat down at the big T-shaped table on stage for our first Monday table read. St. Peter and the director (who for a long time was Don Barnhart) sat at the head of the table, and we began to read through the script. At first, all I could think about was how glad I was that I'd worked hard and graduated from high school early, at sixteen, so that Sidney wouldn't have to stand up at one point—in front of Linda—and announce, "Okay, everybody off to school" and herd me out the door like a little kid in short pants. We read through the entire script, timing it for length—cutting and adding where necessary—laughing at the jokes that worked and "punching up" the ones that didn't. When we finished, we took a fifteen-minute break then returned to block out our positioning on the set for each scene. This is where the director would offer guidance as we moved through each scene and began rehearsing our dialogue.

During the break, all the executives, including Linda, disappeared into their offices, while the actors stayed on stage. Yes, things were definitely back to business as usual. But as I sat there at the table, reading my lines aloud, glancing up into the shadows where I knew Linda was seated, I couldn't help but think about how much things had changed.

So, there I sat in Linda's driveway, the engine of my new Bronco now cold, my thoughts swirling with the possibilities and pitfalls of the unknown. I knew Linda cared about me and had her reasons for extending the invitation for me to visit her at her home. But I also knew that whatever happened inside, we would be forced to maintain a purely professional façade when we returned to work. It was the way it had to be, and I understood the reasons why. That didn't mean I still wasn't a ball of nervous energy. I knew this visit could be the biggest moment of my life. I'd been with dozens of chicks before and stumbled home at night with many a Disneyfinger, but this was a whole new ball game. In fact, this was the majors.

I thought about the time I lost my virginity. It was May 15, 1992 —my fifteenth birthday. It was to a girl I met at—where else? —Disneyland. Her single mom was an employee there, and let me just say this about that magical night: that mom totally let me tap her daughter. The way the whole thing went down, I was convinced that I was pretty slick. I told them both that there was a cool trick I knew that involved kite string, whipped cream, and condoms. I looked at the mom as she shot me a glare of mock sternness, and I said, "Calm down. It's just a prank." So I talked the mom into driving us to the store to buy all three of the aforementioned implements. Back at their house, I filled a condom with water (she had purchased a box of twelve) and whipped cream, tied it off, knotted a length of kite string around the end and then took it outside in the yard. I gave it a few, good bolo swings above my head and released it splattering against their garage. They were delighted. Later that night, before heading up to bed, the mom said, "All right. There are eleven condoms left. There better be the same amount when I wake up in the morning."

There were ten.

Inside Linda's house, she hugged me hello. *No kiss? Kinda weird, but okay.* I played it cool as best I could. Linda gave me the grand tour. I recall my exhilaration as I became increasingly aware of my physical body moving through her house, her private spaces. Especially her bedroom.

In the kitchen, she offered me a glass of chardonnay. I started to relax, deciding I was driving myself crazy by over-thinking everything. I was just going to have fun and enjoy my time with Linda. In the living room, she showed me photos of places she had traveled, awards she had received. She put on some smooth, wine-and-cheese jazz. I lowered myself onto the couch. Linda followed, but leaving more space between us than I had hoped. I couldn't help myself, my insecure thoughts crowded in again as I steeled myself for her to say, "Look, what happened between us was a mistake. You have to understand, this relationship has to stop here . . ." In my head, I rehearsed my easy response wrapped in faux-nonchalance. I would need to fall back on what I knew: acting.

Linda scooted closer. She stroked my hair, asked how I'd been. There was no mention of our rendezvous in New York City, nor any talk of television shows. Instead, we simply talked about each other. Finally, I gathered the courage to own why I was there, in that place,

in that moment. It was time for me to act like a man. I leaned in and kissed her. We kissed for a long time on the couch, groping, fondling, groaning, and fumbling until we began to remove our clothes. I had a flash of recognition: *Wow, this is really happening*. My fantasy was crossing over into reality. But that thought quickly passed as I slipped deeper into the wonder of the living moment.

We moved to the bedroom. I was painfully nervous but thrilled, fully in the experienced, compassionate hands of an older woman. A beautiful, sexy, powerful woman. I may have driven my Ford Bronco to Linda's, but Linda handled all the driving after that. It was a singular, seminal moment in my life, a sensation of intense excitement and emotion that can never be recaptured. It was awesome. Not awesome in the sense that Screech might use the word to describe his robot, Kevin, but awesome like the Taj Mahal. Awesome like Niagara Falls. Awesome like the sun.

Afterwards, we lay tangled in the sheets, talking and giggling. I remember full well the first word I spoke to her: "Wow."

At her front door, she paused, her face suddenly darkening, "Dustin, at work . . ."

I cut her off. "Of course."

Linda smiled. Yes, indeed. The Dust Man was growing up.

Linda and I would steal away for our clandestine meetings and private moments with less frequency as the months, then years, went by. There was never a conversation, never a decision to spend less time together, eventually we simply drifted apart. I got interested in playing my music, the cast split apart as we transitioned from the original show and through the abbreviated season of *SBTB: The College Years*. Then Den and I moved on to *SBTB: The New Class*. I started dating Tiffany Anastasia Lowe, granddaughter of Johnny and June Carter Cash. I would go to Johnny Cash's house in Nashville and The Man in Black used to give me Christmas presents. My favorite was the cologne he gave me called "One Man Show".

When Linda was around thirty-eight, she was diagnosed with breast cancer. I don't know how long she kept it a secret, but when she did decide to share the news I was devastated. We embraced, just holding each other. At that point, it had been a long while since we'd been together.

She lost her raven hair fighting through her first course of chemotherapy. Later, her hair came back gray. She fought hard again as the disease reemerged. Later still she took to wearing a wig as she fought on. For a while, the prognosis seemed positive. The cancer was in remission. She continued to work, becoming head of programming at ABC Family Channel, continuing to attending meetings, finally in a wheelchair, up to her death in 2003 at the age of forty-four. I had already moved to Wisconsin when I heard the news of her passing. It was a shock. I was numb. There were memorial services held in Los Angeles and in her hometown of Chicago. But I couldn't go. My mom had also died of that same disease, when I was nineteen, and I just couldn't go.

ZACK AND KELLY COZY UP TO THE BOSS

I've heard lots of Hollywood hearsay in my day, but I can only vouch for what I saw with my own two eyes and heard with my own two ears. Here is one of the most fucked up things I saw behind the scenes of *SBTB*. Draw your own conclusions because I still don't know what to make of it.

The Golden Child started getting called to St. Peter's office for long meetings. Extremely long. He wasn't in any trouble, there was no Zack Morris spin-off in the works; he just slipped into the office and closed the door behind him. Which was weird in and of itself, because typically Peter kept his office door open for most meetings. But then again, most meetings with the cast only lasted several minutes. So what were these talks? What was going on?

I had heard stories about St. Peter, rumors beyond the dope and party days. Nothing I could verify of course. All I know is what I saw. I used to hang upstairs around the NBC offices at Stage 9 (where *Good Morning, Miss Bliss* started and where the original *SBTB* ended) because I liked to check out all the hot chicks who were cast as extras, the hot extras who were getting bumped up a notch to speaking parts, and, of course, the hot interns. This was during the time when *The Fresh Prince of Bel-Air* was taping next door on Stage 11. We shared wardrobe rooms side-by-side with their show, and I used to play chess backstage with Will Smith, who was a strong player.

I was upstairs one day when the Golden Child had been in St. Peter's office, door closed, for like an hour and a half.

Tiffani also began to be summoned upstairs for long, closed-door meetings with St. Peter. I mean, a couple of hours each time. Then, both Mark-Paul *and* Tiffani (!) were called, together, into St. Peter's inner sanctuary for another mystery marathon behind closed doors.

Just for perspective, I remember when St. Peter called me up to his office for a meeting. At first I was like, "Uh oh, what'd I do to fuck up this time?" It really was like being called to the principal's office, but way worse than Mr. Belding ever gave it to Screech. I entered with great trepidation as St. Peter told me to take a seat. I was scolded for some minor transgression on the Peter Engel morality meter, but St. Peter did leave his office door open the whole time.

Those long, closed-door meetings were all happening in 1992, prior to gearing up for our first movie, *SBTB: Hawaiian Style.* But before the movie was scheduled to begin filming on location in Hawaii for three months, the network was setting up an overseas trip for two cast members to do a press junket in Paris. Our promotional events had evolved over the years from

mall tours and amusement parks to overseas trips as the popularity of the show spread in syndication around the world. The
producers and network suits would decide which characters they
were sending based on the exposure of the trip. Like I said, I got
up to seven thousand pieces of fan mail per week, edging out all
the other cast members by a small margin, but still consistently
the most.

So, based on fan popularity, Mark-Paul and I were selected
to go on the Paris trip together. They were sending the comedy
team of Zack and his trusty sidekick, Screech. I was stoked. I
already had my bags packed when, lo and behold, Princess Tiffani pitched a bitch. She went up to St. Peter's office for another
hours-long, closed-door meeting, and when she re-emerged it
was suddenly her and Mark-Paul now making the trip to gay
Paree.

You bitch!

I mean, I really wanted to go to Paris, but not bad enough to
find out what happened on the other side of St. Peter's closed office door. So Mark-Paul and Tiffani jetted off to the City of Light
for what was supposed to be a week abroad promoting *SBTB*. As
it turned out, the lovebirds were enjoying themselves so much
they wound up convincing St. Peter and NBC to keep putting
them up in Paris for a couple of months. That money didn't just
materialize from thin air; it needed to be pulled from the budgets
of other projects.

So when Tiffani and the Golden Child deplaned in California from their European holiday and it was time to go to Hawaii
to shoot the movie, suddenly our three months on location had
become three days. There was no money left in the budget for
us to film there. All we did while we were in Hawaii was wan-

der around through the scenery shooting B-roll footage with no dialogue. "Okay, you guys, act like you're playing on the beach . . ." "Okay, now walk along that footpath and gaze out over the water . . ." "Okay, stand there for a minute while we get this instantly recognizable Hawaiian landmark squarely in the frame . . ." "And no talking! We have to dub all this shit later." "Okay, that's a wrap. Let's get back to L.A." We ended up filming the movie on the beach in Santa Monica, just down the freeway from Hollywood. *SBTB: Santa Monica Style?*

Tiffani liked to have her fun. Back in the day, guys would stop me on the street and say, "Tell me man, what's Tiffani really like. Can I have her number?" I'd say, "Dude, trust me, you don't want to go near that." Frankly, I just didn't see what the big fuss was about, but maybe that's because I worked so closely with her. I saw what she was like on a daily basis, and my final verdict was, "Meh." Besides, you show me the hottest girl in the world, and I'll show you a guy tired of banging her. Hell, Tommy Lee got sick of nailing Pamela Anderson. It gets old. It's just nature. Out in the forest, I suppose there must be owls sick of banging smokin' hot owls, and so forth.

THE SNIPER

I'm allergic to cats, thus making me not much of a cat guy. But one summer afternoon when I was around nineteen, I was chilling in my backyard by the pool when a cat came around the corner. Not being a cat person has never precluded me from being friendly to all animals, so I said, "Here, kitty kitty . . ." The cat yowled and fell over. I thought, "Holy shit, this strange cat just wandered onto my property and died right in front of me." It wasn't a healthy looking cat, either—scraggly and emaciated with a very labored gait. Turns out it wasn't quite dead yet, so I decided to feed it. I returned from the kitchen with some tuna and milk and encouraged it to eat. The cat seemed pleased by the attention and the meal, and I left it to its own devices while I puttered around inside the house. When I checked on the cat again it was gone. I searched around and finally located it sitting atop the fence separating my yard from the neighbor's. It yowled for some more food and I obliged. And just like that, I owned a fucking cat.

After a few weeks of this animal eating everything I put in front of it right down to—and perhaps beneath—the enamel of the crockery, it started getting rather fat and lethargic. I thought, regardless of its underfed condition when I discovered it, this cat is getting very fat, very, very quickly.

I found out why one day when I came outside to discover it in one of our backyard flowerbeds, in mid labor. The cat had made a little nest for itself and given birth to eight kittens. And I was their dad. The cat fed her kittens, while I provided warmth and shelter and supplemented food and drink for those first weeks. Sadly, the smallest kitten didn't make it.

So now I had eight cats—a mom and her seven kittens. I gave them all names and collars, had them spayed and neutered, that is, all but one. Even though I was allergic, I could still handle them so long as I kept my hands away from my face and washed incessantly after each time I held them. Not a big deal, since I was always right next to our swimming pool. There was one kitten from the litter that refused to come near me. I named him Puss (like Puss in Boots). He wouldn't let me approach him, either. Every time I'd extend my hand to pet him and say, "Hey Puss," I'd get a bop-bop-bop with his razor claws, and he'd bail. Puss was a typical cat, though: he'd give me the ol' figure eight around the legs when I brought his food out, but once he'd been satisfied I couldn't even find him. So, because he was such an elusive dickhead, Puss was the only cat I didn't get fixed. There was a big problem with that decision.

The first problem was that Puss was female. That shows what I know about feline anatomy. The second problem was that when I couldn't find Puss one day, I discovered she had crawled through a space leading into the garage and delivered her own litter of three kittens. Now I had eleven goddamn cats. Me, who's allergic to cats and could take or leave the entire species as a whole. I was now the grand patriarch of three fucking generations of the same cat dynasty, living (and breeding) in every crevice of my backyard life in Orange County.

I also noted that the alpha male of the first litter—Puss's brother—was looking rather scrawny, and his face was scratched up like he had been scrapping with another animal. Turns out what was happening was that some tomcat from somewhere else in the neighborhood was terrorizing my cats and stealing their food. I decided to catch this tomcat in action and scare it off with my pump BB gun. I figured a few pumps should be just enough to give it a good pop in the ass and discourage it from ever coming around my yard again. I didn't want to kill the cat, or even break its skin, I just wanted to scare the shit out of it. So, for a test, I had my buddy Mark stand at the proper range, gave the rifle a few pumps, and shot him. The projectile appeared to hurt Mark more than he had anticipated but, upon review, had not penetrated his skin. My ballistic test a success, it was time to lay in wait for the tomcat. Like any good sniper, I climbed up to the roof of my garage and waited.

One thing I forgot to mention was that my neighbors were a pair of miserable old cranks. They were the neighbors who shared

that fence separating our backyards—the one I had originally returned to find that first cat perched upon, she who was now the
matriarch of a multi-generational brood under my care and protection. This fence was important also because it was over this
fence that my friend, Mark, had recently whipped a pizza crust
into the old farts' yard while they were gardening and pruning
their lemon tree. I was helpless to stop him, being fully lounging
in the pool at the time. Well, this pizza-crust incident exploded
into quite the suburban shit storm. Moments after the pizza-crust
sullied their immaculate landscape, the old man climbed his ladder and stared daggers over the fence. This moment of shared
recognition marked my very first interaction with my neighbors.
The old man then zinged a lemon into my head as I bobbed on
my inflatable pool chair. Such injustice! I had nothing to do with
the pizza crust projectile. I had been wrongly assaulted for an act
I didn't even perpetrate!

"What the fuck?!"

I clambered out of the pool and hoisted myself up so I could
peer over the fence.

"You can't throw lemons at people."

"Fuck you. You can't throw pizza crust."

"First of all, that's not my pizza crust. It's his. For what he
did, I apologize. But there's a big difference between a discourte-
ous guest tossing food in a neighbor's yard and that same neighbor assaulting a person with fruit."

"You're just a troublemaker, that's all."

Which was baseless. I was always very respectful of my
neighbors. In fact, I was the perfect goddamn neighbor. Sudden-

ly, the old lady hurdled a rose bush, ran to the fence, and started brandishing her garden shears in my face hollering, "I'm warning you, buster!" The two of them started swearing at me like sailors with Tourette's syndrome. It was like an unexpurgated DVD of Geriatric Def Comedy Jam.

The pizza-crust incident had seriously escalated. I was confused by this because I felt the advantage in the situation clearly rested with me. Though up to that point I had been respectful of my neighbor's property and privacy, I was still a devious youngster with enormous resources and a fertile mind to plan and execute countless acts of mischief in retaliation. If I felt like it, I could rain all sorts of shit down upon their house. *Were they serious?*

Now where was I? Oh, yes. So there I was, straddling the peak of my garage roof, my eye leveled on the bead of my BB sniper rifle. I was determined to teach a life lesson to the alley cat that was harassing my extended feline family. The operation was a classic bait-and-shoot. I had laid food out for the perpetrator to waltz right into my trap. I observed patiently as my own cats circled the food then scurried away, terrified that the tom might show his menacing whiskers at any moment. Sure enough, a giant tomcat crested the fence. This fucker was mean. He was the Mickey Rourke of tomcats. The big cat pounced into my yard and proceeded to clean house of all my frightened, furry little wards. I understand the laws of nature, but I have a deep sense of quid pro quo. In the animal kingdom of my cul-de-sac the moment had arrived for me to establish dominance. POP! My golden BB flew fast and true. I gave that Tom the shock of his life. He scurried back over the fence like greased lightening, and I descended the roof feeling pretty victorious about the whole affair. Mission accomplished.

Later that day, I found myself inside the house playing video games when Dad entered. He said, "Dustin, are you playing a joke on me?"

"No. Why?"

"The police department just phoned to say they have the house surrounded, and we're instructed to exit through the front door with our hands up."

We looked out the windows and didn't see anything suspicious. We figured it had to be bullshit. Somebody was playing a prank.

How wrong we were.

The phone rang again, Dad answered. He was informed in no uncertain terms that if we both did not exit the house immediately and surrender ourselves they would take the dwelling by force. Holy shit.

We exited through the front door. Somewhere, over a loud speaker, we heard, "Approach my voice. Turn around with your hands up." I was freaking out. I'd never had any trouble with the law. The only thing flashing though my head was what a clusterfuck this was going to be when I had to explain it to NBC, or worse, if someone had tipped off the local news. As we walked down the sidewalk, bodies started pouring out from behind buildings, trees, vehicles—everywhere. There were city and county cops, a SWAT team, black and white cars converging on the area. All our neighbors came out on their front lawns wondering what the fuck was going on while the cops established a perimeter. It was like we were on the FBI's ten-most-wanted list. The cops handcuffed both of us while they explained they were responding to a report of a man on a roof with a gun. They asked us what weapons we owned before they entered and searched our house. Local law enforcement had diverted a lot of manpower to this call. This was high drama for Orange County.

Admittedly, it was one of the stupidest things I'd ever done. My plan to thwart the marauding tomcat was far from foolproof. I explained (sort of) to the cops what I was doing on the roof earlier in the day and that the weapon in question was only a BB rifle. I was informed that, regardless, it was illegal to fire any weapon within the city limits. Good thing they didn't know how often I'd fired off the howitzer in my pants at young extras.

Of course, it was that old bat next door and her lemon-hurling husband that called me in. They had seen me play in the yard with my BB guns for months—setting up targets, shooting Mark at point blank range. They knew when they called the police that I wasn't "a man with a gun on a roof." They did it to fuck me. And it all traced back to that pizza crust.

Gratefully, the cops ended up letting me off with a warning. I was incredibly relieved because, at the time, I was old enough to get in some seriously deep shit. There was no press coverage, but I'm sure the media reaction would have been in measured proportion to the circumstances. The reporters' sense of journalistic integrity would surely have acted as a firewall against any hyperbolic sensationalism. Besides, I doubt anyone would have made a big deal out of learning Screech had been arrested by the SWAT team for perching on a roof with a high-powered sniper rifle.

> INNOCENT BYSTANDER NUMBER ONE: There he is, up in the bell tower! He's snapped!
>
> INNOCENT BYSTANDER NUMBER TWO: Wait, listen . . . Screech is screaming something! He says he's sick and tired of having to deliver corny dialogue.
>
> DUSTIN DIAMOND: (*from bell tower/obscured*) I am *NOT* gay with Mr. Belding!

Making Chicks "Screech!"

Is it bragging to say I've banged over two thousand chicks in my life? Maybe it is, but it's a fact. There were days when I had sex three times with three different, lucky ladies. In the *SBTB* studio alone, I would bang girls in my dressing room or in the prop warehouse and spend the night in my dressing room at NBC. I had a great pickup line. I'd meet a girl out at some club on Sunset and tell her I had an early call the next morning on the set of my hit television show. I'd drive her to the studio, pull right onto the lot, through the security gate—*"Good evening, Mr. Diamond"*—park right beside Will Smith's space and give her a tour of the set (which was the least glamorous part of the evening because we had to squeeze between the chained stage doors.) I banged girls right on the set. Oh yeah, that's right—*on* the *SBTB* set. In fact, there wasn't a bed in any of the bedroom sets from 1992 to the end of the series upon which I failed to complete the deed, except perhaps the top mattress in Screech's bunk-bed set. Can't recall.

In the prop warehouse and set graveyard you could lead a girl through the fuselage of a 747, the drawing room of a murder mystery mansion, past a hot tub, and over the moon. Not a bad first date. It was the land of make-believe. We'd just choose our dark corner, duck in, and have at each other.

Obviously, there was a lot you didn't see on camera that was nevertheless an integral part of the sets and a familiar part of our daily lives while working on *SBTB*. For instance, backstage of The Max's set, to the left of the door, stuck to the wall, was the world's largest, gooiest, most grotesque mound of chewing gum. From the very first episode, someone squished his or her gum on that wall beside the door. Before long it had expanded into an amorphous, sticky rainbow of discarded mastication that just kept growing and growing over the life of the show. At the end, it looked like a seventy-five-pound tumor. It had toothpicks, paperclips, and all sorts of sharp implements and office supplies jammed into it, jutting out willy-nilly like some retarded hedgehog. Surrounding the gum hump was an array of hand-drawn pictures, scribbled notes, jokes, and insults.

Another interesting fact about The Max's set was that the arcade games were real and set to free play, so you could use them anytime you wanted. The jukebox, however, was only a prop. Inside the jukebox, in the little paper windows for each song, the prop guys would often slip in subversive messages without ever breathing a word about what they'd done. Frankly, I don't think they even cared if any of us spotted their inside jokes, they were purely for their own amusement. Like in the window for Zack and Kelly's famous song selection, which if I remember correctly, was A-12, the slip of paper read: "Stereotypical Zack & Kelly song." Or, there would be a little sign with an arrow beneath the glass reading: "Mark-Paul, Push Here." And behind the set of the stairwell in the main hallway, past all the lockers, there were all sorts of crazy drawings and messages scrawled onto that wall.

Anyway, beside the gum tumor is where you would stand and wait with the stage manager who gets the call into his headset from the director in the booth saying, "Cue Screech." The stage manager gently nudged you through the door whispering, "Dustin. Go." But while you were standing there waiting for your cue, you were hanging out, visiting with the extras constantly crossing from left to right and vice versa through the background of the scene. If you watch any episode closely, mostly because of the nature of the various camera angles and how shots need to be set up, you'll often see the same people cross multiple times through the background at ten- or fifteen-second intervals. It doesn't seem like very long, but over the course of a couple days rehearsal and shooting on tape day, those down times were excellent opportunities for me to flirt with the cute extras.

Sometimes, between takes, the crew would have to reset, changing up lighting and camera angles, giving me several minutes to stand around and chat, endearing myself to whichever open-faced starlet I thought I stood the best chance with. This was also the best opportunity for the girls to see firsthand that Dustin Diamond was not the character he played on TV. Screech was a warmhearted, goofball persona he created to make children laugh. Although, as a practical matter, we did both possess identical monsters in our trousers.

Thursdays, or "camera days," were the best days to hit on extras. On Thursdays, all the extras would come in while we blocked out the episode with the cast's marks, the lighting, camera angles, final script changes, etc. It was live action for the main event the next day, but we were not in hair, makeup, or wardrobe, and we were still allowed to carry around our scripts (if there were last minute pages, otherwise we had it memorized by then).

Being a television extra is not a glorious gig. The people you see in the backgrounds of your favorite films and programs, making the scenes come alive, are kind of looked down upon in the industry. It's a really tough way to break in. Extras are considered "biological scenery" or "atmosphere"—basically props with pulses. But without them, the show couldn't go on. They work long, thankless hours. During *SBTB*, the extras would show up early in the morning and leave very late at night—all for a $40 voucher. Many of them were gutting it out to become eligible for the Screen Actor's Guild, but in order to qualify, they had to work their way up to performing at least three lines on camera. That's why you'll always see random, uncredited actors and actresses stroll up to Slater or Kelly or one of the other main characters to deliver a few banal lines of dialogue. Like a nerd who approaches Zack and says, "Excuse me Zack, but I heard you started a new whatever." That kid's an extra who was lucky enough to get upgraded to a speaking role. He just banked his SAG card. Guild membership has perks down the line like collective bargaining, better rates of pay, health insurance, and other stuff. It's a big deal for a new actor.

Which brings us around to the cute girls eager to discover what they could do to make one of the stars take a shine to them so he'd stick his neck out to win them a speaking role. Many sexual encounters with the show's extras were mutually parasitic transactions. The girls wanted to move up the ladder as quickly as possible, and the boys wanted to get their rocks off. In Hollywood—and just about everywhere else on the planet, come to think of it—this process is more commonly known as the Circle of Life.

We'd break for lunch on Thursday and, if things were moving along nicely, I'd share my meal with a lovely lady that afternoon in my dressing room, discussing what we might find ourselves doing after the show. If we hit it off, I'd go to the stage manager or one of the extras wranglers and say, "Hey, is so-and-so coming back next week?" With a knowing nod, they'd always say, "Yeah, I suppose she is coming back."

Like this one chick with terrific boobs. She had a big ass, too, but I could forgive her badonk based solely on the unimpeachable quality of her tremendous rack. She showed me her portfolio of "art" photos; in each one she was totally nude. Outstanding. There was another girl with bulletproof knobs that were toned down by her mousy personality, although she did have a lot of piercings and tattoos. When we met, she had a boyfriend, but of course that didn't stop me. We used to have sex in my dressing room, once even sneaking in to do it on the dressing room couch of this one chick on *The New Class* who was a royal bitch. That was fun.

I scored when we filmed away from the set, too. I had a beach romance with a beautiful blonde extra the casting director brought in during our Malibu Sands stretch. I started talking with her and learned she, too, was a big fan of pro wrestling. Turned out she wasn't just a fan, she was one of the G.L.O.W. Girls (Gorgeous Ladies Of Wrestling). Her name was Jeanne Basone, and she was the "Hollywood" half of "Hollywood and Vine." She must have been around thirty years old at the time, and I was about fourteen. There was an instant attraction between us. Our horseplay together didn't go too far, but in my mental Rolodex of the most gorgeous women I've been with, her image is near the top.

I lusted after more than extras. Soleil Moon Frye appeared on *SBTB* in 1992 as Robin in the "Screech's Spaghetti Sauce" episode. Soleil and I went to school together at Valley Professional in Studio City. It was a school that catered specifically to students who were in the entertainment industry and couldn't attend normal school hours. This may sound cool, but it was actually kind of a drag. On SBTB, we'd work all day for three weeks, then we'd get a week off. For that week, I'd often be sitting in a classroom at Valley Professional, which was much lamer than a typical high school. On the other hand, I was entertaining invites to the *Playboy* mansion. I suppose things did even out in the end. There does tend to be a cosmic balance to the universe.

In my experience, the *Playboy* mansion is not what people assume. Assuming, that is, that you think it's a bunch of hot, naked chicks running around, which it sort of is, but not exactly.

Yes, it's that, but it's also very classy. There's a strict guest list and many rules to obey in the mansion. For example, Rule no. 1: Don't act like an ass (this one had me behind the eight ball from the word go). Rule no. 2: Don't eyeball or flirt with whichever girl/girls Hef is currently banging. Rule no. 3: Don't piss in the grotto (I'm talking to you, Mark-Paul. Sidney can't talk your way outta that one). Actually, I guess there weren't that many rules at Hef's mansion. It was just a fuckfest.

Soleil's turn on *SBTB* came a few years after *Punky Brewster* was off the air. Soleil had to have had the biggest yammers in Hollywood at the time; I'm talking DDDDs. I just wanted to grab them and . . . Wait, where was I? No, this was a serious issue. Soleil suffered back problems resulting from her melonesque guzungas and opted to have them reduced—*twice!* Tsk, tsk. Just another horrific example of man—with all of his blasted modern technology—ravaging the perfectly formed beauty of the natural world. In my opinion she reduced them too much. My informants tell me that today they are the C-cups of a mere mortal. I hope you're happy Soleil. Another girl who fell squarely into this distinguished category was Erin Reed, who played April Newberry on a short-lived series called *Sister Kate*. But I liked Erin for her personality. Honest! If I was Hamlet, Erin would have been my Ophelia. She bewitched me, and I wanted to be around her all the time. I used to wile away many an hour hanging around the set of Sister Kate just to stay abreast of Erin. Also on that show was soon-to-be teen heartthrob, Jason Priestly, who would go on to star in *90210* with my *SBTB* on-screen love interest, Tori Spelling.

But I felt bad during these conquests because all through *SBTB* I just wasn't taking any chick seriously as a girlfriend. I was pretty self-absorbed and obsessed with new sexual conquests. I was having fun, on the hunt for new pussoire. When you get right down to it, I was just being a dick. But I fully embraced that fact by talking a mousy girl into a tag team with me and a friend of mine. She wasn't really into it, but somehow I convinced her. I know now that I shouldn't have done it, but at the time it just felt so right. She said she only did it because she liked me so much, but afterwards things were way too weird. I have to admit, it really tainted my view of her (after letting my friend see her taint). I told her, "Yeah, I can't be with you anymore." I had walked blindly into the ancient riddle of the buddy-girlfriend three-way. To top it off, my friend, whom I now call Captain Douchebag (more on that later), ended up being a real creep. In fact, he went on to filth up one of her close friends who worked for the company that cast the extras every week on *SBTB*. Between my actions and his, I started to become concerned that my steady flow of extras poon might suddenly get pinched off. Had I finally gone too far, putting my smorgasbord in jeopardy? The answer, thankfully, was no. But to this day, I still feel bad about that situation. If I could go back, I wouldn't do it again. And I advise against it for you, too, grasshoppers.

Naturally, there were some psychos, too. One girl started showing up at my house, in addition to hanging around the set of *SBTB* after her role as an extra had ended. She told me she had a new role as a nurse over on *DOOL*, which taped on a nearby set. Later I discovered that *DOOL* wasn't even filming that week.

The damnedest part about avoiding crazy chicks is that,

despite their mental instability (indeed, no doubt because of it), they're consistently the most fantastic lays. Banging crazy bitches is a delicate, complex math requiring the erect male to counterbalance the numerous (and often tragic) consequences of copulating with an insane person against an absolutely mind-blowing fuck. It's not fair.

Sometimes, those innocent first encounters would bloom into serious dating relationships. I started dating a girl I first met as an extra on the show that I soon became convinced was the Perfect Girl. Her name was Anne, We dated for a while, but eventually she dumped me. I was heartbroken because this was *the* girl. I just had this feeling. But alas, our love went sour. Soon after, I fancied another girl I'll call "Laura," who also began as an extra. Just when I thought we might have a future together, she informed me she had a kid. Yipes! An actual child, not a Cabbage Patch doll. I said, "Look, I'm just looking for a good time, sister. Dustin ain't no baby daddy." Not in my teens, anyway. The baby momma also turned out to psychic, or so she said. She was convinced she had ESP and would share with me her all her urgent emanations. For instance, on certain occasions she would receive celestial vibrations informing her that I was out partying with other women (which I was) while she was under the impression our lovemaking was exclusive. She would call me on my big Zack Morris brick cell phone while I was on the town and start admonishing me like I was supposed to feel guilty for my transgressions. I said, "Honey, I just tapped your ass a few times. We are not a couple." She persisted, "Don't lie to me. I know you're out with so-and-so." Which I was.

It wasn't long before I realized I'd have a hard time replacing my love that was Anne, so I tried to reconcile with her, the girl I really liked and thought was perfect for me. But it was too late. She said, "Aren't you involved with Laura?"

I said, "No baby. That's over."

"Really. Did you have sex with her last night?"

"How do you know that? I mean no."

Turns out Laura and Anne had moved in together. Now they were roommates.

The thing that truly sucks is that I was only out banging Laura because I felt so hurt by being dumped by Anne. It was only anger sex. Oh well…

C'est la guerre. So much for the Perfect Girl.

So conversely, if things didn't work out with a girl, a fresh shipment of extras was promptly ordered. Ahhh, the smell of fresh extras, rolling around in their packing peanuts, peeling away their protective coating . . . I almost feel I should write a separate book detailing every boneheaded, hormone-induced misadventure that ended with me hurting someone for whom, however long or briefly, I cared about or who cared about me while I remained oblivious. As the saying goes: I was young, dumb, and having fun. They also say youth is wasted on the young, but I don't feel like I squandered a minute of it. I was given an opportunity to live a different kind of life for a while, and I enjoyed it to the maximum. I wish I could devote an all-out effort to telling all those girls from my less honorable moments how I truly felt about them at the time and how I feel now with the perspective of years, some hard lessons in maturity, and realizing what it means to take responsibility and be a man.

First, I would thank them all for being so clean. In the tens of thousands of times I got it on, with thousands of partners, I never contracted so much as an itchy ballsack. That's not to say there weren't nights of dread anticipation, seated at the edge of my bed cursing myself for the highly questionable hole I had so recklessly entered. If I devoted a book solely to the girls I hurt, and they were the only ones who bought it, it would be still a bestseller. That's how many chicks I've fucked around with. The title could be *Jailbait, Beaters, and Trolls: The Dustin Diamond Story.* (For more on this topic, see Appendix B.)

FAMOUS PEOPLE I'VE MET, OR WHO'S A DOUCHE IN REAL LIFE AND WHO'S NOT

I'm famous, but I try to be an interactive, outgoing, regular guy with everyone I meet. I figure I'm famous in the way that people in, say, Zimbabwe know me by sight; famous in the way that a bum on the street wearing one shoe and smelling of feces (hopefully his own) will approach me and holler, "Screech!" But on the other hand, if fame were a flight from New York to L.A., I'd be seated in Business Class while Sean Penn would be lounging in First Class. If fame was a credit card, I'd carry the Gold Card while someone like Brad Pitt would have the Platinum.

Gary Coleman

I had heard all these stories about how my fellow Gold Card member, Gary Coleman, was a bitter little man with anger issues, so I went out of way to be nice to him. I thought, "Y'know what, everybody always jumps on this guy's case. They treat him poorly. They ram that 'Whachoo talkin' 'bout Willis?' shit down his throat every chance they get. The dude was born in 1968; I'm sure he's sick and tired of being treated like a child." I told him that with me he didn't have to put up with any of that shit and offered to grab a beer with him. I told him we could sit, hang, and talk about pure nonsense for a change. I had heard he was a model-train enthusiast (something I take no interest in whatsoever), so I struck up a conversation about model trains.

The dude was so far gone, he wouldn't let his guard down for an instant. Not even to me, a kindred spirit who has been through the same Hollywood child-star ringer. I felt like I was approaching him like a peer—Screech Powers to Arnold Jackson—and that we'd dealt with a lot of the same hassles over the years for the seminal characters we portrayed on television. People give you shit for why you're famous? People give me shit for why I'm famous, too. Let's hang out. But Coleman was so jaded by that point there was no hope for a friendship. Years of immersion in the Hollywood scene had built a brick fortress around that dude. It was too bad, but I understood.

The Stars of *The Tonight Show*

At NBC Studios, between Stage 1 and Stage 3 (where they taped *The Tonight Show*), the *SBTB* cast occupied a series of adjoining dressing rooms. For some reason or another, we had taped *SBTB* on both stages at different points. That meant we shared the same hallways with *The Tonight Show* and would often run into all the guests, as well as Johnny, Doc, and Ed McMahon. I could simply leave my dressing room door open and watch entertainment-industry icons like Crystal Gayle saunter past. In this way I became friends with legendary NBC Southern California weatherman, Fritz Coleman, who would often take time to stop and chat. Even Michael Landon sat in my dressing room for a nice visit with my dad just before Michael made his famous last appearance on *The Tonight Show.*

I remember how pissed Doc Severinson was when it looked like the network was going to fight him to keep the rights to The Tonight Show Orchestra, even though it was Doc's band. At first, it looked like they were going to keep the musicians, bring in Winton Marsalis (he worked out great) and screw over Doc. Doc wasn't happy.

I wish I'd thought to bring a recorder into that dressing room. Every room received the feed from all the different stages as they rehearsed and prepared for broadcast. On Thursdays, our *SBTB* camera day, I watched the feed of all the NBC stars and casts doing their walk-throughs, camera crews setting up their shots, actors reading their scripts, and talking casually. I could see on-location feeds of the various news affiliates' live shots, rehearsing their heartfelt gravitas: "Our deepest sympathies are extended to the victims of this senseless tragedy. . . Cut! This shit is too technical. How do I look in this shot? Is my hair fucked up? Brenda! Can I get a goddamn coffee please?!" I watched Johnny Carson and Jay Leno practice their monologues. I even watched Jay Leno pick his nose on camera—really getting in there. That's something you'll never find in any DVD bonus footage.

When he first took over *The Tonight Show*, I used to have lunch with Jay Leno in the NBC commissary. Jay, as everyone knows, likes cars. I like cars but didn't know much about them then. Jay used to drive a new car to the studio practically every day, cars like his Lamborghini Diablo and Lamborghini Countach or his Ferrari Testarossa (which he let me sit in). Jay would say, "Oh, I like the Diablo, but the Countach has such a classy look." "Yes," I would agree. Classy look. Yes, indeed, Mr. Leno." But he'd also drive old jalopies to work, too. He had so many cars and motorcycles, and he knew everything about them. He was more than just a casual collector of fine automobiles and motorcycles, he was an encyclopedia of gearhead knowledge. And he was actually just as nice a guy in real life as he appeared to be on TV.

Emmanuel Lewis

I became friendly with Emmanuel (TV's *Webster*) when we did a taping of *Celebrity The Weakest Link*. Back in the day, he used to frequent Michael Jackson's notorious Neverland Ranch. I don't need to rehash the accusations made against Michael Jackson. And trust me, I'm aware that there seems to be a powerful homosexual undertone to many of the stories I'm telling in this book, but I can't avoid it. Why should I be honest about everything else I recall and then avoid being honest about Hollywood's ubiquitous gay subculture. I don't care what someone's preference is. Makes no difference to me.

Emmanuel Lewis told me that when he was at Neverland Ranch, Michael Jackson showed him the room where Bubbles the chimpanzee's cage was situated. He had trees and ropes and all sorts of gymnasium equipment to crawl on and swing from. Emmanuel got the impression that Michael thought it was funny to leave him alone with Bubbles for a few minutes, their statures being relatively equal. As it turned out, Bubbles was actually bigger than Emmanuel, and, when he got a bit rambunctious, Emmanuel was forced to lock himself in Bubbles's cage for protection. What a picture that must have been. Emmanuel didn't mention whether or not, while locked in the monkey cage, he threw his own feces at Bubbles.

The Hollywood Christmas Parade with Pat Boone

One year I was selected from the *SBTB* cast to appear in the Hollywood Christmas Parade. To give another example of how random and bizarre celebrity pairings can be on Planet L.A., I was set to ride in a convertible with *Baywatch Hawaii* heartthrob Jeremy Jackson. Jeremy and I were given a rendezvous point where we were to meet. Then we were to ride together in a limo to the division of the parade where our open car would be waiting. When I arrived at the meet-up, I discovered that, sharing the limo ride with us would be that iconic Christian crooner of my parent's generation, champion of old-fashioned, apple-pie, American values, Pat Boone. I was aware of Pat Boone by name, but as a kid I didn't have any real appreciation for his legend. Pat and I chatted absently while waiting for Jeremy to arrive.

When Jeremy finally showed up, he was a glorious sight to behold: strung out on something, his hair electric purple, smooth *Baywatch* chest exposed through an open, metallic disco shirt, wearing dark sunglasses and having severe trouble remaining vertical. Luckily, hooked around his arm to steady him, was a six-foot porn star wearing sequins, clear Lucite heels and not much else. This chick had the obligatory giant boobs, and ratty hair. She looked like she'd been ridden hard and hung up wet. She also apparently took no issue with holiday revelers along the parade route having a clear view of her moose knuckle. The two of them, together, were a fucking mess. Mr. Boone was not pleased. I knew I had a front seat to an impending disaster, and I was savouring every moment.

"Hey, Dustern . . . Waasup?" slurred Jeremy.

Jeremy and I had known each other for years as child actors making the rounds. I looked at Jeremy's sad, sorry state. I looked at Pat Boone. "Oh boy," I thought. "This will be magnificent."

Inside the limo, Jeremy and his lap dancer squeezed up tight against Pat in the narrow seat at the back of the vehicle while I stretched out along the side. Clearly, Jeremy was getting on Pat's nerves. He was finding it increasingly hard to act Christ-like towards this lunatic rubbing against his left haunch. But Pat has class, so he leaned over and offered his hand to Jeremy's yard troll, "Hello. I'm Pat Boone."

"Charmed," her gum snapped.

"Hey, Bat Poon," mumbled Jeremy, shaking Pat's hand. "Nice to meet you, man."

"It's Pat Boone."

"What is?"

"My name."

"Bat Poon."

"Pat Boone."

"Right on, man."

After we exited the limo, Pat ran for safety while Jeremy and I found our vehicle. He told moose knuckle to get lost while he drove around and waved for a while. Along the parade route, the car moved torturously slow with frequent stops. During one such stop, while bright-faced majorettes twirled batons and did splits on the pavement, Jeremy passed out snoring on my shoulder. Merry Christmas to all, and to all a nice nap.

So, if you're keeping score: Jeremy Jackson is a douche; Pat Boone is not a douche.

Billy Crystal and Danny DeVito

It was dusk, and I was leaving an audition with my dad, walking past buildings on the lot from the casting office when, through an open door, I spotted Billy Crystal and Danny DeVito huddled over a script. I waved at them from the sidewalk, and they waved me in. Dad and I entered the room and introduced ourselves. The script they were kibitzing over was *Throw Momma From the Train*. Danny said, "Don't worry, it's a comedy." We stood and chatted with them for a while. This was when *The Goonies* had just come out and Anne Ramsey, who played Mama Fratelli, was eventually cast as Momma in the picture Danny and Billy were working on (as it turned out, one of her last films before she died).

They asked me if I'd seen *The Goonies* yet, and I was, like, "Of course (duh)." That's when they said it was likely they were casting Ramsey as the momma to be thrown from the aforementioned train. I take no credit for the final casting, but I did sing her praises as a rabid fan of all things Goonie.

Shaq

I was flying first class to the NBA All-Star Game in Texas with my friend Mark. We decided that Mark's looking like Ron Howard would be our "in" with the chicks once we got there: I was Screech from *SBTB*, hanging with my best pal Mark, son of Academy Award-winning director and beloved television icon, Ron Howard. Hey, we were teenagers, it was the best we could come up with on short notice.

On the flight, we sat down the aisle from Shaquille O'Neill. I've never been a big sports fan, but obviously I knew Shaq was a huge star, and I respected that. At the time the SBTB cast was attending and traveling to hundreds of events, meeting loads of famous people in every profession you can imagine. In fact, I'd already met Shaq a few times already. On the other hand, my buddy Mark was blown away. "Whoa!" said Mark. "It's Shaq! We gotta meet him."

Also on this flight, sitting right behind us, was Den. The flight attendant came around to take our drink orders, and Mark and I were determined to have a few alcoholic beverages before debarking for the big basketball game. Truth is, we wanted to be hammered by the time we landed. Even though we were still underage, we were veteran drinkers at that point. My goal in those days was always to appear older than I was.

The airline staff knew the plane was packed with celebrities on their way to party at an event. Regardless, Mark and I knew it was always a crapshoot whether or not we could get served alcohol on board these flights. It all depended on how we approached our liquor order and how cool the flight attendant chose to be. I subscribed to the suave, debonair technique of acting like ordering a glass of booze was old hat. To anyone without severe myopia, I was clearly pre-pubescent, so it was all about the delivery. "What do you have in Johnnie Walker, red or black label? Hm. I'm not a fan of the red label. Very well. I suppose that'll have to do. Rocks, please. Cheers."

This time it worked. The flight attendant didn't blink and moved on behind us to take Den's order. The next thing we heard was, "You guys. You and your shenanigans." *Dude? What the fuck?!* Den had totally cock(tail)-blocked us. I liked Den, and still do, but sometimes he would go way out of his way to be my buzz killer. For instance, when Mark and I turned to getting our Ron Howard's son "facts" straight for later use in the fine art of scoring chicks in Texas, Den leaned forward and asked, "Are you guys talking about Ron Howard?" I told Dennis to never mind. That was a mistake. Later, when Mark and I actually had a couple cowgirls corralled with our phony story, Den came swooping in to kill the fun.

"Sooooo," Den said to Mark, "you're Ron Howard's son, huh? Really good to meet you. Say, I was trying to remember, what's your grandfather's name again?" Mark didn't know. We were just trying to get laid. But the thing is, Den actually did know. That's why he was the Man from Everywhere.

The reason I liked my buddy Mark so much, aside from his striking resemblance to Opie Taylor, was because he was down for anything. He loved a good gag, and he was quick on the uptake when it came to going along with a joke. I knew that if I went with a crazy idea on the fly, Mark could keep pace, whereas most guys would stop and say, "What the fuck are you doing, dude?" When we arrived, stone sober, at the All-Star Game we ran into LL Cool J (Ladies Love Cool James, FYI), Mark Wahlberg (back when he was still Marky Mark), and a bunch of other celebrities. LL had just come out with his FUBU (For Us By Us) clothing line and was out promoting it. Both Mark Wahlberg and LL Cool J are really personable, very cool, very real dudes. I was handed a swag bag filled with all kinds of cool stuff like the new Nike pump sneakers, a mini basketball, disposable cameras for the event, etc. I grabbed Mark and said, "Hey, let's go get that picture with Shaq?"

We approached the big man. Shaq was all smiles; super-cool. Everyone crowded around him, thrilled just to be near him, screaming "Shaq! Shaq! Will you sign this for my kid?! Shaq, can I get a picture?!" I reintroduced myself and asked if Mark and I could get a picture taken. Shaq said, "Sure!" So I handed him my camera, threw my arm around Mark and posed for a picture. Shaq laughed, snapped the shot, and handed me back my camera. When I think about that photo now, I have to chuckle knowing that Shaq Fu was the photographer.

Buddy Hackett

One day Buddy Hackett was appearing on *The Tonight Show*, killing time on our set on Stage 1, visiting with St. Peter, the cast, and crew. He told us how much he enjoyed the show. *Buddy Hackett was a fan of SBTB?*

Buddy wandered around Zack's bedroom set and picked up

a Nerf football. He started tossing it back and forth with us kids and the writers. Buddy waved his hand, encouraging one of us to go long and hurled the ball spiraling high into the technical equipment suspended from the ceiling. SMASH! Buddy had zinged a direct hit into one of the ginormous 20K lights. The glass casing and bulb exploded like a fireworks finale, cascading glass and toxic dust onto the set as everyone scrambled for safety. From under cover, we all heard Buddy say, "Well, I'll see you guys later."

Hanson

One day the MmmmBoppity boy band, Hanson, was appearing on *The Tonight Show* and decided to enthusiastically drop by the set. When I first heard they were coming for a visit, I felt awkward. The Hanson brothers were big fans of *SBTB* and even bigger fans of me and my character, Screech. I didn't know whether to feel honored or goofy. They really went out of their way to meet me and spend time with me that day. The whole encounter left me a little ill at ease because I was *not* a Hanson fan. I was happy when they said, "Hey man, *love* your work!" but it felt weird to reply, "Hey man, thanks!"

Jaleel White

Jaleel White, who played Steve Urkel on *Family Matters* had the closest role to mine on a network sitcom—the annoying, tagalong, nerdy, comic relief. Urkel was the primetime Screech. It's interesting to note that he appeared in the pilot of *Good Morning, Miss Bliss*, playing a character who was in no way a pre-*SBTB* version of Screech. In Jaleel was a kindred spirit, another young actor playing an outrageously over-the-top character on television that was nothing like our real personality.

Jaleel and I met on a film called *The Monster Squad*. The movie was written by legendary action screenwriter, Shane Black (*Lethal Weapon*, *Predator*, etc). The movie was actually filmed between the first two *Lethal Weapons*, and it was my first experience acting in a feature film. Also in the picture was Jason Hervey, who played Wayne, Kevin's older brother in *The Wonder Years*.

Unfortunately, much to my dismay, my scenes ended up on the cutting room floor. I was originally up for the lead role, but the producers didn't think I had enough experience to carry the film (I disagreed, of course). The director, Fred Dekker, still wanted to give me a small role so I wound up playing "Kid With Baseball Cards." My scene had me walk up to the eventual lead, Andre Gower, and say, "Hey, man, you gypped me on this baseball card. It has bird shit on it." Andre's character apologized, traded cards with me, and I ran off. But alas, the scene got cut.

Jaleel also went uncredited in *The Monster Squad*. It was 1986 and neither of us knew what the future held for us. I guess that was just a weird nexus for two kids in Hollywood to briefly connect before going on to become iconic TV comedy geeks of the 1990s. Jaleel was a laid-back dude. He was also nothing like his super-geeky television alter-ego. On *Family Matters*, Jaleel was fortunate when he got to perform episodes where he played his own twin brother, who was a normal, cool guy. He got to play a role closer to his own personality on camera for audiences—

in essence, a slicked-up clone of his real-life self. That was something I never got the opportunity to do.

Frank Zappa and MTV's Kennedy

MTV VJ and host of the 1990s nightly show *Alternative Nation*, Kennedy, was on the set of *SBTB* to do some sort of research for an article she was writing. She said she wanted to talk with me alone, so we ended up going out to dinner together for an interview. I was still too young to drive, so she drove us over to Universal City Walk where we found a restaurant to sit down in and talk. During the meal, she asked me if I wanted to order an alcoholic drink, but I balked because—with NBC fanatical about our public image in the media as cast members of *SBTB* and with Kennedy writing who-knows-what in an article that included me—I didn't want to do anything stupid that could wind up in print. I declined any booze.

Plus, I felt like she was probably trying to ferret out some gotcha moment by being out with me in the first place. She thought *SBTB* was squeaky-clean, conformist bullshit, and she was the cool, punk/grunge/alternative hipster—even though she first came to prominence as an Eastern Orthodox Christian known as "The Virgin Kennedy." I played it safe. The last thing I needed was her writing some expose about "The Dark Side of *SBTB*." (Hey, that's my job! And it's taken me almost twenty years to do it!) The whole thing with Kennedy was very awkward, punctuated by a weird vibe. We were an odd couple indeed to be out for a meal together. Can you imagine being seated in the same restaurant that night? Casually glancing over your shrimp scampi, "Hey, isn't that Kennedy from MTV over there with . . . Screech?" You might think you'd had one too many Long Island iced teas.

After dinner, Kennedy drove us up Mulholland Drive. Final destination: Frank Zappa's house. I was just a stupid kid, and unfortunately it wasn't until years later that I started to fully appreciate Zappa's music. I grew into a connoisseur of the odd and obscure, which eventually put Zappa's style at the forefront in my musical mind. Of the few people on Earth (past or present) that I would completely geek-out on, Frank Zappa was definitely one of them. I wish now that I could have sat and picked his brain until he ran me out the front door at the tip of a sharp object, which he probably would have.

The Zappa house looked like a fractal clinging to the slope of the hill, sections of the organic structure stabbing out into every direction. Kennedy drove up to the imposing security gate, rolled down her window and leaned into the intercom.

VOICE: Can I help you?
KENNEDY: Yeah, we're here to see the Gweech.

There was a long pause, then—Open Sesame! —the gate rolled open.

Inside, Judy Zappa was there. Frank was not up for company. This was in 1993, very shortly before he died of prostate cancer at the age of fifty-two. There was a fireman's pole that extended from the top floor to the ground floor of the house. We spent most of the evening negotiating the abstract architecture inside the family's laundry room, which housed a pool table that Dweezil sat cross-legged on, strumming his guitar, chatting. I'd met him at an audition previously, so I spent the time rekindling our casual acquaintance. Later we would meet again at the NAMM show in Anaheim when I got into playing music, and Dweezil was there, sponsored by Carvin amps, which were the amps I used at the time. Kennedy and I didn't hang long at the Zappa compound. It was just another of those random Hollywood moments that I had come to take for granted.

By the way, the Gweech? He was Zappa's Siamese cat.

Captain Douchebag and the Conspiracy Lawsuit against NBC

I learned the hard way growing up in Hollywood that, in life, there are usually only a few friends you can truly count on. And really, of those few, there's maybe only one, if you're lucky. As a result, I would cycle through friends quite a bit. It's just one of the hazards of the business. On the other hand, you have a yearning to make genuine connections with people who see you as you really are, who enjoy your company because you share common interests, not because you're famous. As a working actor, you spend all day pretending, inhabiting a fully formed personality that is not your own. When you're with friends, you want to feel comfortable enough to drop your guard and be yourself. Unfortunately, it doesn't take long for your idealism about people's motivations and the hopeful possibilities inherent in each budding friendship to give way to skepticism and often cynicism. You develop a sixth sense about people. I got to a point where, if my instincts told me someone's motives were not honest and sincere, I'd drop them instantly and move on.

Even to this day I remain on guard. I've had it happen where I'll be hanging with someone for a while, convinced they're good people, then suddenly something spills from their mouth, and the alarm bells in my head start sounding: ABORT! ABORT! DOUCHENOZZLE ALERT!! Better to be wrong on occasion and live to fight another day than get dragged down by some vindictive psychopath, sinking his claws into your fame, deeper and deeper until you have no choice but to exorcise him entirely in a painful bath of holy hellfire. Of course, the one time my asshole radar failed me, that's exactly what happened. What follows is an all-time classic example of getting mixed up with the wrong dude.

Sometimes, you just click with a person. It's instant and effortless and feels completely natural, like you've always known each other but just never bothered to meet. This happened for me with a guy named . . . No, I'm not going to give him any credit by using his real name. For the purposes of this story, let's just call him Captain Douchebag. Anyway, when I met the Captain, we hit it off from the start. I had just turned eighteen, and I liked him so much as a friend that I started to absorb his lifestyle. I was just getting into playing music with my bass guitar, and he was already in a band. I started hanging with him and his fellow musicians, picking up tips, learning some licks, and doing some backup singing. I adapted instantly. It just felt natural.

After a while, one of the guitar players couldn't afford a good amp rack, his cabinet was going bad, and I decided I would buy a new one for the band. Why not? I was making good money and playing music was just about my only sideline outside working all the time on *SBTB*. So I bought a sweet Marshall amplifier stack (about $2,500), technically for myself, but for all of us to use while we jammed together. That was my first in a series of naïve missteps.

We practiced up in northern California, which was quite a hike from where I was living—over four hours. Looking back now, the music we were playing probably wasn't worth the commute, but I was having fun, and it didn't bother me. After practice one night, I was getting ready to leave, packing up my stack, and the Captain, who was the lead singer, said, "What're you doing?"

"Packing up my amp to go home."

"Dude, we've got a gig coming up. How're we supposed to practice if you take the guitar stack home with you?"

Look, I'm not usually gullible. The fact is, I thought this guy was my friend. So I left my half-cab there for them to practice with. I told them I'd bring it home after the next show. Of course, after the next show, when I reminded him I had to get my stack back. He said, "Sure, sure," then tossed it in his car with the rest of the band's shit and bailed on me. Okay, fuckers. Another lesson learned.

So at the following show, when we were done with our set, I started wheeling my stack off stage. The Captain started giving me a whole song and dance and I was like, "Tough shit. I'm taking it with me this time."

"Fine," he sulked, "then I guess the band is done."

"Guess so."

And it was. But I'm getting ahead of myself.

Captain Douchebag was the craftiest shyster I've ever en-countered—and I've been in show business since I was eight years old! This guy caused more problems for me than anyone else during my time thus far on this planet. He was quick-witted, smooth, conniving . . . Admittedly, this is why I clicked with the guy. He was clever, funny, and keenly observant of the world around him. I thought, "Here's a guy that moves at my speed. We can be friends." Like I said, it's hard to make close friends when you're a kid working all the time in the entertainment industry. I had my best friend, Mark (Ron Howard, Jr.), whom I'd grown up with, but we knew each other so well that half the time we wanted to strangle each other. I was definitely on the hunt for a new pal. I was an easy mark.

I first met the Captain when he landed a role as an extra on *SBTB*. Our early friendship got off with a bang—that is, the two of us banging three chicks at the same time, to be precise. But problems developed soon after, when the Captain started to feel he deserved special treatment on the set and behind the scenes because he was pals with one of the stars. He hung out and kept his stuff in my dressing room, coming and going as he pleased. I didn't see it at the time, but slowly he was making *my* dressing room over into *his* dressing room. In front of the camera, he even started wrangling larger roles on the show. This wasn't unusual, a lot of us tried to get family and friends on *SBTB*. Mario's sister was on the show; so was Tiffani's brother Skyler. Even my dad appeared in some episodes. Mario had a friend named Gil he got a job for on the show as a P.A. (production assistant), who wound up becoming one of Linda Mancuso's roommates towards the end. For some reason, it never occurred to me that the Captain's sole purpose in being my friend was to move up the fame ladder as quickly as possible, no matter what it took. He might have even attained some measure of that ambition if he wasn't such a staggering pothead.

* * * *

Some background on me and weed. My first time smoking dope was totally by accident. Honest. My dad had an old hippie buddy named Gary, who was deep into the ganj. Dad was against pot (and tattoos, and piercings, and all the other stuff most dads are required to be against), but Gary was all for it. One night Gary came down to the house for a visit. Like any veteran pothead, Gary was paranoid. He would take a knitting needle to his cigarettes, push out the smooth tobacco and replace it with weed. Whenever he wanted to partake, he's just snap off the filter, roll the end and have a toke. Another trick of the trade from Gary, a stoner from way back, was to soak a paper towel in vinegar, fold it, use it to shroud the foil wrapper that contained the cigarettes and slide it back into the box. According to Gary, dogs don't like the smell of vinegar, specifically, police dogs. Hey, if Gary said it works, it probably works. Unfortunately for Gary, my buddy Brian and I were no part canine when we unwittingly swiped a couple of cigarettes from his wacky pack of "Marlboro Lights" and went outside to smoke them.

Brian and I sat in the back yard by the pool and lit up. I wasn't really much of a smoker. I was more of an experimental rule breaker, testing boundaries and that kind of shit. I'd only had a few snatched cigarettes at that point and mostly disliked them. Not knowing what to expect, I took a mini-puff and, to my delight, really quite enjoyed it. I said to Brian, "Whoa man, Marlboro Lights are the shit." He agreed. So, the two of us eased back into our deck chairs and killed a couple joints through cigarette filters. It wasn't long before we started feeling very strange. The world took on a new, disorienting intensity as my five senses, one-by-one, were destabilized. Immediately, I assumed the only rational explanation was that we'd been poisoned. After all, a whole jay is a lot of weed for your first time. We staggered back into the house and woke Gary.

"You what?!"

He couldn't believe it. Not only were we underage and high as satellite balloons, we had also bogarted his private stash. In those first moments of realization, Gary ran the gamut of emotions. He explained to us what we had done. My recollection of our reaction is hazy, but I believe we laughed. A lot.

I've heard many a person say he or she didn't get high the first time they smoked pot. Well, I'm here to say Brian and I sure as fuck did. And I discovered that, not only had I survived it, I really enjoyed it. When I woke up the next morning I didn't have a hangover (like when I pilfered beers from the fridge). It was a clean buzz. In fact, I felt fucking great. Why hadn't I tried this sooner? I would probably have never tried it at all if it hadn't been an accident. Then, that next morning, a darkness clouded my thoughts, "Uh oh," I thought, "I've toked up. Does this mean now I'm a loser?" To determine the answer required more field research.

Brian and I decided to get high again, but this time we went into it with the idea that we knew what we were doing, and we were going to go with it, party, and have a good time. We had a blast. We cracked up all night, genuinely puzzled as to why this astonishingly pleasing wonderplant was illegal. Through further field study I discovered the marvelous, ever-deepening effects of this mellow-maker. I also discovered that those supposed pot-head losers who sat around in a grainy-eyed daze at parties were not the proper yardstick for the merits of Mary J. Those clowns were losers to begin with. Pot use had only softened the edges around their loser worlds.

So, to answer the question, was I now a loser? No. Count me as one of the converted. I decided to climb down from the "No Hope With Dope" bandwagon. I was getting off at the next stop: Spliffsville.

The first time I bought pot was arranged indirectly through my friend Paul, who began as an extra on *SBTB* when we were filming at Sunset-Gower Studios. Paul was a gymnast who could do that thing where he runs up a wall and back-flips flat onto his feet. There were always odd and interesting extras filtering on and off the set. One dude from England, whom I called "Beans," actually lived in the house where they shot the movie *Poltergeist*. Anyway, one day Paul brought a buddy named Mike to the set.

After final bows, we were all headed over to the season wrap party at the Gower Grille, a restaurant around the corner from the studio. While I was in my dressing room taking off my makeup and changing I asked Mike (who seemed to know such things) where I could score some weed to get high for the party. He said he had a guy and that he'd make arrangements.

Later, while we were all hanging at the wrap party, in walks this hardcore-looking dude named Jason. It was my first time buying weed from a dealer, and I didn't want to look like a chump, so I summoned up my best game face and told Jason we should retire to the men's room for a minute. He agreed. In the men's room, I suggested we step into a stall. We did. He produced the herb for my inspection. I hefted its weight and smelled it, not really certain what the proper procedure might be. I looked like some backwoods hillbilly struggling to approve of a bottle of fine French Bordeaux. "How much does it weigh?" I inquired.

"Enough," said Jason.

I concurred, and we quickly closed the transaction.

My new pal Jason and I returned to the party. I got us some drinks and started introducing him to the cast members and some of the behind-the-scenes people, as well as some NBC office girls. Jason and I started hitting it off, so I took him, Paul, and Mike back over to the studio, gave Jason a tour of the set, and we climbed to the roof of the sound stage. From our perch we could look down on the wrap party still going on just a half-block away. We decided to toke up. After mellowing out for a while we were laughing, telling stories, and feeling pretty good.

I realized that I had these guys all wrong. They weren't hard-core anything; they were just regular dudes. I said to Jason, "I gotta come clean, man. I was shitting my pants back there at the restaurant. That's the first time I ever bought weed."

"Yeah?" said Jason. "Well, that's the first time I sold it."

We all had a good laugh. I ended up being friends with those guys for years. They were roommates together, and I remember partying with them one night, drinking screwdrivers, when we ran out of orange juice. Wasted, Jason and I piled into his car and drove approximately one block around the corner to the grocery store. We thought that was hilarious until we arrived to find a patrol car parked in the lot. We must've looked pretty sketchy because when we left swinging our bag of OJ, the cop followed us out, climbed into his car and tailgated us all the way back to the house. As soon as we reached the driveway, the prowler's lights flashed, and the siren blurped. Fuck.

The officer approached our vehicle, "Where you headed?"

"Here," said Jason, motioning towards the house.

"You realize you were swerving?"

"Really?" said Jason. "I don't recall swerving. Not unintentionally, anyway."

"You been drinking tonight?"

"Just tons of orange juice."

The officer instructed Jason to get out of the vehicle and administered him a compete field sobriety test. He passed with flying colors. In fact, if there were a medal awarded for Most Outstanding Sobriety Test Performed by an Extremely Intoxicated Person, Jason would have had it pinned to his lapel that night.

The cop said, "So, you live right here, huh?"

"Yep."

Dramatic pause.

"All right. Have a good night."

"Thank you, officer," said Jason.

"Yes. Thank you very much, officer," I echoed as we walked up the sidewalk towards the house.

"Merry Christmas," said Jason.

"Yes," I agreed. "Have a very, Merry Christmas."

"Merry Christmas boys!" said the officers returning our holiday sentiments before climbing back into their vehicle.

"Merry Christmas," I repeated with desperate enthusiasm.

Inside, we leaned against the door and exhaled. Our nuts still lodged in our throats. It was then that we suddenly realized it was only *October*!.

Merry Fucking Christmas?! And they said it *back*!

Good times . . .

In celebration of my new cannabis lifestyle, I started to frequent the head shops in L.A. I enjoyed browsing the different pipes, bongs, screens, cleaners, and other assorted accessories. I liked the ritual of smoking weed. One afternoon I purchased a seven-foot bong that my buddy Mark drove all the way home to Orange County from L.A. with a couple of feet of it sticking straight out the sunroof of his Jetta like a submarine periscope. I also tried to purchase an ounce of weed from this dude who owned a head shop and clothing emporium in L.A. He promised he could score me some excellent shit for a decent price. At the time we were filming the *SBTB* episodes out of Flint Ridge Country Club.

I became friendly with a giant human, our boom operator on set, named Dennis Darby. Dennis was cool; we had music in common, and I hung out at his house a few times. He was very straight-laced and didn't want anything to do with drugs—it just wasn't his scene. During this time I was hanging with Big Dennis (seriously, he was like 6'8"), I was starting to get the runaround from this head shop owner I had forked over $400 to for an ounce of primo greenbud. Days went by as this dude gave me story after story about how he had trouble making his connection, then the stuff was at his house instead of the shop—whatever. I decided to pay him a visit at his place of business with Dennis's massive frame filling the door behind me. Yes, Dustin Diamond from *SBTB* had to roll down Melrose Avenue and shake down his dealer for his bag of weed. To his credit, Big Dennis was extremely reluctant to accompany me. He told me I was just getting what I deserved for dealing with scumbags and smoking dope. He definitely surprised me by offering to come along. Inside the shop, the dude looked up and said, "Oh, hey man. Yeah, the shit still ain't here. Sorry, man."

I said, "That's not gonna work today, dude. I paid you a week ago. I'm leaving here with the weed or the money. Otherwise, things are gonna get ugly."

"No reason to get bent outta shape man. I told you . . . "

And to my amazement, that's about all Big Dennis needed to hear. He stepped right around the counter, picked this dude up by the collar and yelled, "Cough up the fucking shit or you'll be coughing up a lung!"

Wouldn't you know, it was the darnedest thing. The dude had my ounce right there under the counter the whole time. It must've completely slipped his mind until Dennis reminded him. He was even considerate enough to pull out his scale and weigh it right in front of us. Now that's service!

I never thought I was going to be a pot smoker. Hell, I didn't even think I was going to be a beer drinker. My first forays into beer were miserable experiences. I started off with Bud Ice because someone had told me it was smoother and more watered down than other beers. Dad was a Löwenbräu drinker. My first taste of beer was that hoppy German assault on my virgin taste buds. I barely suffered through more than a swallow before I abandoned all hope. As far as I was concerned, beer was disgusting. Of course now, beer is delicious. All sizes and styles. So very, very delicious.

* * * *

The reason I got off on this pot-smoking tangent is because I was leading up to the fact that the Captain and his buddies smoked a ton of dope. Fine. The problem was he was also obsessed with taping everything he and his friends did with his VHS camera. I think you can see where this is headed. He would set up a tripod and tape himself, all his band mates, and their bitches taking huge bong rips. I'd be sitting there sometimes, off camera of course, wondering how I kept getting myself into these situations. Captain Douchebag would pass me the pipe, expecting me to take a hit, and I'd be like, "No fucking way I'm smoking dope on camera, dude" (Michael Phelps? Are you reading this? Too late.) I pushed it even further and said, "Are you trying to set me up or something?"

"Relax, dude," he assured me. "We're all just buds hanging out, smoking buds."

Everybody groaned, acting like I was the big buzz killer. Too cool for school. I was the celebrity dildo too important to hang out with his so-called druggie pals. What I decided to do instead, to have fun with the situation rather than become the group's resident downer, was to create with the Captain a pair of characters called "Weed" and "Shroom." It was a brilliant ensemble with a simple concept at its core: Weed only said "Weed," and Shroom only said "Shroom." It sounds as stupid as it was, but everybody in our glassy-eyed circle agreed it was hilarious. We even decided to make them our band mascots. We took a photo of Weed and Shroom—looking all wacked out and in character—with Shroom staring absently at the flat of his palm with the idea we'd Photoshop miniature versions of the rest of the band standing on his hand. At one point, Weed and Shroom even got their picture taken together with Jay Leno. A typical mock interview with the monosyllabic duo would run something like this:

INTERVIEWER: So, Weed and Shroom, your music is infused with influences from free-verse jazz to glam rock. What's your take on the state of the industry today?
WEED: (barely audible) Weeeeeeed.

INTERVIEWER: Mm hm. And Shroom?

SHROOM: Shroom.

You get the picture. It was humor just how we liked it, straightforward and juvenile. Needless to say, the good-natured antics of Weed and Shroom would come back to haunt me.

The Captain started hanging with some male-model buddy of his who lived on the beach with his weirdly hot girlfriend. You know the type, where there's something not quite proportional about her face and just a tad off about her disposition, but you'd still love to bang her—like one of those razor-thin European runway models with eyes like a hammerhead shark. Anyway, the Captain agreed to house-sit while this model dude was away, then promptly started putting the wood to his slightly irregular girlfriend. Eventually, she left the model, moved in with the Captain and started supporting him financially. Shit like that was par for the course when it came to the Captain. He had no moral compass. His was the type of personality that would do whatever was required to get what he wanted. The dude was pure bad news.

Then it was my turn to get roped in. One night we were all hanging out, smoking and drinking, when the Captain started bitching about how he had no wheels, his parents wouldn't help him get a loan, he had no one to cosign for him, yada, yada. He said he'd finally been offered a really good job, and he was going to be making good money but that he had no transportation. His back was against the wall, and he needed a hand. He laid it out for me. He thanked me for getting him the great background gig on *SBTB*, which was a guaranteed stream of income, he just needed this one favour, closing the deal on a cheap car. He was getting a great deal, and he promised to pay me right back. Yada, yada.

So me, being (a) drunk and (b) stupid, agreed to go down with him to the dealership the next day and cosign on the dotted line. And I did. What a putz I was.

Fast-forward a few months to when the Captain starts missing payments. The lender starts ringing my phone off the hook. I said to the Captain, "Dude, you gotta make these car payments."

"Sorry man. I don't know what happened. I sent the check."

I recognized this. It was the same tired song and dance he gave me when I wanted my Marshall amplifier back. He had played me all over again. After that, he started making threats to common friends of ours that he was going to hop in the car with Hammerhead and slip over the border to Mexico. *Mexico?!* The word itself is synonymous with lawlessness and evasion. I started freaking out, convinced this guy was going to slip down there and make the car disappear, sticking me with the whole bill for a phantom vehicle. On top of that, Captain Shutterbug had amassed all the VHS tape footage from his ubiquitous handheld camera (including "borrowing" all the ones I had in my possession) for some magnum opus music video project he was editing together for the band. When shit looked like it had definitely taken a turn south (literally, to Mexico), I told the Captain in no uncertain terms that he was responsible for all the payments on the car. His response was, "Are you threatening me, man?" I had fallen hook, line, and sinker for this guy's bullshit; the bait was deep in my belly. I decided it was time to act. Luckily, I had already surreptitiously cut my own set of keys. I located the car (that miserable fucking car) and moved it to a secure location.

Meanwhile, Captain Douchebag had been a busy beaver, editing together all the most suggestive footage from his bong circle, combining it with our loveable pals, Weed and Shroom, and sending the tape off to *Hard Copy*, that stalwart of upstanding, hard-hitting television journalism. He told the producers it was exclusive footage of Dustin Diamond, TV's Screech, engaging in elicit drug use.

That's when NBC's lawyers got involved. I don't know how, but they blocked the tape from airing. But the Captain would not be denied. He was a tireless crusader against the apparent injustice of a former friend, who cosigned his loan but had the audacity to ask him to make his own car payments. Next, he captured still photographs from the video footage, printed them on posters and placards and started pick and started picketing outside the front gate of NBC Studios in Burbank hollering, "Screech is a drug user and a liar! Don't let your children be corrupted by *Saved by the Bell!*" At that, one of our producers came down to the set and said, "We've got a problem."

I couldn't believe it. Come to think of it, I still can't believe it. I had been a friend to this guy. I'd gotten him a spot on the show, hooked him up with a place to live, shared clothes—all the stuff pals do for each other. I had been rope-a-doped, and it hurt.

When I moved the car in question to its secure location, I popped the trunk and discovered two garbage bags full of VHS footage he had taken. This shit went back to when he was maybe ten years old. He had video of every friend, every family member, and every passerby he had ever trained his camera on. There was also plenty of footage of him humiliating girls, him pissing on passed-out drunks, committing acts of vandalism, and destroying private property. My dad and I sat and fast-forwarded through hundreds of hours of his mayhem. It was sickening. I came to the conclusion that I was watching a monster. How had I not seen this side of him? Of course, what was conspicuously missing were any images of the band or me. He had found his own secure location for all that footage.

The phone rang. It was Captain Douchebag, "Where's my fucking car?"

"Your car? Excuse me; I'm making the payments. It's my car now."

"We'll see." And he hung up.

You've got to hand it to the Captain, he was tremendously good at being a scumbag—way better than I was. Turns out he arranged for his to be the only name on the pink slip for the vehicle. Under the law, I had no rights to the car.

So, the next day, one of our production managers and producers on *SBTB*, Chris Conte, stepped into my dressing room and said, "Um, Dustin? We have the Burbank Sheriff's Department on the phone, and they're saying they've issued a warrant for your arrest. They're on their way now to take you into custody unless you surrender a certain motor vehicle." When I heard that news come out of Chris's mouth, I swear, I swallowed my heart into my stomach. How could I be arrested for paying the loan on a car I was legally responsible for? Captain Douchebag can stop making payments and shuffle down to Mexico, but I'm a wanted man? There's so much about American jurisprudence that continues to baffle me.

I was forced to return the car to him. I learned later that, at the police station, the Captain went on and on about how I had taken advantage of his trust and abused our friendship. Apparently it was a bravura performance, certainly his finest work outside standing in the background of The Max on *SBTB*. And his girlfriend was there too, balling her wall-eyes out, claiming I had stolen tapes of them ensnarled in their most intimate embraces. It was all bullshit. There were no sex tapes. If there were, my dad and I would have seen all that hot hammerhead action during our all-night, fast-for-warding marathon.

Are you getting as tired of this guy as I was? Well, there's more. In fact, he saved the best for last. All this drama was incredibly embarrassing in front of my colleagues at NBC. I tried to explain that it wasn't my fault, that I gotten mixed up with an evil dude. But I just looked like a clown. At home, the Captain started calling me, taunting me, clearly trying to provoke me into threatening him over the phone, "Ha, ha! I won! I got the car, the tapes. What would like to do to me

if I was there right now, huh? What do you think you could do to me? Tell me all the gory details." At that point I'd finally learned my lesson. I directed his inquiries about whatever potential physical harm I would enjoy inflicting on him to my attorney.

Frustrated by that approach, the Captain changed tactics and sued NBC. He had found some Lionel Hutz-type lawyer to file a $2.5 million conspiracy lawsuit against the network for allegedly conspiring to damage his career by discrediting him and dismissing him from his job on *SBTB*. According to the Captain's lawsuit, everybody at NBC was conspiring to ruin him, from Peter Engel and Tim Shannon (stage manager for the extras) to me, on down to the guy who switched the jugs in the water coolers. My lawyer looked at the suit and said, since there were eight counts and most of them involved NBC (under Douchebag's deep-pockets theory), we should just sit back and let NBC take the lead on the motion. At last, here was something NBC's lawyers could sink their teeth into.

Once again, the red ants descended. In short fashion, they body-slammed the Captain in a flurry of depositions and motions, each landing like a full-on legal roundhouse to his smarmy chops. The Captain's lawyer offered to settle for $250,000. NBC countered with an offer for him to settle his lips around their big corporate balls.

So in the end, Captain Douchebag got nada. But not everybody escaped cheap. I still had to pay my attorney's fees and another $8,000 to get out from under the car that, according to the Burbank sheriff, I didn't legally own. The car was repo'd, sold at deep discount, and I had to cough up the difference. I should just be glad that, when all this went down, the Internet was still in its infancy, and YouTube didn't exist. That would have given him an immediate forum where everyone

could draw his own conclusions before I had any legal recourse to tell my side of the story. I shutter when I think about what celebrities—especially young ones—are up against today in this vicious, instantaneous electronic game of screw your neighbor. Look, I'm a firm believer that the truth should always prevail and that those who do wrong should get their comeuppance. But every so often you encounter a person in which desperation and determination are interchangeable. This dude, Captain Douchebag, was through the looking glass. He's one chapter in my story that I'm glad has ended.

PART IV:

THE DENOUEMENT

Flunking "The College Years"

When *SBTB: The College Years* got cancelled after only nineteen episodes, they handed out T-shirts with the show's title emblazoned across the front. I used white-out to replace the word "years" with "semester." Going into it, nobody expected the show to do well. We had broken the oldest rule in the book: If it ain't broke, don't fix it. We tampered with the formula that had worked for so many years on the original *SBTB* and had failed to transition the format to a broader, more mature audience. We had a terrific, talented director in Jeff Melman, but *SBTB* was just never meant for prime time. The bottom line was: putting a Saturday morning show on prime time was never going to work. It's a different style of humor.

New cast members included Anne Tremko as Leslie Burke, Kiersten Warren as Alex Tabor, Bob Golic as Mike Rogers, and

Patrick Fabian as Professor Lasky. Kiersten (whom I remember mostly as the ditzy, red-haired girl because the show's run was so brief) later appeared in the film *Independence Day* as the scared chick yelling on the roof, "They're coming for us!"

Ken Tucker, the same TV critic from *Entertainment Weekly* who panned the original *SBTB*, gave *The College Years* an "F," under the headline, "Dumb Bell: With Its Insipid Mix of Buff Bods and Maudlin Social Messages, *Saved By The Bell: The College Years* Wears Prime Time's Dunce Cap." He went on, "Given the always stunning amount of idiocy on television, this is probably going out on a limb, but *Saved By The Bell: The College Years* (NBC, Tuesdays, 8:00–8:30 PM) has certainly come to seem like the hands-down stupidest, least worthwhile series on prime-time TV . . . How gratifying it was to hear Drew Carey, costar of *The Good Life*, the NBC sitcom that now airs immediately after *Saved*, say recently that he 'hates' *Saved*, that having to 'follow a show like Saved by the Bell, that's like having to go to the prom with your ugly cousin.' . . . The rest of the actors are glib in the manner of most TV performers who are used primarily to posture attractively. The exception to this is (Dustin) Diamond. During *Saved*'s original run, his Screech became a fan favorite for his wobbly, register-shifting voice. These days, the grown-up Diamond must force his voice to break in order to pull off Screech's trademark sound, and his face is required to maintain a moronic rictus at all times. Diamond could be as good an actor as Dustin Hoffman, for all we know, but rarely has anyone been so utterly trapped by his role. The one good thing that could possibly be said about this show's seepage into prime time is that some parents seeing *Saved by the Bell* for the first time may now realize just how bad Saturday-morning TV programming has become and take steps to shield their children from such dreck. At least, that's my dream, and as Zack recently instructed Kelly, 'If you have a dream, you should go for it.' "

Without question, the biggest story that came out of that short-lived series was Mark-Paul's infamous condom throwdown. It stands as the only time in *SBTB* history when the cast did not return at the end of the night for a final curtain call and to thank the audience. Here's what happened:

One of the production quirks that developed over the short time we did the show was that outtakes would run at the end of each show, highlighting the mishaps, pranks, and bloopers that occurred while taping. It wound up being a popular aspect of the show, and we would wonder throughout the week which outtakes might wind up being selected. Needless to say, we began freelancing a bit, trying to create moments or situations that might make it into the out-takes reel. This time, Mark-Paul decided he was really going to spice things up.

In this episode, Bob Golic—who played Screech, Leslie, and Alex's dorm advisor—entered one of the girls' rooms and closed the door. Suddenly, Mark-Paul knocked, unscripted. When the door swung open, he held up a gum wrapper he had folded to look like a condom and bellowed, "Never fear, Trojan Man is here!" The audience started cracking up as Mark-Paul dashed off stage and frisbeed the wrapper up into the crowd to raucous cheers and applause.

Even though this was *SBTB: The College Years*, technically

geared toward a prime-time audience, that didn't matter to St. Peter. He. Was. Pissed.

Mark-Paul staged his gag in the last scene on a Friday at the end of taping, so after we wrapped the show, we were all back-stage preparing to come back out for our final bow. But before we could, one of our stage managers started making his way up and down the hall announcing in a quick, severe, matter-of-fact voice, "There will be no curtain call. Everybody needs to get back in their dressing rooms. Right now." The audience had already been removed from the studio. Clearly something dark and ominous was headed our way. No one ever spoke to us in that kind of tone. Whatever the issue was, it was some heavy-duty shit.

The next thing we knew, mild-mannered, easy-going, nasally St. Peter came charging up the hallway like a bull in Pamplona behind full-throated screams of "Where is he?! Where is he?!" It was unheard of. Cowering in my dressing room, I realized that in the five years I had worked so closely with St. Peter, never once had I heard him raise his voice. Peter stormed into Mark-Paul's dressing room, slamming the door so hard it cracked. We cast members opened our doors a sliver to hear St. Peter screaming at Mark-Paul, "How dare you! Do you want to ruin my fuck-ing business?! Huh?" Never raising his voice was one thing, but St. Peter—the patron saint of Pollyanna—never, ever swore. The dude was completely unhinged. The cast, the crew—Mark-Paul especially—were all terrified. St. Peter, still consumed by a bib-lical fury, raged out of Mark-Paul's dressing room and disap-peared up into his office. Moments later, Mark-Paul meekly fol-lowed. Without a word, he went straight to his vehicle and sped away.

When our Monday morning table read arrived, we all filed in, took our seats and waited for the other shoe to drop. But it never did. Not a word was said about the condom incident, the fallout, nothing. The light from the Golden Child still shone brightly.

It was the same story all the other times St. Peter accidentally thought he was mad at Mark-Paul, only to realize later that his star could do no wrong. Like when Mark-Paul ignored the dangerous-activities clause present in all our contracts and started riding a motorcycle. St. Peter got pissed but eventually got over it. Or when Mark-Paul got into skydiving. St. Peter found out and, citing the contract, forced him to quit. Of course Mark-Paul still went skydiving, he just didn't talk about it anymore. Mark-Paul rebelled against everything St. Peter told him he had to do. Just because he was granted Golden-Child status, that didn't mean Mark-Paul was immune to the other growing pains we were all suffering through, coming of age in front of network suits, fellow cast, crew, and millions of viewers around the globe.

The only time St. Peter brought the hammer down on Mark-Paul—and all the rest of us for that matter—was when his Golden Child almost died during training for *Circus of the Stars*. The producers of the show asked us what circus talent we wanted to learn, and Mark-Paul, Mario and I suggested trapeze. They set up a training area atop Universal Studios in Hollywood complete with trapeze and nets. It was actually quite terrifying because the trapeze, when you swung through the air, extended beyond the edge of the building, leaving you out in the hinterland, staring down at a twenty-story drop. There was a net, but even so it was freaky. Mark-Paul's training began first. The trapeze artists hooked him up to a rope-and-pulley system to assist him in learning how to do flips and to work his way up to doing them on his own. The ropes and pulleys helped him get used to the disorienting feeling of being upside-down. He learned that wherever his head looked, that's where his body would follow. So, if he wanted to do a proper back flip, he had to trust that by throwing his head straight back, his body would follow in correct form. Once his body rotated over his head, he had to focus straight down on the ground to complete the flip. Up high in the air, the whole experience was a scary, awkward feeling.

Mark-Paul graduated past the ropes and pulleys and began to train freely with only the net below to protect him. I was there one day during training and watched while Mark-Paul, executing a flip, suddenly missed the bar, fell, missed the net below and landed on the back of his head with so much force he crushed his sternum with his chin. *He broke his own sternum with his chin!* He tore ligaments throughout his neck and lay on the ground howling and screaming in sickening pain. He couldn't move or breathe. His injury put Mark-Paul in a hospital bed, closing down production of SBTB for six months.

That horrific event also shut down any plans for my performance on the trapeze. In the fallout, producers asked me what other event I'd like to try, and I suggested the high wire. That was an immediate, "No." So I suggested taming lions. I got pulled into St. Peter's office one day and he said, "Look, you're not doing anything dangerous for *Circus of the Stars*." As a result, I wound up doing the dog-training act. *Whoopee!* The dogs are already trained, they have a routine, so they just learned to take their commands from me. They also made me perform the act like Screech, letting the dogs do shit like steal my hat and making me chase them all around the ring. The dogs kept passing the hat to one another until, exhausted, I sat down on their pedestal as one came over and sweetly placed it back atop my sweaty brow. *Best pals again.* The dogs were the stars of that routine, while I took second billing once again as the comic relief. And it was all because the Golden Child broke himself in half on the flying trapeze.

For my part, I suffered two major injuries while I was on *SBTB*—one of which forced me to wear an eye patch for an episode of *The New Class.*

The first incident occurred at my home away from home, the Diz—Disneyland. It was in the evening, and I was hanging with my buddy Brian. I just want to say this: Disneyland wasn't always just about poontang hunting. Sometimes my pals and I would also go there simply to get super-high, laugh at people, and do stupid shit. We'd bring a pipe with us and sneak little tokes here and there throughout the day until we were good and stoned. For some reason, in our baked torpor, Brian and I decided it would be an excellent idea to hurdle the waist-high chain-link fences that cordoned off the line to Pirates of the Caribbean. *Fantasmic* had just opened, which was a fireworks and water show that played at the Hollywood Hills Amphitheater inside the park. Thousands of people crowded towards the display like vertical sardines. Bombs were bursting in the air; there were dragons and all sorts of shit rising out of Tom Sawyer's Island; there was a Peter Pan battle;

and Mickey Mouse and Mark Twain floated past on Colombia, Disney's full-scale replica of the first American ship to circumnavigate the globe. It was pure bedlam.

In the midst of all that, Brian and I were stoned and running full speed, bounding over those fences like Edwin Moses (the American Olympic gold medalist in the 400-meter hurdles in 1976 and 1984. Truly a god on wheels). Like him, we were just floating to the roar of the crowd.

My dad was there with us, hanging back, allowing us to act like maniacs. That was his way. If we met chicks or hatched a plan to do something juvenile, he'd chill and catch up with us later. Because of the spectacle of *Fantasmic*, the line to Pirates was uncharacteristically short. I leapt a few barriers, full speed, with ease until my back foot caught the crossbar on something and sent my face rotating towards the pavement with the full weight of my body behind it. SPLAT! My arms splayed off to my sides as I absorbed the full force of the impact with the center of my face.

As I struggled to push myself away from the ground I heard whimpering. A voice, somewhere nearby, was in tremendous pain. I realized it was my voice. I pushed against the ground with all my might, only to realize that the ground wasn't there. I opened my eyes to find my head resting on Brian's lap as he knelt beside me. My father hovered over us as a crowd gathered. I heard someone whisper, "Is he dead?" Regaining consciousness, I became aware that I'd been out for more than a minute. My face was bleeding profusely, and Brian told me that my head had twisted violently to the side in the fall.

Brian and my dad assisted me through the melee that was *Fantasmic*. Throngs of people stopped cold and gawked at my mangled face. "Look away," I mumbled. "Look away. I am not a monster!" The only first-aid station was located on Main Street. We had to walk from New Orleans Square, through Adventureland, to the center of Disneyland near the castle on the main strip while the giant Main Street Electrical Parade was going on to the delight of thousands. The parade had to come to a full halt while we crossed Main Street, I with my bloody, famous face and my feet scraping on the pavement, towards the aid station. I heard the chatter as we passed, "Is that Screech? Holy shit, he's fucked up! Quick! Take a picture!"

When we finally reached the nurse, she called an ambulance, and I was rushed to the hospital. Fortunately, my bone structure remained intact. But back on set, I had to have layer after layer of pancake makeup slathered onto my scabbing face to get through that week's taping.

The second incident occurred while I was playing bass for Captain Douchebag's band. We were opening for the L.A.-based punk band NOFX in front of a crowd of ten thousand at a concert I booked for us at UC–Santa Barbara. While we performed on stage, a mosh pit formed below us. This fat dude down front stripped off his shirt, exposing his milky man-tits, and started helicoptering his T-shirt over his head, moshing against the circular flow of the pit. He made it a point to ram head-first into everybody he passed. I noticed this nonsense developing, when suddenly, out of nowhere, I was struck in the left eye with an unopened, glass beer bottle. KACHUNK! It was a perfect fucking hit.

The only way I can describe the next moments is to say that, from my perspective, the world around me melted into an orange dreamsicle. All I could see, in the middle of the afternoon, were fluid, pulsing forms shifting in a thickening ooze of orange and white. Despite the shock and creeping insanity of the pain, I had the full awareness that I was in deep, deep doo-doo. I didn't know if I was blind or crossing over to the afterlife. I staggered backward as my head drooped. I raised my left hand toward my eye, terrified of what I would discover. Halfway to my face, my hand was bathed in so much blood I almost passed out. I touched what felt like my eyeball on the outside of my head. My right eye, frozen open in terror, scanned the stunned faces of the crowd—many of whom appeared poised to hurl. Douchebag and the band, of course, kept on playing. After all, this was a big gig that could further their careers—fuck the dying band member.

In the emergency room, their first order of business was to administer a monstrous hypodermic needle into my eye. That didn't suck or anything. All of this happened on a Thursday during the season, which meant the next day I had to be on set to tape before a live audience. When I rolled into the studio, I could hear the collective gasp of, "Ohhh, fuck." There was no getting around it: my face was a ten-car pile-up. No amount of makeup could fully cover the damage that had been done. But here's the ingenuity of network television for you—because, after all, the show must always go on: In no time flat, they slapped an eye patch on me and wrote a couple lines of throwaway dialogue into the script to cover for it. It was Belding saying something like, "Screech . . . Explain." Then I said something stupid like,

"The marching band has a new trombone player. All I can say is, look left and right before crossing the grass." *Boing!* So, when you catch that episode where I'm wearing an eye patch, it's because I was assaulted by a half-naked blob from the mosh pit while I opened for NOFX.

I heard later that after I was beaned and spirited off to the hospital, NOFX drummer Erik Sandin stood up and hollered at the crowd, "Whoever did that to my buddy Dustin is a fucking asshole, and you better not let me find you." Ultimately, Erik's indignation didn't accomplish anything. But my swashbuckling eye patch and I did appreciate the sentiment.

* * * *

After the original SBTB, Mark-Paul grew up in more ways than one. When we started filming *SBTB: The College Years*, he suddenly exploded with manliness, loading twenty-five pounds of muscle onto his once-scrawny frame in, oh, about a month.

Everyone was like, *Whoa! What the fuck is up with you, dude?* Acne had spread all over his face and body, he suddenly had a short fuse and was completely into weight lifting, Arnold Schwarzenegger, and slick, glossy mags packed with oiled-up muscley dudes. It was clear he was on the juice. I asked him to level with me but he denied it emphatically. It was his phony blonde hair secret all over again. Watch *The College Years* and you can plainly see how massive he became. It reached a point where he had so noticeably gotten so freakishly humungous that St. Peter finally said, "You have to stop this." In the end, Mark-Paul admitted to everyone on set that he had made a mistake by taking steroids. He said he'd gotten carried away with his fitness obsession and had made a bad choice. He apologized to everyone for intimidating them for so long with his meaty, rippling buffitude.

Tiffani wasn't even supposed to be around for *The College Years*. She and Elizabeth had refused to sign new contracts after the network ordered more shows. *The College Years* was supposed to be the three guys—Zack, Slater, and Screech—go off to party at Cal U. All of a sudden, Tiffani is locked again in those troubling closed-door meetings in St. Paul's office and, voilà, she's off to college with the guys. From then on the show's writing became all about Zack and Kelly. I was like, "We've played this shit out to death already." We had made the big move to prime time, and viewers who had stuck with us had outgrown that pap; they were hungry for new story lines. But no.

Soon we were off to film the TV movie *SBTB: Wedding in Las Vegas*, and it was all about Zack and Kelly, Zack and Kelly, blah, blah, blah. I was seventeen years old when we shot Wedding in Las Vegas at the Stardust on the Vegas strip. The shoot was only a few weeks, but the pace of making a film is dramatically slower than taping a weekly TV show. One big difference was that we only had to memorize the script a few scenes at a time instead of in its entirety because each set-up and shot took so long.

While in Vegas, I had a fabulous relationship with a twenty-eight-year-old dancer in the Stardust's review at the time, *Enter the Night*. In the movie, when the guys come out on stage dressed as showgirls, that stage, all the wardrobe and all the girls are from the *Enter The Night* show at the Stardust. The girl's name was Melissa, and she was a stunner—she taught at a dance studio and was super flexible. I have a photo of us together under a low-roofed archway where my arm is around her waist and she has one foot flat on the floor and the other flat against the ceiling.

I invited dad and my friend Mark to join me for one of Melissa's performances. This may amaze you for my apparent naiveté, but before the show began, I had no clue it was performed topless. It took a little while to settle into the sight of a sea of tits (including my girl's) passing before my father's eyes. Melissa was sure to offer us a wink, a smile, and a shake of the ass for good measure. *Dad, this is Melissa. Melissa, dad.* I did discern a sense of "That's my boy" from Dad's expression. He turned to me and said, "I approve."

We all went out to eat together at the Peppermill on Las Vegas Boulevard. That's a nice, quiet restaurant where you can get away from all the clang-clang-clang and flashing lights of the casinos. There's a very classy step-down area, like a big, circular living room, with a fireplace. It's a great place to have a low-key meal and some drinks. The trick to spending any amount of time at the Peppermill, however, is to remain aware that there are no clocks or windows to the outside world—it's always nighttime. You easily lose track of the hours that pass; it can be like stepping into a wormhole and reemerging into the blinding sunshine of a bright, new day.

Melissa didn't think dad would like her because she was so much older than me.

An absurd notion, considering her phenomenal rack. I used to have a little game I'd play with older women I was interested in when it came to revealing my age. I refused to blatantly lie to them, so I would use misdirection to sidestep the issue. Usually when I would ask a girl her age, she would respond, "How old do I look?" I was like a carnival barker when it came to this question. I had an uncanny knack for guessing ages to within a year (always, wisely, trying to come in younger than her actual age). With Melissa, she didn't make me guess. She said, "I'm twenty-eight. How old are you?" In her case, I just reversed the game. I said, "How old do I look?"

I don't know why, but chicks always guessed high for my age. Very high. Maybe it was wishful thinking on their parts. Melissa said, "I think you're twenty-six." To which I responded, "Aw. You've been talking to people. Cheater." Then I quickly changed the topic. I didn't lie; I just never answered the question. It all goes back to my interview-grooming regimen for NBC affiliate days: Make a statement of fact ("You've been talking to people." Everybody "talks" to people) then discuss your opinion surrounding that fact ("Cheater." Fake incredulity directed at the statement of an irrelevant fact). Sounds stupid, but this technique consistently worked like a charm. Later, I came clean and told Melissa my real age. At that point she didn't really give a shit because she'd already been seduced by my writhing trouser snake.

As a cast, we didn't hang out much together in Vegas. The Mark-Paul contingent partook of strolling the strip, smoking cigars, and waxing philosophic on the rigors of the Hollywood life. Meanwhile, I was busy banging a topless, contortionist showgirl.

I would never have traded my experiences with theirs.

As much fun as I had in Vegas (and I did have a lot of fun), my underage status did make trying to party there a real pain in the ass, especially at the casinos. Even though I was filming a movie and banging one of their showgirls, I was constantly being approached by security to show ID and getting booted off the gambling floor because I was a minor. After getting kicked off the floor of the Luxor, my buddy Mark and I decided to launch a covert reconnaissance mission to steal every single plastic cup in the casino that all the blue-hairs used to cart around their coins for the slot machines. Mark and I made trip after trip for hours, each time snatching a stack of a dozen or two cups before making our way out the exit. On each pass, we would deposit the cups in my father's green minivan until we had completely picked the Luxor clean of every single plastic cup. In total, we stuffed close to three thousand plastic slot-coin cups into that vehicle. We had so much fun that we decided to take our show on the road and did the same thing at Excalibur. We dropped the Luxor cups at the hotel and proceeded to make three packed minivan trips back from Excalibur for a haul of close to ten thousand cups. When we returned home, Mark and I split our take and stacked the towers of cups high in our garages. For years afterward, no matter the situation, I always had a cup for the job.

At the Bellagio, I met a pit boss and "cheat-spot" named Sal Piasanti. Sal had the most remarkable memory I have ever witnessed first hand. Sal could recall tens of thousands of faces and names, most of them people he'd met only once. He would have me create a list of fifty items, take one look at the page and be able to remember everything on the list, in order, hours—even days—later. He could probably still remember everything on that list this many years later. He could stare at a page of a magazine for five seconds then read me back, word-for-word, the entire page from memory. Sal could read The Catcher in the

Rye in three minutes with total comprehension. He was a student of all those Howard Berg (The World's Fastest Reader) and Kevin Trudeau (Mega Memory, Mega Math, etc.) courses and a firm believer in the word/picture association technique. He said numbers were easy to remember: the number one looks like a melting candle, two looks like a skier hunched over, three looks like a nice pair of tits, four looks like an upside-down chair, five looks like a wheelchair, six is a pregnant woman, and so on. "It sounds stupid," Sal said, "but if you do it, it works. What do you think of when you hear my name?"

The Catcher in the Rye in three minutes with total comprehension. He was a student of all those Howard Berg (The World's Fastest Reader) and Kevin Trudeau (Mega Memory, Mega Math, etc.) courses and a firm believer in the word/picture association technique. He said numbers were easy to remember: the number one looks like a melting candle, two looks like a skier hunched over, three looks like a nice pair of tits, four looks like an upside-down chair, five looks like a wheelchair, six is a pregnant woman, and so on. "It sounds stupid," Sal said, "but if you do it, it works. What do you think of when you hear my name?"

"Well," I said, "Sal makes me picture a salad. Piasanti makes me think of peeing in the sand."

"There you go," encouraged Sal. "From now on, whenever

you think of me, you'll see a salad peeing the letter T in the sand. Sal Piasanti."

He was right. Here it is, fifteen years later, and I never forgot.

Like I mentioned, at some point towards the end of *The College Years* and the filming of the *Wedding in Las Vegas*, Mark-Paul did stop being such a dick. He was maturing, settling into his true skin, his authentic personality, and a lot of his douchebag ways had fallen away. I think he just got tired of being the focus of everyone's adulation. He'd grown weary of it.

* * * *

Those old studios at Sunset-Gower didn't only have trap doors dropping down into labyrinthine tunnels; they also had ladders that climbed to the roof. I used to go up there and look down over Gower Gulch, an area adjacent to the studio complex. In the Gulch there was a store that sold bottles of Yoo-Hoo and Bosco, an old-school chocolate drink. The Yoo-Hoo came in flavors like coconut and strawberry, but Mark-Paul, ever the trend-setter, went on a fierce kick of drinking—exclusively—a Mexican cinnamon-rice milk drink called *Horchata*. It was sweet-tasting and came in original flavor, chocolate, cherry, and vanilla. The consistency of Horchata was like drinking a bottle of tapioca pudding. It was all right, but certainly nothing to go nuts over. Mark-Paul went through a phase where he drank that shit by the metric ton. There was always a bottle of Horchata at the end of his arm. I would see him wandering around, sucking down the last gulp of a bottle of Horchata, then moments later emerge from his dressing room—fresh bottle of

Horchata in hand! I don't even want to imagine what rumblings he experienced in his large intestine on a steady diet of a Mexican rice drink. Of course, Mark-Paul's obsession-du-jour led everybody backstage to also start drinking Horchata.

The Gulch store also sold good, hand-rolled cigars. For a time, Mark-Paul had become a bit of a connoisseur, so we bought a couple of fine cigars together and climbed up to the studio rooftop to watch the sun set over the Hollywood Hills, gazing at the iconic Hollywood sign and twinkling bulbs of the Sunset Strip. Standing there, chatting and not chatting, our faces were obscured by a swirling cloud of blue smoke. Me drinking Bosco, Mark-Paul guzzling an ice-cold bottle of thick Horchata, we pondered the random physics that led us to that spot. In that moment, it was almost like we were buddies. But in truth, he had come up to the roof to be alone. And so had I.

* * * *

In 1992, Mark-Paul, Tiffani, Elizabeth, Mario, and Lark were looking beyond the beyond the end of *SBTB* to what projects might be next. It seemed that at every year's wrap party the tears flowed as everyone stood convinced we wouldn't be back for another season. Tiffani and Elizabeth refused to sign on for the final half-season of the original SBTB. They both probably tried to hold St. Peter over a barrel for a bunch more cash, and he said, "No dice." Eh, who could blame them? One thing you could say about St. Peter, he was plenty tight with the purse strings. I'm surprised he didn't commence each workday by kicking dirt in Bob Cratch it's eyes, mumbling, "Bah. Humbug." Without going into any forensic accounting details, let's leave it at this: nobody on *SBTB* was making what they should have. Nobody. Except maybe Peter Engel.

At some point someone in fact suggested that the kids on *SBTB* weren't making enough money. The parents started to compare notes on the issue and decided to raise a stink to St. Peter as a united front. They agreed that they would force an audience with Engel and demand that we be treated better and paid more. They reasoned that, in the face of their unity and determination, St. Peter would have no choice but to fold. *He would never fire the entire cast, right? That would be insane, right?* But we never found out because on the day all the parents were supposed to convene to march upstairs together and carry out their bloodless coup, only my dad and Mario's mom showed up.

Tiffani cried as we wrapped the final episode of *SBTB*, but they were actress tears. Tiffani was remarkable for her ability to cry on demand, which, as a performer, is huge because it makes every take believable. Only in real life does it get somewhat confusing. At the time, Tiffani was dating Brian Austin Green (remember his groundbreaking portrayal of an early '90s, *8-Mile*, Beverly Hills-ghetto gangsta?), and she knew she was already in with Aaron Spelling. As a side note, Brian Austin Green was in the original pilot of *Good Morning, Miss Bliss*, as well as Jaleel White (later of Steve Urkel infamy) and Jonathan Brandis. Tiffani-Amber had met Brian Austin at one of our celebrity events. In *SBTB*, Tori Spelling played Violet Anne Bickerstaff, Screech's girlfriend. Tori's dad, Aaron Spelling, would drop by the set to chat with St. Peter.

I overheard him say, "Y'know, Peter, you've got a really good thing going here. I wish I'd thought of it. Who would've thought that teenage kids and their exploits would be the hot new market?" Next thing I knew . . . New, from Aaron Spelling, in prime time, teenage kids and their exploits in Beverly Hills . . .

Tori was nice, but this was before she had her "work" done. Have you ever seen a girl who had negative boobs? Breasts that actually grew inward? That was Tori, holed up in the east wing of her dad's hundred-room mansion with ingrown boobs. Tori was Hollywoodized before she ever left the womb. Her brother Randy lived up the lifestyle of a millionaire's kid, too. He zipped around in his new Ferrari, spending gobs of cash. Look at me! I mean, I can't blame them. I would've probably acted the same way coming from so much money. And the Spellings were always nice people to me. When Aaron died, the sadness of his passing was compounded by the surprise of Tori's stunning and mysterious disinheriting—which you can read her book to learn the truth or fiction about. But that was definitely the talk around town. At the time, many assumed it was Aaron's final act of wisdom: not rewarding all the years of partying and general irresponsibility. When you're born like they were—with a set of limited-edition, collectible platinum spoons in your mouth—and you're not careful, you run the risk of pissing it all away.

While she was on *SBTB*, Tori was trying to hook up with Mark-Paul, and I was playing half-assed matchmaker. I would talk to Tori on the phone at night, letting her phone at night, letting her depose me for any morsel of information about the Golden Child while she asked, "Did you talk to him today? Did he ask about me?"

Mark-Paul wasn't interested in chicks with negative boobs.

Come to think of it, another weird thing about Mark-Paul was that he was always extremely reserved when it came to sharing his exploits chasing ass. A more mild way of characterizing it might be to say he didn't kiss and tell. I don't know if he was just an early incarnation of Niles Crane or what, but he never talked about the girls he was banging. And he was never on the prowl at events like Mario—and later I—was. I mean, the whole excitement of going to these things was new town, new ladies. The road events were subsidized trips to Assylvania. All-you-can-bang buffets. I was busy seeing how many girls I could squeeze into my hotel bathtub while Mark-Paul was relaxing in his alone, shaving his legs. Seriously, for a while he shaved his legs. He said it was because he liked to jog. Reduced his wind drag.

But the point I was trying to make about Tiffani's fake crying at the season wrap party was that she already knew she had a role waiting for her on *90210*. And when she started over there, her first order of business was to dump Brian Austin Green before the ink was dry on her contract. (I wonder if she actress-cried for him, too?)

Elizabeth cried at the end of *SBTB*, but hers seemed like genuine tears. In the graduation episode, the tears you see on screen pouring from Elizabeth's eyes were very real—she couldn't stop bawling on set. She was extremely emotional because she knew she was leaving and would never be back. They were tears of sadness mixed with fear and concern. I'm convinced she wasn't so sure she was making the right decision. *Showgirls* had already tanked at the box office. I mean, not just tanked—it's still an industry- and pop-culture punchline for all-around shittyness. She knew there were probably no career prospects for her beyond SBTB, outside the minor, odd role as a slutty temptress. Turns out she was correct.

The reason everyone was so convinced the show was finally finished once and for all was because we had already filmed the graduation episode. But then the network decided to order another half-season. The resulting incongruity in the episodes of the final season of the original *SBTB* was what resulted in the Tori paradox. The *Tori paradox* is a term credited to Chuck Klosterman from his essay "Being Zack Morris" *in Sex, Drugs and Cocoa Puffs: A Low Culture Manifesto* (Scribner, 2004). It describes the bizarre format in the final season of *SBTB* of alternating episodes between those starring Tiffani and Elizabeth and those starring Leanna Creel, whose character was a leather-clad rogue named Tori Scott who rolls into Bayside on her motorcycle. She began as a foil to Zack but, of course, soon became his main love interest. The paradox was that viewers were supposed to believe that, in the episodes where Tori roamed the halls, Kelly and Jessie were simultaneously in some other class somewhere else in the building. But then, after firmly establishing Tori's character in the series, she was nowhere to be found in the graduation episode, because it had already been taped long before the final half-season began. It was a lazy solution on the part of the network and the producers to the quandary created by Tiffani and Elizabeth's decisions to leave the show early, but, on the other hand, viewers never seemed to get very worked up about it.

During that graduation episode, there was a song that accompanied the emotional finale as the gang at Bayside hugged their goodbyes. Tears flowed (real and Tiffani's) on set and at the wrap party, but, like I said, I knew we'd be back. We had a lot of alleged wrap parties. Everybody said, "How can you not be sad, Dustin?" The answer was that I knew we were coming back, because we always came back, no matter what people told us.

THE NEW CLASS LETS OUT

SBTB: The New Class was initially an attempt at a carbon copy of the original *SBTB*, just putting new faces on those timeless character archetypes that previously worked so successfully: handsome/mischievous male lead, cheerleader, feminist, jock, socialite, and geek. If it ain't broke, don't fix it! Well, that was the theory, anyway. A young actor named Isaac Lidsky was cast as the Screech clone, a character named Barton "Weasel" Wyzell. They even tried to match the physical features of the new character to mine. It was very strange, but of course nothing new. When Tiffani and Elizabeth bailed at the end of *SBTB* (before Tiffani materialized again on *The College Years*), the producers said to themselves, "Hm, we just lost Jessie, who has curly hair and is a feminist, and Kelly, who has dark hair and is Zack's primary love interest . . . Just spitballing here, but how about a new character named Tori who has dark, curly hair, is a tomboy (i.e., feminist) with a motorcycle and instantly becomes Zack's love interest? Genius!"

It was like some cheeseball, *Island of Dr. Moreau* creation. Leanna Creel was one of triplets. She and her identical sisters, Joy and Monica, starred in the NBC/Disney show *Parent Trap Three*. Leanna was awesome—beautiful, fun, and friendly. She wasn't around long enough for the lure of Hollywood to really taint her. She grew up near Fullerton, California (close to where I grew up), and she knew Todd McFarlane, the comic book artist who created Spawn. Knowing I was a huge comic-book fan, Leanna, sweetheart that she was, went out of her way to score me a couple of autographed copies of Spawn, issue no. 1. I still have them today.

After *SBTB*, Leanna went on to create a couple of successful production companies (one was purchased by Lionsgate) and brought about ten successful indie films to completion. She also wrote and directed the critically acclaimed short film *Offside*, about the Germans and Allies in World War I playing a friendly soccer game against each other in No Man's Land on Christmas Day. I think these days she's a filmmaker and photographer.

I was still playing Screech in *SBTB*: The College Years when *SBTB*: *The New Class* began production, so there was a brief gap in time when I was still part of the original *SBTB* and hadn't yet transitioned all the way with Den into the new format. When I started with *The New Class*, that's when all the weird scripts started getting handed down to Den and me—scripts with all sorts of blatant homosexual innuendo between Mr. Belding and

Screech. It was clear that the writers were either getting bored or had a bone to pick and were taking it out on us. Den was the first to vocalize his objections to whoever would listen. Stage directions started to be inserted into scripts that said things like, "Screech and Mr. Belding embrace and stare into each other's eyes." Weird shit like that. Look, I don't care anything about people's sexual preference. As far as I'm concerned, people can hit any hole they choose. But in the context of the long-standing relationships and backstories that had been established over years of creating the characters in *SBTB*, the shit they were handing us was totally inappropriate, and they knew it.

Maybe it all was to get back at Den, who seemed to always be up in the writers' room lecturing them on how he wanted Mr. Belding to be written. Maybe Den had told each of the writers that he was from their individual hometowns, and they'd finally compared notes with each other, deciding he was full of shit. Den was telling them how to do their jobs, and they were like, "Okay buddy, we're the writers; you're the actor. We'll write the lines, you memorize them, and everybody will be happy." I think Den just got on their nerves after a while, and they started taking it out on us in the scenes we had together. They'd write action like, "Screech gets scared and wraps his arms around Belding for safety." It was a comedy show with a number of slapstick, cartoonish set pieces, so that wasn't so bad. But then when scenes weren't coming off as the writers envisioned, they started getting more graphic.

Eventually, Den went to the director, Miguel Higuera. Miguel had been with the show since *Good Morning, Miss Bliss*, working as assistant director under Don Barnhart before Don moved on, and staying with the entire run of 260 episodes. Den said, "I'm tired of this shit, Miguel. I'm not doing it. Screech and Belding are not fucking hugging each other." I thought it was bullshit, too, but Den was clearly fed up, because he never spoke like that to anybody. Eventually, Den and I just started working around it in the walk-throughs, and if the writers questioned why we weren't following directions, we just said that it was inappropriate, and we weren't fucking doing it. I mean, despite all the backstage intrigue, wasn't *SBTB* supposed to be a morning television show for kids?

Later, Ron Solomon and Brett Dewey's partnership ended after Ron went on to other projects. Brett stayed with *SBTB*, sitting up in the seats of the darkened studio during rehearsals, uncorking that high-pitched, *Revenge of the Nerds* laugh of his whenever we performed one of the overtly gay gags he'd written into the script. You always knew which writers had written which jokes by who laughed the loudest. Den started mumbling, "It's fucking Brett. He's the one who thinks this shit's so funny."

Again, that's Hollywood. Brett had been one of my buddies since the beginning of the show, letting me hang with him, supplying me with comic books while regaling me with ribald tales of St. Peter's hard drug use and sexcapades in a former life. Just another lesson that nobody in that town is ever really your friend.

But Den could be pushy with people. I remember him marching upstairs on many a crusade barking, "I need to speak to Peter!" As the years went on, that shit got old, and I think it reached a point with St. Peter where he started giving Den the shaft. One day we were called down to have merchandising shots taken of the entire cast together for the *SBTB* board game. We were all in full makeup and wardrobe. After a few shots, the photographer asked Den to step out.

"Why?" asked Den. "What possible use could you have for photos without the full cast?"

"Well, let's try a few with just the kids."

We all knew what was happening. I thought it was downright shitty and cold-hearted. Dennis had put his time in just like the rest of us and deserved to share the recognition. I announced that I wasn't going to do the photo shoot if Den wasn't included in the pictures. It caused this big ruckus. Everybody started scurrying around, making phone calls. St. Peter came storming down onto the stage, "What's going on?!"

I said, "This is bullshit. I'm not gonna do this shoot if the idea is to cut out Dennis. This isn't right. You're shitting on him."

To my surprise, St. Peter directed his ire at Dennis. "What did you say to Dustin?"

But it was already a done deal. Den saw the futility of fighting the powers that be that day and finally acquiesced. He told the photographer to go ahead and finish his photo shoot. Den went out of his way to assure us he was fine with the decision. Of course, he wasn't. Afterward, he came to me and said, "Dustin, I really appreciate what you did here this afternoon. You stood by me when no one else would."

One day on the set of *The New Class*, we got a visit from Kareem Abdul Jabbar. I wasn't a huge basketball fan, so my first reaction was, "Wow, you trained with Bruce Lee. *Game of Death*. That big foot mark on Bruce Lee's chest, that's yours!" One of the kids on the show, Anthony Harrell, who played Eric Little, casually mentioned that Kareem's "birth name" was Lew Alcindor. Kareem spun around, leaned down, grabbed poor little Anthony by the shoulder with one of his gargantuan folding lawn chair hands and said, "The name is Kareem Abdul Jabbar. Get it right!" In the long shadow of this skyscraper of a man, it was all Anthony could do not to soil himself. "My God," I thought, "Kareem Abdul Jabbar is gonna eat Anthony Harrell." It was definitely a shit-your-pants moment.

Apparently the kid who played the Zack reincarnation in the first season of *The New Class* was an outspoken, radical neoconservative. That kind of ideology goes over like a bad entrée at a bar mitzvah in Hollywood. Once his views were fully fleshed out for all on set, he was promptly replaced. He was long gone by the time I arrived for the second season.

Richard Lee Jackson was cast as Ryan Parker (the second Zack reincarnation) in season two to replace their barking little pundit. After I transitioned over to that set from *The College Years*, Richard and I went bungee jumping together about forty miles north of L.A. in Angeles National Forest. We took along Ryan's sister and Ann, the Perfect Girl I was dating at the time. The jump was from the Bridge to Nowhere, which was a two¬hour hike in and spanned a river between two steep canyon walls. The drop shot you out over a huge rock and was, like, twenty stories in the air and, let me tell you, it felt that high. The whole time, I just kept thinking about how St. Peter would shit his britches if he knew two of his stars were so flagrantly breaking their dangerous-activities clause in their contracts.

At the second-season wrap party for *The New Class*, all the new kids in the cast were crying and hugging each other goodbye, just like everyone had done so many years earlier for the original *SBTB*. Again, I knew better. I stood back, drinking a beer, knowing we were coming back for at least two more seasons. The reason the producers brought Screech back was to liven up the show and help push the episode total into syndication. Again I was asked, "Dustin, why aren't you sad?" I just had to shake my head. They had no concept of how many *SBTB* wrap parties I had been to—or would continue to go to. I finished my beer and said, "Well, see you in four months."

When *SBTB: The New Class* was cancelled in 2000, and it was clear the long run of *SBTB*, in all its formats, was over, Den and I looked at each other and said, "Finally!" Everybody else, especially the kids, were crying and upset all over again, but we were laughing. I knew that this wrap party was the real deal. *SBTB* had officially come to an end. After attending so many wrap parties where everyone was convinced we weren't coming back and then we did, it was sort of a relief to know, in my heart, after ten seasons and 260 episodes, that my long run playing Screech had finally reached its end.

Truth is, when I knew it was over, I was sad. It was the end of an era, and I knew I would never get those moments back. For me, *SBTB* was more than just a TV show—it was my youth. I played Screech from the time I was eleven to the time I turned twenty one. From my first kiss to my first (legal) beer. I lost my virginity while I was on *SBTB*, bought my first car, got my first bank account, graduated from high school—you name it. St. Peter always touted *SBTB* as a show of firsts: first kiss, first date, first dance, first love, first fight, first breakup. I always mocked that until I was older and it all had a chance to sink in. For me, you see, *SBTB* really was all that and so much more. As much as I never wanted to play Screech for the rest of my life, I do miss it.

* * * *

As I look back now, I want to address a criticism I often receive from people about why Screech had grown so excessively corny and grating by the end of *SBTB: The New Class*. The bottom line is: I wasn't a happy camper. Not only were the writers pulling that shit with Screech and Belding acting increasingly gay together, I just felt like the writers were out of material for Screech. The comedy moments simply weren't as good. *The New Class* had a completely different feel from the original series— not just on screen, but from top to bottom. Den and I would look through the scripts and come to the sad conclusion that to a large degree that it was up to us to punch up our scenes together, adding as much funny as we could, because if we didn't, it wasn't going to happen.

Toward the end of *The New Class*, I started thinking to myself, "It's gonna be awfully hard as an actor to go anywhere from here after playing Screech for so long." I knew it was going to be extremely difficult to transition to new, more challenging, and (most importantly) different roles as an actor after we wrapped the series for good. I often thought of the transition Jim Carrey made from *In Living Color*, but of course that was a completely different situation. Obviously Carrey is a much different talent from mine, but he also had the freedom to play a variety of roles on a single television show (instead of being locked into one character). But more specific to my situation, he made the leap into other acting opportunities by getting to play himself. I mean, he created outrageous characters, but they were all channeled through Carrey's innate and unique sense of humor, which is pretty much the Thousand Faces of Jim Carrey. The power of his humor and the draw for the audience—regardless of the outlet—is that it originates from Jim Carrey. Audiences got to know him first and foremost as Jim Carrey. That's why, in my opinion, Carrey was so easily accepted and commercially successful right out of the gate in *Ace Ventura Pet Detective*.

As for me, I wanted to conspire a way to become known as Dustin Diamond in the waning days of *SBTB: The New Class*. I was always a fan of Buster Keaton and pure physical comedy: rubbery faces, slapstick, and exaggerated stage movements. I was hyper aware that I was deeply pigeonholed as Screech, having played the character for over a decade. That's not bad in and of itself (see Kelsey Grammer as Dr. Frasier Crane), but I had other aspirations, and I knew it wasn't going to be easy to change people's set impressions about my range and abilities as a performer.

I knew that whatever comedy acting I branched off into and tried after *SBTB*, whenever I made a face or hammed up a line, audiences would say, "Look, he's doing Screech," instead of,

"Dustin Diamond's pretty funny." That is, if I could even get past casting directors and be given the opportunity to stretch in more challenging roles. It's a common lament: the double-edged sword of early success as a child actor. Screech has certainly been my Sword of Damocles (my attempts to crawl out from under him and stay in the game have been well documented). But that's the price I've paid for playing a single role too well for too long. You can say what you want about it, but it's tough to argue that I didn't take the ball and run with it when handed the role of Screech. I employed all my resources to make as indelible an impression as I could with the tools I had to fully realize that character. A character, mind you, whose only distinguishing characteristic at my first audition was that he "speaks in a high, squeaky voice."

Some actors have been able to transition into second lives as iconic characters. I think of the late Bob Denver. A previous generation only knew Denver as Maynard G. Krebs from *The Many Loves of Dobie Gillis*. But of course he was later able to go on to larger fame—Hollywood immortality, really—as Gilligan.

I think what has surprised me most since *SBTB* is how many people seem to truly dislike Screech. Some go far out of their way to spew vitriol about the character. Perhaps it's a poisonous mixture of their opinion of me in real life coupled with a television character whose personality was intended to be aggravating and annoying to the "cooler" kids who ruled the high-school roost. I'm not ashamed to say that I've always viewed Screech as an Everyman, and that's how I tried to play him (especially in the original *SBTB*). I saw Screech as a wide-eyed innocent, an outsider cast away from the hipster crowd—an observer and reporter of what were purported to be the important happenings of the high-school hierarchy while maintaining his individuality by never wavering from his unique eccentricities or so-called nerdish pursuits. The Screech I tried to portray in the 1990s prodded millions of viewers across the globe (and still does) with the question, "Is it really better in the long run to be captain of the chess team or captain of the football team? When you grow up, would you rather be Bill Gates, the richest man in the world, or Trent Dilfer, with a Super Bowl ring, a couple of hobbled knees and a decent five-iron shot to a tight pin? And, when it's all on the table, who's really sexier: the ex-jock or the billionaire?"

Screech was a champion of the underdog. He stood for any kid who got bullied or singled out for being different because Screech achieved "popularity" and acceptance within the group by remaining true to himself. Yes, *SBTB* was the Pollyanna concoction of an idealized high school sprung, fully formed, from the mind of St. Peter Engel (like Athena from the forehead of Zeus).

St. Peter himself described Bayside as "the school we all wish we could go to." But within the world of that super-stylized fiction, I worked to play Screech with honest sincerity. To be blunt about it, *SBTB* played to a world that labels people—the jock, the nerd, the slut, the girl next door. But labels only simplify life for those who, for whatever convenient reason, choose to pigeonhole for others, often casting them as negligible or inferior, all for the ease of being able to catalogue themselves advantageously in society's vast Rolodex. But those people do not define you. Rather, they define themselves through the labels they choose to apply to others.

At the end, I think I overdid it with Screech, much to my detriment. My plan was simple, though far from brilliant. I had convinced myself that if I went way, way overboard with the character as the series wound down towards its finale, it would be easier in the aftermath of the show to separate the actor Dustin Diamond from the outrageously cartoonish, cheesy, obnoxious character of Samuel "Screech" Powers as a young adult. I believed that anything I did comedy-wise after playing Screech at a volume of eleven for the final season would ease my transition into more subtle roles. Surely, I reasoned, casting directors would be able to see that I was basically aping around like a Looney-Tunes character instead of revealing any aspects of my depth as a person or a professional performer. I was trying to widen the gap as I approached the finish line.

During that final season of *SBTB: The New Class* I even altered my appearance more by growing out my hair. The stylists stuffed it all up into a hairnet and picked it through to create that helmet of wild, curly hair I was sporting. I wanted to do whatever I could to divorce me, Dustin Diamond (the person and performer), from Screech the character on *SBTB*. My goal, as I said my final goodbyes to good ol' Screech, was to leave him in the realm of the absurd.

How I Missed Out on the *Scooby Doo* Movie

In 1991, Casey Kasem was on set all week for the rise and fall of Zack Attack in the "Rocumentary" episode. Casey and his wife, Jean, were amazing human beings. Jean became famous playing Loretta Tortelli on *Cheers* ("Hi, gang at Cheers!") and then again on the short-lived spinoff *The Tortellis*. In a side note, her son on The Tortellis, Anthony, was played by Timothy Williams (also a writer on that show) who appeared as Brett in the "Blind Dates" episode of *SBTB* in 1990.

One evening, the *SBTB* cast members were invited to the Kasems' house for a celebrity charity silent auction Casey was hosting for one of his many philanthropic causes. Also there was that Siamese Dr. Frankenstein creation, the Coreys (Corey Haim and Corey Feldman when they were at the height of their fame). Of course this was long before Corey Haim was trying to sell his teeth for a slice of pizza on the streets of Santa Monica. The Coreys strolled around Casey's house like God's twin gifts to the Earth, truly believing they were the cat's nards because they graced the covers of *Bop* and *Tiger Beat*.

I was in awe of Casey as the voice of my all-time favorite cartoon character, Shaggy, in my favorite cartoon, *Scooby Doo* (remember, I named my dog Scooby). In fact, years later it was me who got the ball rolling on what would become the Scooby Doo feature film—a project I was cut out of at the end. What happened was this:

I decided I wanted to play Shaggy in a *Scooby Doo* movie adaptation. Toward the end of the original *SBTB*, I contacted Kasem about it. I asked if he would coach me on pitch, cadence, phrasing—anything he was willing to teach me in my quest to become Shaggy in live action and get my project off the ground. Of course, the ever-gracious Casey agreed and invited me to his home, where we sat together as he taught me the voice dynamics he'd perfected over the decades. I then talked to my friend Wally Wingert, who later played Don Lewis, radio DJ, in a 1996 episode of *SBTB: The New Class*, and had made a great career in voiceover work (including various characters on Family Guy now). Wally put me in touch with Iraj Paran, who was an art director at Hanna-Barbera Studios on various projects, including *Scooby Doo*. Iraj brought me to meet directly with Joseph Barbera. Joe Barbera loved the idea of a *Scooby Doo* feature film. I began to work with his team, taking pictures of myself in a Shaggy shirt and wig with Shaggy facial hair. I re-created the hunched-over Shaggy posture—I had Shaggy down. Then Joe Barbera hand-drew Shaggy and several other visual aspects of the project in a proposal that pictured me (in real-life, human form) looking into a mirror with a *Scooby Doo* backdrop, while reflected back to me was a drawing of Shaggy (in Joe Barbera's own hand) that looked disturbingly familiar—to me! I was elated. At last, I had completed my transformation into Norville "Shaggy" Rogers!

Supplementing the artwork was a book we created that was an elaborate, bulleted pitch for the film project. The book itself was an ingenious work of art. It was constructed with illustrated cut-outs, including a pair of drawings that folded out to support the book upright when you set it on a table. One drawing was of me as Shaggy while the other was of the original, animated Shaggy character. I carted this pitch under my arm all around town while producers and studio development execs kept shuffling me off to different meet-and-greets. One exec told me there was already a script in development, while others said there was no interest in doing a *Scooby Doo* feature, especially one that included live action.

I relayed all my trials and tribulations back to Casey, who nodded knowingly. It was all old hat to him. He had always felt they had under-marketed the *Scooby Doo* franchise. For instance, he wondered why they had never even done the simplest and most obvious idea of licensing Scooby Snacks to dog food makers and receiving royalties from the packaging. Of course they did sell the rights eventually, but you're always left to wonder why things like that take so long. It doesn't take a fucking marketing visionary to make that deal happen.

Anyway, I was beating every bush in town with my pitch

book in tow when I was encouraged to meet with Jean McCurdy, president of Warner Brothers TV animation and head of Kids' WB. (McCurdy headed up Hanna-Barbera after it was absorbed by Time Warner in the Ted Turner takeover around 1996.) She also oversaw animated series, like *Batman: The Dark Knight*, and had a big say in what projects got fast-tracked and which died a slow, agonizing, Hollywood-development death.

My whole pitch for the film revolved around the idea of Rotoscoping. That's when animators trace over live-action film movement (think *Roger Rabbit*). At least, that was the original technique before the advent of computer animation. Now the term refers to the technique of manually creating a matte for an element on a live-action plate so it can be composited over another background. That sounds complicated, but my idea was even cooler. I wanted to employ a sort of reverse Rotoscoping. I wanted to preserve the integrity and feel of the original *Scooby Doo* episodes, so my idea was to transpose the live action over the animation. I wanted the finished product to look identical to the Hanna-Barbera creations. That would eliminate any chance of actors' cheesy interpretations of the animated characters movements and gestures. So when I met with Jean McCurdy and spread out my materials and notes and pitch book and danced around talking about how I had Casey Kasem (the voice), Joseph Barbera (the creator), Iraj Paron (the art director), and the *Scooby Doo* animators on board for the project, I thought she had to see it was a slam dunk. I went as far as to present a voice comparison presentation, matching my voice characterization back-to-back with Casey Kasem's. I even mixed them up so, hard as they tried, they couldn't discern which was the original and which was me. But none of it seemed to impress them. They told me nothing was moving forward with a *Scooby Doo* feature. They told me if it did, I'd be the first to know. They told me a lot of stuff.

Everybody on the set of *SBTB* knew that the *Scooby Doo* feature project had become my obsession. Den came up to me one day and said that he'd heard there was a script for *Scooby Doo* going around town and that Mike Myers was attached to play Shaggy. Fucking Hollywood, man. The way I heard it explained was that Myers had got wind of the project, bought the rights (which I could never afford), and written a script with him as Shaggy. I don't know if that is exactly how it went down, but that's how I heard it, and this is my story. I also heard that it was getting red-lighted (very much the opposite of green-lighted, the Hollywood term for a "go" movie) because there was content in it about Nazis. *Nazis?!* That may have worked for Mel Brooks, but America wasn't quite ready for Scooby and the gang to motor the Mystery Machine into Berlin to take on the Third Reich—*and I would've gotten away with the Holocaust if it wasn't for you meddling kids!*

Time went by. Joe Barbera passed away. Jean McCurty wouldn't return my calls. Then the talk around town was that Myers had let the rights lapse and that the *Scooby Doo* project was available again. Next thing I knew, Kevin Bacon was on *The Tonight Show* telling Jay Leno he wanted to play Shaggy in the new Scooby Doo film. He got up and did his version of the Shaggy walk (which was horrible), and of course everybody hooted and cheered and loved it. I thought, "Shit, I can't compete

with Kevin Bacon. Plus, he's like twenty years older than me."
Then I heard Jim Carrey announce he wants to play Shaggy in
the new *Scooby Doo* movie. At that point I knew I really couldn't
compete. Bacon may have been twenty years older, but Carrey
commanded $20 million a picture. Suddenly the project was the
talk of the town. In the end, of course, the script wasn't green-
lighted until 2001 with a cast of douchey teen heartthrobs led
by Sarah Michelle Gellar and Freddie Prinze Jr. Their first order
of business was to make sure their best pal, Matthew Lillard,
was given the role of Shaggy. I got the freeze-out on my dream
project. And it was cold.

People can say whatever they want about how the *Scooby
Doo* movie came to be, but they won't convince me that I wasn't
the one who got it started. All the people who should know, and
who were the point people for anything that had to do with the
Hanna Barbera property of *Scooby Doo*, had me in their faces for
years before that project got green-lighted. I met with everyone
from Casey Kasem to Joe-fucking-Barbera himself and tried to
convince them all that Scooby needed to be in a live-action, hy-
brid film on the big screen.

The most disappointing part of all was when I learned that
they had cast my favorite comedian of all time as the bad guy
in the role of Spooky Island owner Emile Mondavarious—*Mr.
Bean* himself, Rowan Atkinson. My favorite comedy sitcom is
the British series *Blackadder*. I would've given my left nut to
work with Atkinson. Instead, it's Matthew-fucking-Lillard acting
scenes with my hero. Yeah, Hollywood can be a rough town, and
I've had my share of ups and downs, but that one really stung.
Still does.

AFTER THE *BELL*

I'll be the first to say I was one lucky sonuvabitch landing the role of Screech on *SBTB*. We were all lucky. Acting is a tough way to make a living—to make a life—and for those of us who were fortunate enough to land this gig, even though we didn't always show it, we were grateful. Dennis Haskins and I stuck around for *SBTB: The New Class*, but our other co-stars each had tough rows to hoe after *SBTB* ended, beating the streets and casting offices for new opportunities after being typecast as Zack, Kelly, Slater, Jess, and Lisa. After we wrapped *SBTB: The College Years*, it took Mark-Paul nearly five years to land a decent role, starring in the comedy feature *Dead Man on Campus*. And in 2001, when he was cast on *NYPD Blue* to replace another child star, Rick Schroeder, critics and fans howled.

I think your adult life is just an extension of high school. High school is that period when you're forming your personality, discovering what sort of person you really are, or want to work to be. The people in your proximity—for good or for ill—are powerful influences on the adult you will one day become. High school presents to you daily your first real-world relationships with other people: friendship, conflict, love, anger, betrayal . . . I could go on, but it's hardly necessary. We were all there at one point, and many still are. There were times in my high-school days when I was bullied for being Screech on *SBTB*. I turned to martial arts for the emotional balance and physical skills that could protect me from harm when verbal ridicule led to physical aggression. I was a slender, birch-branch of a kid (don't forget, the camera doesn't exclusively add ten to fifteen pounds to Tiffani's ass), but I made it clear early on that I would fight anybody who thought it might be fun to verbally assault me, or even threaten me physically, simply because they had issues with a character I once played. I decided very early on that I wasn't gonna take no shit from nobody. I told many a wannabe bully, "Look pal, you're gonna look pretty stupid tomorrow when you have to tell everybody you got your ass kicked by Screech." This attitude of never backing down from bullies has imbued me with a lifelong commitment to sticking up for the little guy—except for that one time when I beat *Welcome Back, Kotter*'s Arnold Horshack (Ron Palillo) senseless on Fox's *Celebrity Boxing 2*. But I swear, that's the only exception.

Life after *SBTB* turned out to be harsh on Den, too. Sometime after we wrapped the last season of *The New Class*, I ran into him, and we went out for a drink. Den wasn't looking tip-top; he had put on a bunch of weight. That's when he told me he'd been released by his agency, summarily shit-canned by his agent. That was a pretty low blow. Hollywood is a town where most actors fire their agents with the same frequency I used to fire my BB gun in my back yard. It's not supposed to work the other way around.

After *The New Class*, I started doing comedy on the college circuit. I was traveling and doing a lot of dates for The National Association for Campus Activities (NACA), an organization that arranges appearances of speakers, performers, and celebrities for on-campus events. It wasn't long before Den had a new agent who was booking him for the same events in direct competition with me. I was doing my comedy act, while Den was presenting some sort of motivational speechification. Admittedly, it was annoying that Den was trying to go up against me for bookings. I was of the opinion we could combine forces for double-bookings to bring Screech and Belding to schools with some sort of play off of our TV characters with a spin into our new gigs. But whatever. He wanted to do things his way, and he didn't really have much else going on.

I don't do the NACA circuit anymore. It was a fun experience, but I had to learn to accept it for what it was. The students who organized the events were often the outcasts: the theater kids and hall monitors—the real life Screeches. It was pretty amusing, though only because I could see how they relished the authority and decision-making power they possessed in the organizing and facilitating of the events where I would perform. As they tried to maintain a tenuous air of executive authority, and I would think to myself, "You guys realize I'm older than all of you, right?" In reality, most of the gigs were pretty bare bones and unprofessional—as one might expect from any student-organized, cob-job event. Sometimes they wouldn't even be able to provide me with something as basic as a secure room for me to store my cell phone, keys, and other personal items while I was on stage. They'd just point to a chair in some common area for me to sling my coat over and drop my bag. Maybe this sounds like celebrity-prima-donna, groomed-by-NBC, hissy-fit bullshit and no big deal—but it's not, really. Once, while I was performing, my road manager had his cell phone stolen. It was loaded with his contact list of celebrity clients, along with backstage passes for different events and other personal items. It wasn't funny, actually. So there are certain standards all performers need to maintain for ourselves.

Like I said, Den was at these events to deliver a rousing motivational speech about clean living to exactly the wrong demographic. He was serving up the high school *SBTB* credo to college students already deep into their investigations of casual sex, casual (or even hard-core) drug use, binge drinking, and the practiced dual arts of biting sarcasm and bitter irony. You can image how that crowd received the message Den was pitching. This was a post-*SBTB* generation of college students that viewed the show's incessant reruns with snarky cynicism and ebullient irony. Case in point: the *Saved by the Bell* drinking game (see Appendix A.).

I haven't kept real close tabs on what all the other cast members are up to post *Bell*. It's certainly far from the forefront of my mind, but if it ever happened, I'd love to see the gang reunite in a film where everyone plays against type. Let's give everyone a real test, push their acting chops to their outermost boundaries. I'd like to see Mario play a mentally ill person, Mark-Paul play a homosexual struggling against his true self. Um, I want to see Tiffani play a crack whore. Man, this is hard. Okay, still just spitballing here: Lark can play a homeless person with rags for clothes. Elizabeth can play a prim and proper schoolmarm with skirts cut at the ankles. I'll play the serial killer. Twenty minutes into that film, if everyone is doing his and her jobs, no one in the audience would recognize anyone from the gang from Bayside.

ON BEING A CHILD STAR

I mentioned earlier that the pay for the principle cast members of *SBTB* was below what it should have been. St. Peter acted like he was such a nice guy *(Heeey, there's my stars. I'm looking out for you guys)*, but the fact in Hollywood is that when it comes to pay, kids get raked over the coals. The way it worked at that time was that there was a mandatory pay increase of ten percent per year. The producers would lock us into multi-year contracts (usually three years), so we didn't have the power to negotiate if the first season was a hit. That was part of the logic behind the standard increases each year, as protection for the actors. This provision wasn't great, but it was still better than nothing. Then one year, from a clear blue sky, word was handed down that the standard annual increase had been sliced in half to five percent, which is barely a cost-of-living increase. It may sound like griping, but when you're starring on a successful program, your window to parlay that success into fair remuneration is a small one. I know everyone thinks, "Oh, you television stars, you're making so much money. Quit your goddamn belly-aching." Well, everything is relative. If you're not maximizing your opportunity when it's in your grasp, it's the same frustration whether you're an actor, an entrepreneur, or a shift worker down at the mill. Your job is your job, and you want to be compensated comparably to your peers.

That's another topic: your peers. Actors on Saturday-morning shows are graded on a much different scale from actors in prime-time (regardless of viewership share). We were paid much, much less than cast members of prime-time shows and, frankly, looked down upon as the slumdogs of the industry by the arrogant elite. *(What time slot are you in? Oh, how terrible for you.)* The cast's parents were aware of it; they bitched about it, and most of them talked big about their plan to approach St. Peter. But, like I said, ultimately they chickened out. Look at Tiffani and Elizabeth. They bailed rather than remain for the second half of the last season. For the right money, I bet they would have stayed.

Stage parents are whole other breed of human, anyway. Many are living vicariously through their children, channeling a career they failed to achieve for themselves. It's a fact that tends to contribute to the fucked-up nature of the industry as a whole—everything is inverted. The whole pyramid of logic has been obliterated. I didn't have an allowance as a kid; I was pulling down the main income. But it wasn't like I was doing the family banking at eleven years old, either. That job fell to my parents. They cashed my checks, deposited what they saw fit, spent how they saw fit, and didn't feel they owed me any explanations. People could look at my life at that age and assume I was doing very well financially. I was forced to make that same assumption because I had no power over my earnings or the decisions being made for the investment and saving of my income. It would be different, I suppose, if I had had the option of blowing my own money; but I didn't. With very little oversight or obligation to me as the principal wage earner, my parents blew or lost my money for me. That's why today, I'm no longer on speaking terms with my dad.

I had no choice but to trust my parents to make the best decisions for my financial future. But most parents are not financial wizards, and mine let it be known that they were making sacrifices to move and commute everyday so that I could build a career as a performer. *Everything we've done has been for you so that you can have a bright future.* But the bottom line was, my parents just weren't that good with money. That's a tough situation for all kids in the entertainment industry: ninety-five percent of all work done by children is done without court-approved contracts, and eighty percent of all the work in the entertainment industry is located in the state of California. If your money as a child actor wasn't being protected, then why were you working so hard? What was it all for? It became such an issue for children in the industry that sixty years ago they passed a law known as the *Coogan law*, which exists only in California. This law was named for the 1930s child actor Jackie Coogan (who later achieved a second round of fame as Uncle Fester on the 1960s show *The Munsters*), whose parents had burned through $4 million (think of it, in the

1930s!) by the time Jackie reached the legal age to take charge of his financial affairs.

The Coogan law required that fifteen percent of my earnings be deposited into a special, protected account that neither my parents nor I had access to until the day the I turned eighteen. If it hadn't been for that law, by the time I turned eighteen, all that money would have been gone, wasted, just like the other eighty-five percent. But keep in mind, the Coogan law only comes into play when contracts are called into court for approval. Yes, the child star definitely plays against a stacked deck.

Take my dad, for instance. He brought me to the set most of the time because my mom worked such odd hours. What were his responsibilities all day? I had to attend school on set, memorize lines, do run-throughs, blocking—you name it. I missed most of the extracurricular activities and field trips offered through my program at Valley Tech. Meanwhile, he was shooting the shit with the crew, playing Sega Genesis inside an air-conditioned studio on a movie lot. To be fair, sometimes he had to walk all the way down to Kraft Service to make himself a sandwich (actually, they made it for you). All complimentary, of course. I had my down time, but my job was far from just hanging out all the time—it was a serious job. On top of all that, I'm playing the "nerd" character on the show, so I have that to contend with every day of my professional and personal life. I'm the skinny guy with the curly 'fro struggling to find where I fit in beside the Golden Child and the muscle-bound, permed mullet when it came to trying to stand out as a real individual rather than the character I portrayed on TV. I scored my share of coochie backstage at *SBTB*, but it wasn't easy, walking around all day cracking my voice while sometimes wearing a yellow chicken suit. Hey, I played the number one nerd in the world, for all kids, for a decade.

There were a number of professional and personal obstacles I had to overcome while my dad kicked back playing Super Mario Brothers. But the suits didn't care about what I was up against, nor did my parents. The bottom line was, I had a job to do. Their opinion—all of them—was, *"You're making good money, learn your lines, do your shit, don't bitch."*

Another odd aspect of being a child star is that I was constantly aware of wannabe actor adults who either openly resented my success or angled to get close to me so that I might rekindle their long-extinguished aspirations. I had a third-grade teacher at Lincoln Elementary School in Anaheim. She was an actress—er, I mean, failed actress. She made it abundantly clear that my very presence in her vicinity annoyed her to no end. She, and teachers like her over the years, would send me home with up to five hours of spiteful homework just to exercise whatever authority they had over my time and attention. I got sick and tired of it. That's why I worked hard, accelerated my studies, and graduated from high school at sixteen.

I'm well aware that many of you will have no sympathy for this situation. But this was my life; this was my experience. And if I have kids of my own one day, I will never let them get involved in the entertainment industry. I'm just too jaded, and there's too much I would be frantic to protect them from. I know what I had to endure, and still endure, and I wouldn't want it for them. Simply put, I don't think Hollywood is a good place for children.

The industry uses you when it's convinced it can gain something from you and drops you when it thinks it can't. Hollywood is like a friendly, open embrace that squeezes you tight, then reaches around and picks your pocket. All you feel in the moment is the warmth of that hug. You have no premonition of what selfish forces are maneuvering around you in that window of your usefulness. And even then you think, "Hey, he stole my wallet! Mmmm, but I still miss that warm, snuggly hug."

The kids of the industry are often the victims of their parents. But it's the parents, in fact, who go through a more serious withdrawal than their children when the money dries up and the perks of the Hollywood lifestyle are history.

When I step back and look at it all, I ask myself, "Was it all worth it?" The answer is yes. But I know that I grew up tougher than most kids, especially on an emotional level. I grew a thick, iron skin, numbed my emotions (when required), and taught myself how to suck it up and soldier on. Those factors, coupled with my experiences with people who tried to take advantage of my friendship, forced me to build walls between the world and myself and to never show vulnerability. It's an odd sensation. I always assume a camera is watching.

EPILOGUE

If the end of *SBTB* was the end of an era, then the best way to usher in a new era, from my point of view, was to create new memories. I had to decide what direction I wanted acting to take me in after the *Bell*. I decided I wanted to go into stand-up comedy. It's a tough second act—no overnight process—and it has taken me a lot of hard work and long hours of performing and travel to reach a point where I feel I'm delivering a strong, entertaining stage act. It has certainly made me appreciate a whole new art form. The acting gigs aren't gone forever, I'm just more careful now about what I choose. After *SBTB*, I received a lot of scripts and offers to rehash a cloned version of the Screech character. I rejected all of them. I'd done the Screech thing, and I wanted to push myself to expand in a different way—as a professional artist and as a person. Most recently, playing the villain on reality television has been liberating. It's helped me shake that image of the one-trick pony.

In my career now, doing stand-up comedy and making notorious appearances on reality TV shows, I feel like people have begun to embrace me as a completely separate entity from the character of Screech. In my comedy, people judge me on my material and whether or not I can make them laugh. In my role as a reality-TV villain, people appropriately hate me as the whiny, spiteful scumbag I portray.

For those who have yet to receive the memo, reality TV is anything but. The producers work with you to create characters to—again, not unlike *SBTB*—fill out a list of archetypes that viewers at home are looking for in each new installment. I have embraced the role of bad guy/asshole. By the way, it's way more fun to play the villain than any other part. The producers help you create your character, carefully crafting his (or her) personality to create conflict in the group dynamic, and then they let you know when it's "go time"—time to jump in there and stir the turd soup. They want the bad guy to generate a ton of negative feedback; they want people's fingertips smoking as they dash to their keyboards, filling fan sites and discussion boards with thick, noxious venom for the one character they hate the most, the one wrench in the works without whom—if he would just get kicked off the show—everyone would get along so well, spontaneously locking elbows and swaying as they sang "Kumbaya." Reams and reams of malicious chatter fill the Internet; viewers spew and froth about how much they hate that dopey motherfucker on *Celebrity Fit Club*. My only response is: keep those great e-mails coming. It means I'm doing what I was paid to do.

The funniest part to me is that the producers didn't believe at first that I could pull off the bad-guy routine. They didn't want to give me a shot, because they thought I was too typecast as squeaky clean and dorky from all my years as Screech. They were leaning towards Warren G being the bad guy that season. I had to convince them I could do it. But if there's one thing I know, it's the television industry. It's been my life and livelihood for twenty-four years (I'm now thirty-two). I knew I could dig deep, push buttons, and make millions of people really, really hate my fucking guts.

Like that blowout I (supposedly) had with Harvey (that's Gunnery Sergeant Harvey Walden of the U.S. Marine Corps for the uninformed) on *Fit Club*. None of that was scripted, but we both knew what we were trying to accomplish in that scene. We conferred with the producers backstage and then rolled with the punches on camera. When the director yelled cut, I turned to the crew and said, "That was pretty harsh." They laughed and said, "It's gonna look great on TV." Then I returned after what was supposed to be a week wearing a T-shirt that read "Star of the Show" . . . Hello? Are there really television viewers in America who don't think wardrobe approved that shirt? Who believes that I could walk onto the set of a network television show wearing whatever I brought from home? I also wasn't allowed to tell the other cast members that the producers from Granada Productions for VH1 were paying me more money on the side, under the auspices of my own "development deal." Since the show wrapped, and I was able to gauge the reaction to my performance, I have

felt like I should have played it safer on *Fit Club* and perhaps portrayed a "nice guy." I had a lot of fun playing the asshole, but I
dramatically underestimated how seriously viewers take "reality"
television.

In a way, where public perception and sentiment is concerned,
I think non-actors have an advantage over professionals in the format of reality television. In my case, I was groomed by NBC and
was in full-on, network-combat mode for more than decade in a
career spanning twenty-four years. I approach every new set as a
character role, even for talk-show appearances. When the camera
is on, so am I. I consider the sensibility of the audience; I play
a scene with the host balancing wit, charm, and attentiveness;
and I respond with interesting, effective, concise, and informa-
tive answers while ever-conscious of my perceived "likeability."
I approach all those aspects of my performance while balancing
my rapport with the host, because it's important to maintain a
specific role while being interviewed, especially for an international broadcast. There are many factors at play during talk-show
appearances, a format that the viewing audience might consider
the ultimate example of natural, candid, reality-based television.
But it, too, is an acting process that requires professional focus.
When there's a camera, there's an audience; when there's an audience, there's awareness; and when there's awareness, reality
breaks down.

My transition to comedy has been a similar endeavor to my
turn on *Fit Club* and my other reality-TV appearances. Nobody
thought I could pull it off. I know people come to my stand-up
shows wondering if I'm just going to do a whole set about being

Screech or about shit from *SBTB*. I know they're curious about whether I even work blue (in the industry, that's the term for an act that includes profanity and racy content. And yes, I work very blue).

Bob Saget earned a reputation with a large television audience as a total cornball for his roles as Danny Tanner on *Full House* and as host of *America's Funniest Home Videos*—two programs so sicky-sweet and family-oriented they practically gave you cavities by watching them. Saget experienced a big blowback after those shows ended, and he continued his stand-up career as a comedian who works extremely blue. In fact, Bob Saget is such a down-and-dirty sonuvabitch. He doesn't just work blue, he practically works brown. I think Saget's return to his first love—being an insanely dirty and wickedly absurd comic—was a big mental implosion for millions of people who believe everything they watch on television, who believe actors actually are the characters they portray. Saget paid his dues for years as a comic on the road. His big break was his appearance on *Rodney Dangerfield's 9th Annual Young Comedian's Special* in 1984. That was three years before *Full House* premiered.

Or take for instance the *Saturday Night Live* parody of Screech, which by the way, I thought was very funny. Will Farrell plays James Lipton, and Toby Maguire plays Screech in a send-up of the Bravo Channel's *Inside the Actor's Studio*. Funny as this skit is, it simply reinforces the mentality that I'm up against. Maguire plays an over-the-top rendition of the character Screech, but the "interview" is billed as being with the actor Dustin Diamond. For many, there is no separation between the actor and the icon. I get the gag (trust me, I understand taking creative liberties in performing humor), but clearly Maguire isn't playing me, he's playing Screech—the character I created to entertain children and drunken college students. That's just the professor inside me trying to come out and logically analyze a comedy sketch that essentially doesn't make sense. Eh, it's just the way the business works. It's still flattering—and it was funny.

Of course movie actors are free to play whatever role they please and rarely ever get the stink of caricature or typecasting. Movie actors are *artistes* while television actors (especially in the years I worked the most) are all about locking into recognizable patterns that can be consistently repeated to build a growing audience so the network can charge ever-increasing ad rates. Moving from film to TV is in vogue these days—there are buckets of cash to be made for known actors (i.e., commodities) who have staked their claims and built loyal followings with audiences. But sadly, when Elizabeth Berkley made the jump in the to film in the '90s with *Showgirls*, the fact was that the primary audience for that rotten tomato was a perverse curiosity to see the snatch of that chick on *SBTB*. And, as I alluded to before, when she popped up more recently as Horatio Caine's love interest on *CSI: Miami*, millions of viewers reflexively said, "Hey, there's Jessie Spano." There's nothing evil about it, it's just become second nature in a culture that insatiably consumes, then evacuates, its media entertainments like so much caramel corn.

The pattern of recognition is even more profound for actors like myself and my fellow cast mates on *SBTB* because our target demographic was watching us in their formative years. The imagery of us on their television sets is burned into their collective generational psyche. Not only that, but we were aging in pace with those kids who were watching us. That concept may seem odd, now since we are forever frozen in time through syndicated reruns, but during the period when we had the most influence on those young minds, we were, for all intents and purposes, a living organism that was as much a part of their lives as their older brother or their best friend at school. Think about it from our perspective: most kids have static photo albums they look at to review their transition from adolescence through puberty and into young adulthood. I have a live action document that chronicles my development just about every Friday from the time I was eleven to the time I was twenty-one. It's a bizarre document, indeed. When I watch myself now I feel entirely foreign from that person, body and soul—it's me but it's not me. It's me pretending to be someone else. And it's the same lament for all my cast mates on *SBTB*. No matter what else we do, till the day they plant us in the ground, for millions we will always be Zack, Kelly, Slater, Jess, Lisa, Screech, and Mr. Belding.

Fame does seem to come with more curses than blessings. But I wouldn't have changed a thing. For me, part of the curse is being so inextricably linked to the character I brought to life on television, a character that still invites frequent ridicule and mockery. I'll go to a theater with my girl, and as the lights dim, some jackass will begin to moan, "Screeech." If my washer breaks, and I need to get wash done, I can't be spotted at the local laundromat some afternoon or ten web sites will be up by dinner time, breathlessly announcing "Screech Hits Rock Bottom!" If I get pulled over for speeding, the ticket will be posted on thesmokinggun.com. One of the side effects of that sort of exposure is that, as a result, every nut job with an Internet connection has your home address. As it is, it's hard enough to keep that information private. When people learned my address in Wisconsin, they started driving past at all hours, honking the horn and screaming, especially on the weekends. In the summer time, or on New Year's Eve, forget it. That shit makes me weep for humanity. Point is, my social faux pas are magnified. But alas, assholes are everywhere in daily life. Only when you're famous, you're an asshole magnet.

People have come up to me feeling they have free rein to be rude because they "know" me and are entitled to get anything and everything off their chest. I can't act irritated, I need to be all smiles, otherwise people will dismiss me as just another arrogant celebrity. Say I'm at dinner, sitting in a quiet restaurant with my girl, off in a corner, minding my business. Maybe it's Valentine's Day. Maybe we just had a fight. Maybe we're discussing how her grandmother just died or how the world just sucks at that point, and we're both on the edge of tears. Sometimes people will recognize me and be very respectful and friendly. They'll say they're a big fan and ask for a photo or an autograph. Then there are others that have no sense of decorum or class. They'll walk right up to my table, throw their arm around me without a word with their camera phone poised in their outstretched hand and snap a shot—while I'm eating!

"What the fuck, dude?!"

"Oh, well excuse me, Mr. Hollywood."

People will come right up to me and ask, with all sincerity,

"So, what's it like being the biggest fucking idiot on TV?" Behavior like that is tough to tolerate, but if I say anything derogatory in response, I'm the asshole.

Parents have approached me, telling me they want to get their children started in acting. They ask me if there's anything I can do to help and, with many of them, I'll recognize that ravenous "stage-mom" glare in their eyes. I see that hunger some parents have to live vicariously through their children's fame. Sometimes I'll ask these kids, "What do you really want to do? What are your interests?" They tell me everything from wanting to be a writer to becoming a jet-engine mechanic. I encourage them to follow those dreams, not the dreams of their parents. Because sacrificing your childhood for the adventure of acting has its price. For some, that price is too high.

I felt protective of the kids who comprised the shifting casts of *SBTB: The New Class.* I always wished I could turn back the clock and try a few things again, knowing what I then knew as a young man already with years in the industry under my belt (that sentiment is, if anything, stronger with what I know now). I was in a unique position, having earlier lived through those kids' exact experiences first hand, so I tried to counsel them on what to expect and how to avoid certain pitfalls. Unfortunately, much like myself at the same age, they already "knew it all" and didn't want to hear what I had to say. So, in much the same way as I watched Tiffani discard the sweet, bright-faced "knew it all" and didn't want to hear what I had to say. So, in much the same way as I watched Tiffani discard the sweet, bright-faced enthusiasm of her first days on the set of the original *SBTB* as she was seduced by "fame, I watched the kids of *The New Class* embrace the poisonous attitude of, I'm a star!" A strange outlook indeed, considering they were riding in on the coattails of something I had helped to build from scratch. And I don't know if it was just my new perspective of being older and more mature, having been around the block a time or two, but the process seemed to be accelerated with those kids. I can't blame them for living the good life while it was there for the taking (I did the same, myself), and there were some great kids in those *New Class* casts. I just wanted to give them a big brotherly heads up that it wasn't going to last forever. For the vast majority of young actors, the perks of fame— the money, the attention from fans, the doting from the network—all come to an end sooner than they ever expect. I shared my concerns with Den. He smiled and said, "Dustin, just let 'em make their mistakes. I let you make yours."

The blessings of fame can be tremendous, far exceeding much of the drudgery or ridicule that result from living in the public eye. Working on a television or film set, seeing everything come together, getting along with the cast and crew, vibing off the whole creative environment of making entertainment, knowing your job, and performing like a pro—that's an amazing experience. Few experiences in life come close to the total reward of doing one thing extremely well.

I've never heard another actor discuss this, but there's a moment when you realize you're a professional actor. Maybe it's a realization that you're doing what you were born to do, but whatever it is, it's an odd, slightly unsettling sensation when it occurs.

I remember the when it first happened for me. It was a hallway scene on *SBTB* where the whole gang was grouped together. I spoke my line of dialogue first then waited while the others began to exchange their lines. As I stood there, my mind began to wander. I had no dialogue, but I was still on camera, so my body language was reacting to whatever Zack and Kelly were yammering on about. Meanwhile, my eyes searched the studio audience, I made eye contact with the camera guys, stared through the glass of the bustling beehive of the booth, gazed at the boom-mike operator . . . I realized, in that moment, that everyone was focused, one hundred percent, on us. Suddenly, without the slightest awareness of my dialogue queue, I began to speak. I delivered my lines exactly as they appeared in my script, but I wasn't regurgitating them from memory—no, I was speaking them as my own conscious words. I was responding to what Zack was saying, unconsciously, in what felt effortlessly like my own, fully formed thoughts. As I was doing this, I remained fully aware that I was in the process of acting on a television show. I was on autopilot. It was like I had torn myself in two, and one half was speaking while the other stood a half-pace away, observing myself as the spectacle played itself out. Inside, I was freaking out, terrified there was no possibility I could know my lines as simultaneously I was speaking them with full confidence and inflection. It's almost impossible to describe the sensation I felt that day—like some bizarre, seamless marriage of utter unconsciousness and hyperawareness. I was both in the moment and of the moment. And after that day, it was like I had turned a corner in my professional career. From then on, I became increasingly aware of my ability to be both fully involved in the delivery of my character's dialogue in a scene while simultaneously remaining coolly detached from the rudimentary logistics of the acting process. It was as though I had arrived. It was a mystical invitation to relax and enjoy the ride.

These days it's especially gratifying when I can see the positive affect my work has had—and continues to have—on fans around the world. There were many fun moments over my decade-long run on *SBTB*, but nothing—nothing—trumped the excitement of Friday nights. Nothing could equal that anticipation of gearing up to perform before a live audience, knowing the taped broadcast would be aired to millions of viewers around the planet. Before every Friday taping, we would huddle up backstage for a pre-show powwow: director, cast, guest stars—everybody. On stage we could hear Phil Stellar wrapping up his warm-up act. The director would give us his final notes, telling us what a great week of rehearsals we'd had, cautioning us to take things slow on stage, hit our marks, have fun, and knock it out of the park (like Mark-Paul at that infamous cast-and-crew softball game). We'd all throw our hands over his at the center of our circle, count to three, and holler the word of the night—whatever quirky word had bubbled to the surface through the week's run-throughs and had become that episode's catchphrase, almost like a good luck charm. One week I remember the word was a punch line delivered with typical verve by Screech himself. So, with hands stacked together, and comically cracking voices, we'd chant, "One, two, three . . . GADZOOKS!"

Then we'd break and head out for our opening bows (after Mario did a few sets of donkey presses). They'd announce, "Ladies and gentleman . . . Dustin Diamond!" I'd run out, bow, wave, and the audience would go fucking bananas. They were so excited to see us. And we were thrilled to see them. The tarps still shielded the first set, and the cameras were rolled away to the sides. It was just us standing before the audience. I would look out to see all the crew, our parents and friends, the director, the writers, the network suits, Peter Engel, Linda Mancuso—everybody. All the hard work of that week had culminated in that glorious moment. The rehearsals and rewrites, the business, the wardrobe, the makeup, the cast squabbles, and all the bullshit—it was all set aside for that next hour and a half while we created something new in the supercharged energy of that room. Those were the best of times.

Yeah, I got to play Screech—the comic relief at the center of a situation comedy. What was endearing about Screech's character was that the audience would always get the joke while Screech didn't. Hopefully, in this book, I've revealed the behind-the-scenes drama that Screech knew and the audience didn't. But in the end, the best part is that I got to make people laugh, for many years. And I hope it's the laughter that people remember most.

The tarps fall away. The first set is revealed. A nervous murmur ripples through the audience. The director calls out, "Positions everyone. Quiet, please. Quiet."

Silence envelops the studio.

"Background."

The extras appear as the scene comes alive, crossing back and forth, taking their seats at The Max.

"In five, four, three, two, . . ."

APPENDIX A:

THE *SAVED BY THE BELL* DRINKING GAME
Created by Bill King and Brad Valentine

ONE DRINK

* Zack talks directly into camera
* Slater calls Jessie "Momma"
* Belding is fooled
* Any teacher is fooled
* Screech in locker

TWO DRINKS

* Any of the kids sing
* The girls cheer
* Zack sent to Belding's office
* We see one of the kids on the job
* Zack uses giant cellular phone
* Slater wrestles
* Audience goes "WooOOOoo"
* Slater calls Zack "Preppie"
* Commercial break
* Scene in locker room
* Belding reminisces
* Nerd or Jock gets a throwaway line
* Students buy something Zack is selling
* Lisa mentions shopping
* Lisa bitches at Screech
* Somebody actually ingests food at The Max

* Jessie calls Slater "Poppa"
* Jessie calls Slater "Sexist"

THREE DRINKS

* Zack freezes time
* "Zack Attack" plays
* Zack's plan fails
* Character has a fantasy
* Parent sighting
* Kelly wears a skirt cut below knees

FOUR DRINKS

* Open locker without entering a combination

FIVE DRINKS

* Any slapping
* "To be continued . . ."
* Tori Paradox episode
* Cineplex music plays
* Kevin the Robot sighting
* Belding says "Hey, hey, hey . . . What's going on here?!"

FINISH THE GLASS

* Screech dresses as a woman

APPENDIX B:

To All the Chicks I Banged Before:
An Open Letter

Dear Ladies,

No doubt many of you were just filthy. You'd hook up with me, with my buddies, or any dude you thought might advance your career. You just didn't care. But there were also those of you who suffered full mental breakdowns as a result of the depraved sexual shit we did together in my younger, dumber days.

Look, those were crazy times, and I did a lot of stupid stuff back then. There are a lot of things I did as a young man that I'm not proud of, and if I could go back, I would change them. Please allow me to explain, in all modesty, that a lot of the shit I did was in an effort to make memories and simply live in the moment. I spent my formative years working full-time in an industry that consumed any chance I had at a normal childhood. With my pubescent hormones raging, many— perhaps most—of my decisions were guided by my monster and dirty thoughts. Dirty, dirty thoughts.

Now, as a grown man, I've had time to reflect on some of my more immature sexual escapades, and I regret many of them. Not for the women I was with, but more for my actions leading up to (and during) our bang sessions and for how I conducted myself afterward.

With heartfelt sincerity, deepened by years of more worldly experiences in a search for substantial meaning and wisdom in my life,

I offer my apologies to anyone I filthed up, back in the day. I was a (willing) victim of the whirlwind of Hollywood, and I tried my hot damnedest to make the most of it.

Don't get me wrong, there were a lot of great moments, too. I've reflected upon all of them. Unfortunately, remembering so many other moments, I just have to shake my head and say, "D-Man, what were you thinking?"

So, for every one of you I ever hurt (unless you begged me to hurt you because that's what you were into), from the bottom of my heart, I'm sorry.

Sincerely yours.

Dustin

P.S.: Call me.

APPENDIX C:

A FAN'S TOP EPISODES (a very unofficial list)

This might disappoint many hard-core *SBTB* fans, but when I look back on the taping of the individual episodes and try to recall strange backstage happenings and juicy tidbits of Bayside trivia, each show just seems to blend together with the next into one long blur. At the time, I tried to key in on one aspect of each week's show that made that show unique and fought the monotony, and sometimes boredom, of retreading the same plots and storylines for the principle characters. But there are only so many trials and tribulations that characters can realistically (or even unrealistically) face in a make-believe high school in Southern California. As I've mentioned, we did often pull pranks on one another to keep the week fresh. Each of us handled the occasional ennui of network television in our own unique fashion.

What follows is a brief selection of episodes that nonetheless still stick out in my mind.

"DANCING TO THE MAX" (Air date: August 20, 1989)

Casey Kasem hosts a dance contest at The Max. Kelly demands a dance-off between Zack and Slater because she can't decide whom to attend the dance with. Jessie teaches Zack his dance moves, so when Kelly picks Slater, Zack convinces Jessie that they were meant to be partners all along. Lisa Turtle sprains her ankle and is stood-up by her date. Screech comes to the rescue with his new dance, the "Sprain."

The Sprain was another dance routine coordinated by Maria Henley. It's amazing to me how many people still ask me in person to do it. If you see me on the street, please don't ask me to do the Sprain anymore.

Now that I'm in my thirties, it's more likely than not I'll suffer an actual sprain in the process. What's interesting, though, is that the plot calls for Screech to save Lisa (who has injured her ankle) from disappointment and failure by performing his triumphant improvisational dance—a concept that pre-dates by fifteen years Napoleon Dynamite's heroic effort to save Pedro from embarrassment through the power of funky movement. I think Joseph Campbell, the eminent scholar of storytelling, would have agreed that it's a classic mythological plot construct for the nerd archetype: The nerd hero completes his journey into the unknown by poppin' a nut on the high school dance floor.

Also, I must say that I felt it patently unfair that Screech, who pined for Lisa Turtle all those years, never had any romantic satisfaction in that relationship, indeed, no closure at all. Quite the opposite. When Lisa made out with Zack at her house in "The Bayside Triangle," and then again backstage at her fashion show (which Zack organized for her, of course), and Screech was made to watch this transgression backstage in tortured silence, that episode struck a low point for me. From a storytelling perspective, Zack has maintained a friendship with Screech since the beginning of *SBTB* and is well aware of Screech's infatuation—his love—for Lisa, but he goes ahead and scumbags him anyway. He is stealing away the only girl Screech has ever been after. Meanwhile, the main story and character arcs for the series as a whole are in total service of the epic on-again/off-again romance between Zack and Kelly, culminating in their eventual marriage in the Las Vegas movie. This seemingly insignificant plot point—Zack choosing to make out with Lisa—(I mean, insignificant as far as the producers and writers were concerned), solidifies Zack Morris as a blue-ribbon douchebag, who gives not one shit about anyone but himself. For the viewers of *SBTB*— the target demo being primarily pre-pubescent young people—there's the core personality of your lead character revealed, there's the face of the whole Peter Engel franchise, there's the Golden Child. He's a self-absorbed pretty boy who makes no bones about nailing the one girl his "best pal" adores with all his heart and soul and, further, is convinced he can talk, grin, and "Aw shucks" himself out of any situation, no matter how intentionally vindictive.

"CREAM FOR A DAY" (Air date: October 7, 1989)

Kelly is nominated for Homecoming Queen but doesn't want to leave her room when she discovers a zit at the end of her nose. Meanwhile, Zack and Screech accidentally invent a cream in chemistry class that clears up acne. They begin selling it at school. Only one problem: it turns everyone's face purple. Bayside plays Valley in the Homecoming football game. News footage provided at the end by KNBC shows number 3, A.C. Slater, scoring the winning touchdown.

My dad played the chemistry teacher in this episode. Screech was in the miserably hot Bayside Tiger mascot costume.

"HOUSE PARTY" (Air date: October 6, 1990)

Screech's parents leave him in charge of the house while they go on a vacation to Graceland. The boys break Mrs. Powers's explicit "no parties" rule and, in the process smash her prized Elvis statue. The gang has to find a way to replace the statue before she returns.

Guest starring: Ruth Buzzi as Mrs. Roberta Powers, Patrick O'Brien as Mr. Dewey, Jeffrey Asch as Maxwell Nerdstrom, and Tori Spelling as Screech's love interest, Violet Bickerstaff.

This episode featured *Laugh In's* Ruth Buzzi as Screech's mom, and the producers tried to get Michael Richards (a.k.a. Kramer) to play my dad. It was only the first season of *Seinfeld*, but Richards passed on the role, claiming he didn't want to get locked into comedy roles so he could branch out into more serious material. I thought that was strange, because a few years later he played Doug Beech in *Airheads*, a guy who basically crawls around inside the air ducts of a radio station. It may have been a minor role, but apparently it was an important, serious one. I would have loved teaming up with Richards as Screech, Sr., patriarch of the Powers clan. Oh, well.

During the party scene in that episode, when Screech's mom returns and they drop a surprise "Happy Anniversary" banner from the ceiling, standing beneath the banner is a girl (I think she has dark hair and is wearing pink overalls) who was appearing on the show because, somewhere in America, she was awarded first prize in a "Win a Chance to Be In the Background of an Episode of *SBTB*" contest. You can tell from her body language that she isn't nearly as comfortable on camera as the other extras.

This was also a Tori Spelling/Violet Bickerstaff episode while she was lobbying hard to get with Mark-Paul, using me as her inside informant. *Did he mention me today? Did he? Did he?*

"THE GLEE CLUB" (Air date: December 23, 1990)

The gang joins the Glee Club trying to win a trip to Hawaii. Violet Bickerstaff (Screech's girlfriend) is the only one who can sing. Screech bombs with Violet's parents, and she quits the Glee Club. He's told to stay away from Violet, but later, when she chokes onstage, Screech comes to her rescue. Also in this episode, Zack uses a "time out" to freeze the space-time continuum.

Guest starring: Tori Spelling again, Jack Angeles as Mr. Tuttle (our real-life NBC accountant) and another uncredited Scott Wolf appearance.

Every time I sang the song in this episode, the director kept encouraging me to do it louder and louder and more over-the-top, until I belted out the outrageous version that made the final cut.

"THE LAST DANCE" (Air date: September 14, 1991)

Zack and Kelly plan to go as Romeo and Juliet to the big costume ball. Kelly's new boss at The Max, Jeff, comes between her and Zack, and they break up. At the ball, Zack Attack sings "Love Me Now" and "How Am I Supposed to Live Without You?" Jessie's knee has not yet been split open, so she is the band's lead singer. Kelly isn't in the band at all. In one scene, on drums, is Ollie Creekly, a minor, African American nerd character with a deep, gravelly voice.

Guest starrng: Patrick Muldoon (*Starship Troopers*) as Jeff Hunter and an uncredited Scott Wolf (*Party of Five, Go*).

In this especially cheesy episode, Slater and Jessie are singing at the costume ball for Zack's eponymous band, Zack Attack. Not for nothing, but did everything have to be named for Zack? And another thing: how did this apparent schemer and ne'er-do-well, who was always involved in some half-baked plot to skirt authority and shirk responsibility, manage to earn a near-perfect score on his SATs? I'll tell you how—magic. (For more on this brand of magic, refer back to the section on Ed Alonzo and Neil Patrick Harris.)

Stage coordinator Maria Henley, who was with *SBTB* forever, would choreograph all our dance routines, like for the Zack Attack music performances or for the "Buddy Bands" episode. Slater and Elizabeth's Zack Attack performances were lip-synched to professional performers, whose voices were intentionally paired with theirs because, supposedly, they mirrored what Mario and Elizabeth's real singing voices might sound like if they possessed the talent to sing. Our music was usually arranged by Scott Gale, though there were others whose names now escape me. The music guys would come down whenever they had a number to arrange and then disappear just as quickly. They would give us cassette tapes (because that was the technology back in the day) along with our scripts to be read and listened to over the weekend.

They were also in charge of matching up the voice-over talent for the musical performances—all performers we never met. So, if it was Tiffani singing, she would lip synch while the voice track played, and not only were the vocals supposed to sound excellent as music, they were also intended to sound like Tiffani's voice if she were singing in real life. It was apparently important to at least attempt to pull this trick off, though in my opinion it failed miserably and sounded ridiculous. Just listen to Mario as he opens his mouth for the first stanza of "How Am I Supposed To Live Without You?" It's an all-time classic moment in the annals of lip-sync-dom, resting somewhere in that golden pantheon alongside Milli Vanilli and C & C Music Factory.

Speaking of music, a lot of people don't remember—or never knew—that *SBTB* had two recorded versions of the theme song. For one season, St. Peter commissioned a new theme from Michael Damian. (Remember "Rock On," the hit from his *Dream a Little Dream* album?) I don't think it ever became popular with the fans or, most importantly, the powers that be, and it didn't last long. I don't even know if the new theme ever aired on television or made it to the DVDs, but it would play in studio as the intro to the show's Friday tapings.

Another factoid about the music on *SBTB*: there wasn't any played on set. If there was a dance scene or band scene, it was silent on set because any music would have stepped on the dialogue. All music was mixed in during post-production.

"CHECK YOUR MATE" (Air date October 5, 1991)
Zack and Slater bet $300 that Screech will defeat his Valley High opponent in the chess championship. When Valley students steal Screech's lucky beret, Zack and Slater steal Screech's opponent.

This episode is a direct result of those questionnaires the writers and producers made us fill out. Since I was a chess player, they designed this episode around Screech competing with a wager laid down on the results. There's a bogus, campy chess move in this episode called the "Spassky bishop block." Boris Spassky is a real guy, but the chess move is pure fabrication. I only mention it because I'm a chess player and kind of a stickler for such things, but it's all in the service of *great* comedy—I suppose.

When it came to Screech, the producers and writers of *SBTB* insisted on a number of stock geekoid clichés (i.e., a high-stakes high school chess championship). They gave him the wacky, loud clothes, the bunk beds, the ant farm, the robot, chess—the only affectation they fell short of was the plastic pocket protector. It was always important to me from day one to understand and portray the emotional side of Screech, but there was only so much I could do within the confines of how the character was written. Screech was gullible with a big heart and had his fair share of eccentricities.

But what was interesting to me was that, as time went on, the writers would introduce new, minor nerd characters (like Maxwell Nerdstrom, who played the wealthy love interest trying to lord over Violet Bickerstaff) who were the proto-stereotypical nerdy-nerds with the white tape wound around glasses, the high-waters with bright white socks, etc. It was interesting because, in the main cast, Screech filled the role of the nerd archetype, yet when other nerds were portrayed in minor roles (like Ollie, Alan, or the lazily named Nerdstrom), there was never any depth to their characters; they were total, unabashed cartoon caricatures. It always made me wonder if that put Screech in the same category of nerd as those other, throwaway characters in the mind of the viewers. My question was: If Screech defined the nerd archetype in the fictional universe of *SBTB*, then why were actual nerds portrayed so utterly different from him in both appearance and mannerisms? I think this conflict between the societal concept of nerdiness and the stock television portrayal of nerdiness is what made Screech the most realistic of all the main cast members. I received numerous letters from fans that said my portrayal of Screech helped them "get through high school." Many of the letters were heartbreaking because, while all the ridicule and disappointments I faced as Screech were through a character I played on TV, the letters I read were filled with the troubles these "nerdy" kids were actually experiencing in their real lives.

This dichotomy bothered me. I was worried that the producers had designs on getting rid of Screech and replacing him with a more archetypal nerd. This may seem far-fetched now, but at the time I was consumed by it. We were engaged in negotiations over my contract renewal. My initial three-year contract was up, and I was smack in the middle of the conundrum of whether I should demand more money and risk getting canned from the show or play ball and simply go along to get along. Sometimes in the industry, when you feel your leverage is weak, you have to take a little screwing on the money side to ensure that you have steady work. I certainly didn't want to be the next Denise Crosby. She played Lt. Tasha Yar on *Star Trek: The Next Generation*. In 1994, she was unceremoniously shit-canned when she held out for more dough. Denise may live long, but, thanks to that decision, she will not prosper.

My negotiations stretched out, and at one point it didn't look like the network was going to come through with what I was asking. Meanwhile, the writers had all sorts of new nerds stepping to the fore on *SBTB*. I was happy for the extras who were getting more lines, but at the same time I couldn't help feeling a bit hinky about where it was all headed. Fortunately,
my contract was settled favorably, but I always thought it was interesting that when they brought their gaggle of new nerds to Bayside, they

were all ridiculously over-the-top. One kid was named Kevin (in the show and real life). He had the blonde, frizzy hair and used that urgent, nasally stock nerd voice. Then there was Nerdstrom and low, robot-voiced Ollie. They all made their bid to grab the laughs, but I knew my audience better than all of them.

"PIPE DREAMS" (Air date: October 26, 1991)

Zack and the gang adopt "Becky," an injured duck (named after Mr. Belding's wife), during a biology project in the pond beside Bayside High. Workers strike oil while digging for a new goal post on the football field. As a result, an evil oil company wants to destroy the pastoral pond. This episode features the cast doing their high-fives shown in each show's opening credits.

In "Slater's Friend," Mario lost his pet chameleon Artie, and in this episode Mark-Paul loses his new friend Becky the duck. This episode is most amusing to me for the lengths of absurdity the writers would go to make Zack Morris a little slice of pretty much every vocation and bleeding-heart cause a human being can be involved in on planet Earth. This time: animal activist.

"ROCKUMENTARY" (Air date: November 30, 1991)

The great Casey Kasem narrates the rise and fall and rise again of Zack Attack. It starts with their garage-band beginnings and progresses into their days of fame and fortune. The band breaks up over Zack falling for their publicist and arguing with the other members. The others branch out into solo careers. In this episode, Kelly is the lead singer.

Guest starring: Casey Kasem as himself, Stacie Foster as Mindy Wallace, and Nick Brooks as Brian Fate.

Notice that Elizabeth Berkley does not appear in this seminal episode. However, She was supposed to, however. The episode had to undergo an emergency, last-minute rewrite after Elizabeth tripped and fell during rehearsals and camera blocking the day before shooting. She stumbled and split her knee open like a soft-boiled egg on the metal floorboard between the stage doors that led out to the dressing rooms. Screaming and writhing, blood everywhere, she was rushed to the hospital, and it was soon clear that she would be out of commission for a while. The writers had to scramble and write out her part, distributing all her dialogue to the other cast members. In this episode, when Zack Attack is performing on stage and the camera cuts away to a shot of the audience, in the audience sits a kid with an oily forehead, glassy eyes, and a tiny nose. That handsome chap is Skyler Thiessen, Tiffani's little brother. Somewhere in there too, I believe, sits Lauren Engel, St. Peter's daughter (she also appeared in *SBTB: Hawaiian Style* and a bunch of other episodes). Cast parents often made it onto set in small roles as well. My dad played a chemistry teacher and a study hall teacher who once told Mario, "Mr. Slater, this is study hall, not Soul Train." And yes, my dad did walk away with a SAG card.

"MYSTERY WEEKEND" (Air date: December 28, 1991)

The gang travels to a murder-mystery weekend in an old mansion. Strange things start happening and people start disappearing.

Guest starring: Christopher Carroll as Bartholomew, Larry Cedar as Steven Jameson III, and Lisa Montgomery as Jeanette.

Here's a weird, random tidbit: the actress who played the French maid with the over-the-top accent in this episode—she had the line, "You ayrr a seeef and a mayrdayrarrrr" (Translation: "You are a thief and a murderer")—was dating Jon Lovitz at the time.

This was the only episode we ever did that was written as a mystery and the first set we filmed on that was not the Bayside school setting. Showing up on Monday and seeing a completely different set for the first time was, quite frankly, awesome. It was a much welcomed relief and breathed life into the usual monotony. Every Friday when the crew would remove the black tarps to reveal the *SBTB* set, the audience would oooOOOOOoo and cheer, but for us it was painfully boring. The "Mystery Weekend" set had couches and chairs we could lounge around on during breaks when we went over notes, rather than school chairs, The Max booths, Belding's desk, or the stairs in the main hallway.

By the way, whenever you saw different classroom sets on *SBTB*, they were all the same set with interchangeable components swapped around and redecorated. For instance, if a door was written to be on the opposite side of a room, the crew would just switch the rollaway walls to give it the feel of a new space. The lockers in the main hallway remained the same as well. On *Good Morning, Miss Bliss* they were red, then they were painted orange, etc. Also, keep your eyes on the main stairway. In early episodes, sometimes it's on the left, then inexplicably it appears on the right. Another inconsistency in that squished-together first season, which combined the totally different show and cast of *Good Morning, Miss Bliss* with the revamped *SBTB*, was that the school relocates from Indiana to Palisades, California, without a whiff of explanation. Apparently, the original high school was set in Indiana because that's where Brandon Tartikoff grew up.

SCREECH'S SPAGHETTI SAUCE" (Air date: September 19, 1992)

Screech invents a recipe for a new spaghetti sauce. This wins him the attention of an uppity girl who just wants him for his money. In communications class, the gang makes a show for cable access. In a commercial for Screech's sauce, Slater says, "We're saved by the bell!"

"The sauce, you can have. But the secret, she's-ah mine." I've still got one of those beakers with the picture on it somewhere in my vast archives. Soleil Moon Frye's epic rack makes an appearance in this episode. I can't
recall for certain, but quite possibly those beauties were still pre-reduction.

"THE FIGHT" (Air date: September 12, 1992)

This is the episode where Zack and Slater have it out in a full-on hallway brawl. A beautiful new student, Joanna Peterson, transfers into Bayside from Idaho. Zack and Slater come to blows over her affections.

Guest starring: Shana Furlow as Joanna Peterson, Jon Clair as Darren Brooks, Vaughn Armstrong as Mr. Breskin, and Bel Sandre as Martha.

Here's how the fight went down, blow-by-blow: A.C. Slater quickly descends the stairwell of Bayside's main hallway. He approaches Zack as he stands at his open locker.

A.C.: Zack, last night at the movies, you went too far.

Zack: Just helped a mother get together with her son. What's so wrong about that?

A.C.: Wrecking my date with Joanna wasn't funny.

Zack: Oh? Like it was funny wrecking my study date the night before?

A.C.: Hey, you started it, man—making me look like a jerk at The Max.

Zack: Well. That's what you are.

Audience: WoooOOOOOOOoooooo.

A.C.: What did you just say?

ZACK: You heard me. Get outta my face.

A.C.: And what if I don't? Punk.

ZACK: Then I'll just have to make you. Punk.

Zack pushes Slater. Slater pushes back. Zack lands a devastating right cross to Slater's left cheek, sending him crashing to the floor. Slater recovers, charges Zack. He wraps up Zack and throws him to the floor. Now straddling him, Slater lands a powerful right cross to Zack's eye. Zack seizes two fistfuls of Slater's lustrous hair as they wrestle back to their feet.

A crowd circles the action as a teacher steps forward, struggling to break them apart . . .

"THE BAYSIDE TRIANGLE" (Air date: September 26, 1992)

This is the lesser-known fight episode where Screech finally stands up to Zack when his heart is broken. Zack helps Lisa put on a fashion show in an attempt to impress an admissions emissary from the Fashion Institute of Technology in New York City. When Zack and Lisa fall for each other, Screech lashes out.

Before ripping open Zack's silken shirt in a fit of rage and despair, Screech says to Zack, "Why'd you have to steal my dream? I hate you."

AUDIENCE: WoooOOOOOOOOooooo.